Christianity

Its Evidences, Its Origin, Its Morality, Its History

Annie Besant

Christianity: Its Evidences, Its Origin, Its Morality, Its History

The present edition is a reproduction of previous publication of this classic work. Minor typographical errors may have been corrected without note, however, for an authentic reading experience the spelling, punctuation, and capitalization have been retained from the original text.

ISBN: 978-1-61895-989-8

CONTENTS

SECTION I

ITS EVIDENCES UNRELIABLE

The origin of all religions, and the ignorance which is the root of the God-idea, having been dealt with in Part I. of this Text-Book, it now becomes our duty to investigate the evidences of the origin and of the growth of Christianity, to examine its morality and its dogmas, to study the history of its supposed founder, to trace out its symbols and its ceremonies; in fine, to show cause for its utter rejection by the Freethinker. The foundation stone of Christianity, laid in Paradise by the Creation and Fall of Man 6,000 years ago, has already been destroyed in the first section of this work; and we may at once, therefore, proceed to Christianity itself. The history of the origin of the creed is naturally the first point to deal with, and this may be divided into two parts: 1. The evidences afforded by profane history as to its origin and early growth. 2. Its story as told by itself in its own documents.

The most remarkable thing in the evidences afforded by profane history is their extreme paucity; the very existence of Jesus cannot be proved from contemporary documents. A child whose birth is heralded by a star which guides foreign sages to Judæa; a massacre of all the infants of a town within the Roman Empire by command of a subject king; a teacher who heals the leper, the blind, the deaf, the dumb, the lame, and who raises the mouldering corpse; a King of the Jews entering Jerusalem in triumphal procession, without opposition from the Roman legions of Cæsar; an accused ringleader of sedition arrested by his own countrymen, and handed over to the imperial governor; a rebel adjudged to death by Roman law; a three hours' darkness over all the land; an earthquake breaking open graves and rending the temple veil; a number of ghosts wandering about Jerusalem; a crucified corpse rising again to life, and appearing to a crowd of above 500 people; a man risen from the dead ascending bodily into heaven without any concealment, and in the broad daylight, from a mountain near Jerusalem; all these marvellous events took place, we are told, and yet they have left no ripple on the current of contemporary history. There is, however, no lack of such history, and an exhaustive account of the country and age in which the hero of the story lived is given by one of his own nation—a most painstaking and laborious historian. "How shall we excuse the supine inattention of the Pagan and philosophic world to those evidences which were presented by the hand of Omnipotence, not to their reason, but to their senses? During the age of Christ, of his apostles, and of their first disciples, the doctrine which they preached was confirmed by innumerable prodigies. The lame walked, the blind saw, the sick were healed, the dead were raised, demons were expelled, and the laws of nature were frequently suspended for the benefit of the Church. But the sages of Greece and Rome turned aside from the awful spectacle, and, pursuing the ordinary occupations of life and study, appeared unconscious of any alterations in the moral or physical government of the world. Under the reign of Tiberius the whole earth, or at least a celebrated province of the Roman Empire, was involved in a preternatural darkness of three hours. Even this miraculous event, which ought to have excited the wonder, the curiosity, and the devotion of mankind, passed without notice in an age of science and history. It happened during the lifetime of Seneca and the elder Pliny, who must have experienced the immediate effects, or received the earliest intelligence, of the prodigy. Each of these philosophers, in a laborious work, has recorded all the great phenomena of nature—earthquakes, meteors, comets, and eclipses, which his indefatigable curiosity could collect. Both the one and the other have omitted to mention the greatest phenomenon to which the mortal eye has been witness since the creation of the globe. A distinct chapter of Pliny is designed for eclipses of an extraordinary nature and unusual duration; but he contents himself with describing the singular defect of light which followed the murder of Cæsar, when, during the greatest part of the year, the orb of the sun appeared pale and without splendour. This season of obscurity, which cannot surely be compared with the preternatural darkness of the Passion, had been already celebrated by most of the poets and historians of that memorable age" (Gibbon's "Decline and Fall," vol. ii., pp. 191, 192. Ed. 1821).

If Pagan historians are thus curiously silent, what deduction shall we draw from the similar silence of the great Jewish annalist? Is it credible that Josephus should thus have ignored Jesus Christ, if one tithe of the marvels related in the Gospels really took place? So damning to the story of Christianity has this difficulty been felt, that a passage has been inserted in Josephus (born A.D. 37, died about A.D. 100) relating to Jesus Christ, which runs as follows: "Now, there was about this time Jesus, a wise man, if it be lawful to call him a man, for he was a doer of wonderful works—a teacher of such men as receive the truth with pleasure. He drew over to him both many of the Jews, and many of the Gentiles. He was [the] Christ; and when Pilate, at the suggestion of the principal men amongst us, had condemned him to the cross, those that loved him at the first did not forsake him, for he appeared to them alive again the third day, as the divine prophets had foretold these and ten thousand other wonderful things concerning him; and the tribe of Christians, so named from him, are not extinct at this day" ("Antiquities of the Jews," book xviii., ch. iii., sect. 3). The passage itself proves its own forgery: Christ drew over scarcely any Gentiles, if the Gospel story be true, as he himself said: "I am not sent

2

but unto the lost sheep of the house of Israel" (Matthew xv. 24). A Jew would not believe that a doer of wonderful works must necessarily be more than man, since their own prophets were said to have performed miracles. If Josephus believed Jesus to be Christ, he would assuredly have become a Christian; while, if he believed him to be God, he would have drawn full attention to so unique a fact as the incarnation of the Deity. Finally, the concluding remark that the Christians were "not extinct" scarcely coincides with the idea that Josephus, at Rome, must have been cognisant of their increasing numbers, and of their persecution by Nero. It is, however, scarcely pretended now-a-days, by any scholar of note, that the passage is authentic. Sections 2 and 4 were manifestly written one after the other. "There were a great number of them slain by this means, and others of them ran away wounded; and thus an end was put to this sedition. About the same time another sad calamity put the Jews into disorder." The forged passage breaks the continuity of the history. The oldest MSS. do not contain this section. It is first quoted by Eusebius, who probably himself forged it; and its authenticity is given up by Lardner, Gibbon, Bishop Warburton, and many others. Lardner well summarises the arguments against its authenticity:—

"I do not perceive that we at all want the suspected testimony to Jesus, which was never quoted by any of our Christian ancestors before Eusebius.

"Nor do I recollect that Josephus has any where mentioned the name or word Christ, in any of his works; except the testimony above mentioned, and the passage concerning James, the Lord's brother.

"It interrupts the narrative.

"The language is quite Christian.

"It is not quoted by Chrysostom, though he often refers to Josephus, and could not have omitted quoting it, had it been then in the text.

"It is not quoted by Photius, though he has three articles concerning Josephus.

"Under the article Justus of Tiberias, this author (Photius) expressly states that historian (Josephus) being a Jew, has not taken the least notice of Christ.

"Neither Justin in his dialogue with Trypho the Jew, nor Clemens Alexandrinus, who made so many extracts from Christian authors, nor Origen against Celsus, have ever mentioned this testimony.

"But, on the contrary, in chapter xxxv. of the first book of that work, Origen openly affirms, that Josephus, who had mentioned John the Baptist, did not acknowledge Christ" (Answer to Dr. Chandler, as quoted in Taylor's "Diegesis," pp. 368, 369. Ed. 1844).

Keim thinks that the remarks of Origen caused the forgery; after criticising the passage he winds up: "For all these reasons, the passage

3

cannot be maintained; it has first appeared in this form in the Catholic Church of the Jews and Gentiles, and under the dominion of the Fourth Gospel, and hardly before the third century, probably before Eusebius, and after Origen, whose bitter criticisms of Josephus may have given cause for it" ("Jesus of Nazara," p. 25, English edition, 1873).

"Those who are best acquainted with the character of Josephus, and the style of his writings, have no hesitation in condemning this passage as a forgery interpolated in the text during the third century by some pious Christian, who was scandalised that so famous a writer as Josephus should have taken no notice of the Gospels, or of Christ their subject. But the zeal of the interpolator has outrun his discretion, for we might as well expect to gather grapes from thorns, or figs from thistles, as to find this notice of Christ among the Judaising writings of Josephus. It is well known that this author was a zealous Jew, devoted to the laws of Moses and the traditions of his countrymen. How then could he have written that Jesus was the Christ? Such an admission would have proved him to be a Christian himself, in which case the passage under consideration, too long for a Jew, would have been far too short for a believer in the new religion, and thus the passage stands forth, like an ill-set jewel, contrasting most inharmoniously with everything around it. If it had been genuine, we might be sure that Justin Martyr, Tertullian, and Chrysostom would have quoted it in their controversies with the Jews, and that Origen or Photius would have mentioned it. But Eusebius, the ecclesiastical historian (i., II), is the first who quotes it, and our reliance on the judgment or even the honesty of this writer is not so great as to allow of our considering everything found in his works as undoubtedly genuine" ("Christian Records," by Rev. Dr. Giles, p. 30. Ed. 1854).

On the other side the student should consult Hartwell Horne's "Introduction." Ed. 1825, vol. i., p. 307-11. Renan observes that the passage—in the authenticity of which he believes—is "in the style of Josephus," but adds that "it has been retouched by a Christian hand." The two statements seem scarcely consistent, as such "retouching" would surely alter "the style" ("Vie de Jésus," Introduction, p. 10. Ed. 1863).

Paley argues that when the multitude of Christians living in the time of Josephus is considered, it cannot "be believed that the religion, and the transaction upon which it was founded, were too obscure to engage the attention of Josephus, or to obtain a place in his history" ("Evid. of Christianity," p. 73. Ed. 1845). We answer, it is plain, from the fact that Josephus entirely ignores both, that the pretended story of Jesus was not widely known among his contemporaries, and that the early spread of Christianity is much exaggerated. But says Paley: "Be, however, the fact, or the cause of the omission in Josephus, what it may, no other or different history on the subject has been given by him or is pretended to have been given" (Ibid, pp. 73, 74). Our contention being that the supposed occurrences never took place at all, no history of them is to be looked for in the pages of a writer who was relating only facts. Josephus speaks of James, "the brother of Jesus, who was called Christ" ("Antiquities," book xx., ch. ix., sect. 1), and this passage shares the fate of the longer one, being likewise rejected because of being an interpolation. The other supposed reference of Josephus to Jesus is found in his discourse on Hades, wherein he says that all men "shall be brought before God the Word; for to him hath the Father committed all judgment; and he, in order to fulfil the will of his Father, shall come as judge, whom we call Christ" ("Works of Josephus," by Whiston, p. 661). Supposing that this passage were genuine, it would simply convey the Jewish belief that the Messiah—Christ—the Anointed, was the appointed judge, as in Dan. vii., 9-14, and more largely in the Book of Enoch.

The silence of Jewish writers of this period is not confined to Josephus, and this silence tells with tremendous weight against the Christian story. Judge Strange writes: "Josephus knew nothing of these wonderments, and he wrote up to the year 93, being familiar with all the chief scenes of the alleged Christianity. Nicolaus of Damascus, who preceded him and lived to the time of Herod's successor Archelaus, and Justus of Tiberias, who was the contemporary and rival of Josephus in Galilee, equally knew nothing of the movement. Philo-Judæus, who occupied the whole period ascribed to Jesus, and engaged himself deeply in figuring out the Logos, had heard nothing of the being who was realising at Jerusalem the image his fancy was creating" ("Portraiture and Mission of Jesus," p. 27).

We propose now to go carefully through the alleged testimonies to Christianity, as urged in Paley's "Evidences of Christianity," following his presentment of the argument step by step, and offering objections to each point as raised by him.

The next historian who is claimed as a witness to Christianity is Tacitus (born A.D. 54 or 55, died A.D. 134 or 135), who writes, dealing with the reign of Nero, that this Emperor "inflicted the most cruel punishments upon a set of people, who were holden in abhorrence for their crimes, and were commonly called Christians. The founder of that name was Christus, who, in the reign of Tiberius, was punished as a criminal by the procurator, Pontius Pilate. This pernicious superstition, thus checked for awhile, broke out again; and spread not only over Judæa the source of this evil, but reached the city also: whither flow from all quarters all things vile and shameful, and where they find shelter and encouragement. At first, only those were apprehended who confessed themselves of that sect; afterwards, a vast multitude discovered by them; all which were condemned, not so much for the crime of burning the city, as for their hatred of mankind. Their executions were so contrived as to expose them to derision and contempt. Some were covered over with the skins of wild beasts, and

5

torn to pieces by dogs; some were crucified. Others, having been daubed over with combustible materials, were set up as lights in the night-time, and thus burned to death. Nero made use of his own gardens as a theatre on this occasion, and also exhibited the diversions of the circus, sometimes standing in the crowd as a spectator, in the habit of a charioteer; at other times driving a chariot himself; till at length these men, though really criminal, and deserving exemplary punishment, began to be commiserated as people who were destroyed, not out of regard to the public welfare, but only to gratify the cruelty of one man" ("Annals," book xv., sect. 44).

This was probably written, if authentic, about A.D. 107. The reasons against the authenticity of this passage are thus given by Robert Taylor: "This passage, which would have served the purpose of Christian quotation better than any other in all the writings of Tacitus, or of any Pagan writer whatever, is not quoted by any of the Christian Fathers.

"It is not quoted by Tertullian, though he had read and largely quotes the works of Tacitus: and though his argument immediately called for the use of this quotation with so loud a voice, that his omission of it, if it had really existed, amounts to a violent improbability.

"This Father has spoken of Tacitus in a way that it is absolutely impossible that he should have spoken of him had his writings contained such a passage.

"It is not quoted by Clemens Alexandrinus, who set himself entirely to the work of adducing and bringing together all the admissions and recognitions which Pagan authors had made of the existence of Christ or Christians before his time.

"It has nowhere been stumbled on by the laborious and all-seeking Eusebius, who could by no possibility have missed of it....

"There is no vestige nor trace of its existence anywhere in the world before the fifteenth century.

"It rests then entirely upon the fidelity of a single individual. And he, having the ability, the opportunity, and the strongest possible incitement of interest to induce him to introduce the interpolation.

"The passage itself, though unquestionably the work of a master, and entitled to be pronounced the chef d'oeuvre of the art, betrays the penchant of that delight in blood, and in descriptions of bloody horrors, as peculiarly characteristic of the Christian disposition as it was abhorrent to the mild and gentle mind, and highly cultivated taste of Tacitus.

"It is falsified by the 'Apology of Tertullian,' and the far more respectable testimony of Melito, Bishop of Sardis, who explicitly states that the Christians, up to his time, the third century, had never been victims of persecution; and that it was in provinces lying beyond the boundaries of the Roman Empire, and not in Judæa, that Christianity originated.

"Tacitus has, in no other part of his writings, made the least allusion to Christ or Christians.

"The use of this passage as a part of the 'Evidences of the Christian Religion,' is absolutely modern" ("Diegesis," pp. 374—376).

Judge Strange—writing on another point—gives us an argument against the authenticity of this passage: "As Josephus made Rome his place of abode from the year 70 to the end of the century, there inditing his history of all that concerned the Jews, it is apparent that, had there been a sect flourishing in the city who were proclaiming the risen Jesus as the Messiah in his time, the circumstance was one this careful and discerning writer could not have failed to notice and to comment on" ("Portraiture and Mission of Jesus," p. 15). It is, indeed, passing strange that Josephus, who tells us so much about false Messiahs and their followers, should omit—as he must have done if this passage of Tacitus be authentic—all reference to this additional false Messiah, whose followers in the very city where Josephus was living, underwent such terrible tortures, either during his residence there, or immediately before it. Burning men, used as torches, adherents of a Jewish Messiah, ought surely to have been unusual enough to have attracted his attention. We may add to these arguments that, supposing such a passage were really written by Tacitus, the two lines regarding Christus look much like an interpolation, as the remainder would run more connectedly if they were omitted. But the whole passage is of more than doubtful authenticity, being in itself incredible, if the Acts and the Epistles of the New Testament be true; for this persecution is said to have occurred during the reign of Nero, during which Paul abode in Rome, teaching in peace, "no man forbidding him" (Acts xxviii. 31); during which, also, he wrote to the Romans that they need not be afraid of the government if they did right (Romans xii. 34); clearly, if these passages are true, the account in Tacitus must be false; and as he himself had no reason for composing such a tale, it must have been forged by Christians to glorify their creed.

The extreme ease with which this passage might have been inserted in all editions of Tacitus used in modern times arises from the fact that all such editions are but copies of one single MS., which was in the possession of one single individual; the solitary owner might make any interpolations he pleased, and there was no second copy by which his accuracy might be tested. "The first publication of any part of the 'Annals of Tacitus' was by Johannes de Spire, at Venice, in the year 1468—his imprint being made from a single MS., in his own power and possession only, and purporting to have been written in the eighth century.... from this all other MSS. and printed copies of the works of Tacitus are derived." ("Diegesis," p. 373.)

Suetonius (born about A.D. 65, died in second century) writes:

7

"The Christians, a race of men of a new and mischievous (or magical) superstition, were punished." In another passage we read of Claudius, who reigned A.D. 41-54: "He drove the Jews, who, at the suggestion of Chrestus, were constantly rioting, out of Rome." From this we might infer that there was at that time a Jewish leader, named Chrestus, living in Rome, and inciting the Jews to rebellion. His followers would probably take his name, and, expelled from Rome, they would spread this name in all directions. If the passage in Acts xi. 20 and 26 be of any historical value, it would curiously strengthen this hypothesis, since the "disciples were called Christians first in Antioch," and the missionaries to Antioch, who preached "unto the Jews only," came from Cyprus and Cyrene, which would naturally lie in the way of fugitives from Rome to Asia Minor. They would bring the name Christian with them, and the date in the Acts synchronises with that in Suetonius. Chrestus would appear to have left a sect behind him in Rome, bearing his name, the members of which were prosecuted by the Government, very likely as traitors and rebels. Keim's good opinion of Suetonius is much degraded by this Chrestus: "In his 'Life of Claudius,' who expelled the Jews from Rome, he has shown his undoubted inferiority to Tacitus as a historian by treating 'Christ' as a restless and seditious Jewish agitator, who was still living in the time of Claudius, and, indeed, in Rome" ("Jesus of Nazara," p. 33).

It is natural that modern Christians should object to a Jewish Chrestus starting up at Rome simultaneously with their Jewish Christus in Judæa, who, according to Luke's chronology, must have been crucified about A.D. 43. The coincidence is certainly inconvenient; but if they refuse the testimony of Suetonius concerning Chrestus, the leader, why should they accept it concerning the Christians, the followers? Paley, of course, although he quotes Suetonius, omits all reference at this stage to the unlucky Chrestus; his duty was to present evidences of, not against, Christianity. Most dishonestly, however, he inserts a reference to it later on (p. 73), where, in a brief résumé of the evidence, he uses it as a link in his chain: "When Suetonius, an historian contemporary with Tacitus, relates that, in the time of Claudius, the Jews were making disturbances at Rome, Christus being their leader." Why does not Paley explain to us how Jesus came to be leading Jews at Rome during the reign of Claudius, and why he incited them to riot? No such incident is related in the life of Jesus of Nazareth; and if Suetonius be correct, the credit of the Gospels is destroyed. To his shame be it said, that Paley here deliberately refers to a passage, which he has not ventured to quote, simply that he may use the great name of Suetonius to strengthen his lamentably weak argument, by the pretence that Suetonius mentions Jesus of Nazareth, and thus makes him a historical character. Few more disgraceful perversions of evidence can be found, even in the annals of controversy. H. Horne refers to this passage in proof of the

8

existence of Christ (Introduction, vol. i., page 202); but without offering any explanation of the appearance of Christ in Rome some years after he ought to have been dead.

Juvenal is next dragged forward by Paley as a witness, because he mentioned the punishment of some criminals: "I think it sufficiently probable that these [Christian executions] were the executions to which the poet refers" ("Evidences," p. 29.) Needless to say that there is not a particle of proof that they were anything of the kind; but when evidence is lacking, it is necessary to invent it.

Pliny the Younger (born A.D. 61, died A.D. 115) writes to the Emperor Trajan, about A.D. 107, to ask him how he shall treat the Christians, and as Paley has so grossly misrepresented this letter, it will be well to reproduce the whole of it. It contains no word of Christians dying boldly as Paley pretends, nor, indeed, of the punishment of death being inflicted at all. The word translated "punishment" is supplicium (acc. of supplicium) in the original, and is a term which, like the French supplice, derived from it, may mean the punishment of death, or any other heavy penalty. The translation of the letter runs as follows: "C. Pliny to the Emperor Trajan, Health.—It is customary with me to refer to you, my lord, matters about which I entertain a doubt. For who is better able either to rule my hesitation, or to instruct my ignorance? I have never been present at the inquiries about the Christians, and, therefore, cannot say for what crime, or to what extent, they are usually punished, or what is the nature of the inquiry about them. Nor have I been free from great doubts whether there should not be a distinction between ages, or how far those of a tender frame should be treated differently from the robust; whether those who repent should not be pardoned, so that one who has been a Christian should not derive advantage from having ceased to be one; whether the name itself of being a Christian should be punished, or only crime attendant upon the name? In the meantime I have laid down this rule in dealing with those who were brought before me for being Christians. I asked whether they were Christians; if they confessed, I asked them a second and a third time, threatening them with punishment; if they persevered, I ordered them to be led off. For I had no doubt in my mind that, whatever it might be which they acknowledged, obduracy and inflexible obstinacy, at all events should be punished. There were others guilty of like folly, whom I set aside to be sent to Rome, because they were Roman citizens. In the next place, when this crime began, as usual, gradually to spread, it showed itself in a variety of ways. An indictment was set forth without any author, containing the names of many who denied that they were Christians or ever had been; and, when I set the example, they called on the gods, and made offerings of frankincense and wine to your image, which I, for this purpose, had ordered to be brought out, together with the images of the gods. Moreover, they cursed Christ; none of which acts can be extorted from those who are really

9

Christians. I consequently gave orders that they should be discharged. Again, others, who have been informed against, said that they were Christians, and afterwards denied it; that they had been so once but had ceased to be so, some three years ago, some longer than that, some even twenty years before; all of these worshipped your image, and the statues of the gods; they also cursed Christ. But they asserted that this was the sum total of their crime or error, whichever it may be called, that they were used to come together on a stated day before it was light, and to sing in turn, among themselves, a hymn to Christ, as to a god, and to bind themselves by an oath—not to anything wicked—but that they would not commit theft, robbery, or adultery, nor break their word, nor deny that anything had been entrusted to them when called upon to restore it. After this they said that it was their custom to separate, and again to meet together to take their meals, which were in common and of a harmless nature; but that they had ceased even to do this since the proclamation which I issued according to your commands, forbidding such meetings to be held. I therefore deemed it the more necessary to enquire of two servant maids, who were said to be attendants, what was the real truth, and to apply the torture. But I found that it was nothing but a bad and excessive superstition, and I consequently adjourned the inquiry, and consulted you upon the subject. For it seemed to me to be a matter on which it was desirable to take advice, in consequence of the number of those who are in danger. For there are many of every age, of every rank, and even of both sexes, who are invited to incur the danger, and will still be invited. For the infection of this superstition has spread through not only cities, but also villages and the country, though it seems possible to check and remedy it. At all events it is evident that the temples, which had been almost deserted, have begun to be frequented, and the sacred solemnities, which had been intermitted, are revived, and victims are sold everywhere, though formerly it was difficult to find a buyer. It is, therefore, easy to believe that a number of persons may be corrected, if the door of repentance be left open" (Ep. 97).

It is urged by Christian advocates that this letter at least shows how widely Christianity had spread at this early date; but we shall later have occasion to draw attention to the fact that the name "Christian" was used before the reputed time of Christ to describe some extensively-spread sects, and that the worshippers of the Egyptian Serapis were known by that title. It may be added that the authenticity of this letter is by no means beyond dispute, and that R. Taylor urges some very strong arguments against it. Among others, he suggests: "The undeniable fact that the first Christians were the greatest liars and forgers that had ever been in the whole world, and that they actually stopped at nothing.... The flagrant atopism of Christians being found in the remote province of Bithynia, before they had acquired any notoriety in Rome.... The inconsistency of the supposition that so just and moral

10

a people as the primitive Christians are assumed to have been, should have been the first to provoke the Roman Government to depart from its universal maxims of toleration, liberality, and indifference.... The use of the torture to extort confession.... The choice of women to be the subjects of this torture, when the ill-usage of women was, in like manner, abhorrent to the Roman character" ("Diegesis," pp. 383, 384).

Paley boldly states that Martial (born A.D. 43, died about A.D. 100) makes the Christians "the subject of his ridicule," because he wrote an epigram on the stupidity of admiring any vain-glorious fool who would rush to be tormented for the sake of notoriety. Hard-set must Christians be for evidence, when reduced to rely on such pretended allusions.

Epictetus (flourished first half of second century) is claimed as another witness, because he states that "It is possible a man may arrive at this temper, and become indifferent to these things from madness, or from habit, as the Galileans" (Book iv., chapter 7). The Galileans, i.e., the people of Galilee, appear to have had a bad name, and it is highly probable that Epictetus simply referred to them, just as he might have said as an equivalent phrase for stupidity, "like the Boeotians." In addition to this, the followers of Judas the Gaulonite were known as Galileans, and were remarkable for the "inflexible constancy which, in defence of their cause, rendered them insensible of death and tortures" ("Decline and Fall," vol. ii., p. 214).

Marcus Aurelius (born A.D. 121, died A.D. 180) is Paley's last support, as he urges that fortitude in the face of death should arise from judgment, "and not from obstinacy, like the Christians." As no one disputes the existence of a sect called Christians when Marcus Aurelius wrote, this testimony is not specially valuable.

Paley, so keen to swoop down on any hint that can be twisted into an allusion to the Christians, entirely omits the interesting letter written by the Emperor Adrian to his brother-in-law Servianus, A.D. 134. The evidence is not of an edifying character, and this accounts for the omission: "The worshippers of Serapis are Christians, and those are consecrated to the god Serapis, who, I find, call themselves the bishops of Christ" (Quoted in "Diegesis," p. 386).

Such are the whole external evidences of Christianity until after A.D. 160. In a time rich in historians and philosophers one man, Tacitus, in a disputed passage, mentions a Christus punished under Pontius Pilate, and the existence of a sect bearing his name. Suetonius, Pliny, Adrian, possibly Epictetus, and Marcus Aurelius, casually mention some people called Christians.

The Rev. Dr. Giles thus summarises the proofs of the weakness of early Christian evidences in "profane history:"—

"Though the remains of Grecian and Latin profane literature which belong to the first and second centuries of our era are enough to form a library of themselves, they contain no allusion to the New

Testament.... The Latin writers, who lived between the time of Christ's crucifixion and the year A.D. 200, are Seneca, Lucan, Suetonius, Tacitus, Persius, Juvenal, Martial, Pliny the Elder, Silius Italicus, Statius, Quintilian, and Pliny the Younger, besides numerous others of inferior note. The greater number of these make mention of the Jews, but not of the Christians. In fact, Suetonius, Tacitus, and the younger Pliny, are the only Roman writers who mention the Christian religion or its founder" ("Christian Records," by Rev. Dr. Giles, P. 36).

"The Greek classic writers, who lived between the time of Christ's crucifixion and the year 200, are those which follow: Epictetus, Plutarch, Ælian, Arrian, Galen, Lucian, Dionysius of Halicarnassus, Ptolemy, Marcus Aurelius (who, though a Roman emperor, wrote in Greek), Pausanias, and many others of less note. The allusions to Christianity found in their works are singularly brief" (Ibid, p. 42).

What does it all, this "evidence," amount to? One writer, Tacitus, records that a man, called by his followers "Christ"—for no one pretends that Christ is anything more than a title given by his disciples to a certain Jew named Jesus—was put to death by Pontius Pilate. And suppose he were, what then? How is this a proof of the religion called Christianity? Tacitus knows nothing of the miracle-worker, of the risen and ascended man; he is strangely ignorant of all the wonders that had occurred; and, allowing the passage to be genuine, it tells sorely against the marvellous history given by the Christians of their leader, whose fame is supposed to have spread far and wide, and whose fame most certainly must so have spread had he really performed all the wonderful works attributed to him. But no necessity lies upon the Freethinker, when he rejects Christianity, to disprove the historical existence of Jesus of Nazareth, although we point to the inadequacy of the evidence even of his existence. The strength of the Freethought position is in no-wise injured by the admission that a young Jew named Joshua (i.e. Jesus) may have wandered up and down Galilee and Judæa in the reign of Tiberius, that he may have been a religious reformer, that he may have been put to death by Pontius Pilate for sedition. All this is perfectly likely, and to allow it in no way endorses the mass of legend and myth encrusted round this tiny nucleus of possible fact. This obscure peasant is not the Christian Jesus, who is—as we shall later urge—only a new presentation of the ancient Sun-God, with unmistakeable family likeness to his elder brothers. The Reverend Robert Taylor very rightly remarks, concerning this small historical possibility: "These are circumstances which fall entirely within the scale of rational possibility, and draw for no more than an ordinary and indifferent testimony of history, to command the mind's assent. The mere relation of any historian, living near enough to the time supposed to guarantee the probability of his competent information on the subject, would have been entitled to our acquiescence. We could have no reason to deny or to doubt what such an historian could have had no

12

motive to feign or to exaggerate. The proof, even to demonstration, of these circumstances would constitute no step or advance towards the proof of the truth of the Christian religion; while the absence of a sufficient degree of evidence to render even these circumstances unquestionable must, à fortiori, be fatal to the credibility of the less credible circumstances founded upon them" ("Diegesis," p. 7).

But Paley pleads some indirect evidence on behalf of Christianity, which deserves a word of notice since the direct evidence so lamentably breaks down. He urges that: "there is satisfactory evidence that many, professing to be original witnesses of the Christian miracles, passed their lives in labours, dangers, and sufferings, voluntarily under-gone, in attestation of the accounts which they delivered, and solely in consequence of their belief of those accounts; and that they also submitted, from the same motives, to new rules of conduct." Nearly 200 pages are devoted to the proof of this proposition, a proposition which it is difficult to characterise with becoming courtesy, when we know the complete and utter absence of any "satisfactory evidence" that the original witnesses did anything of the kind.

It is pleaded that the "original witnesses passed their lives in labours, etc., in attestation of the accounts they delivered." The evidence of this may be looked for either in Pagan or in Christian writings. Pagan writers know literally nothing about the "original witnesses," mentioning, at the utmost, but "the Christians;" and these Christians, when put to death, were not so executed in attestation of any accounts delivered by them, but wholly and solely because of the evil deeds and the scandalous practices rightly or wrongly attributed to them. Supposing—what is not true—that they had been executed for their creed, there is no pretence that they were eye-witnesses of the miracles of Christ.

Paley's first argument is drawn "from the nature of the case"— i.e., that persecution ought to have taken place, whether it did or not, because both Jews and Gentiles would reject the new creed. So far as the Jews are concerned, we hear of no persecution from Josephus. If we interrogate the Christian Acts, we hear but of little, two persons only being killed. We learn also that "many thousands of Jews" belonged to the new sect, and were propitiated by Christian conformity to the law; and that, when the Jews rose against Paul—not as a Christian, but as a breaker of the Mosaic law—he was promptly delivered by the Romans, who would have set him at liberty had he not elected to be tried at Rome. If we turn to the conduct of the Pagans, we meet the same blank absence of evidence of persecution, until we come to the disputed passage in Tacitus, wherein none of the eye-witnesses are said to have been concerned; and we have, on the other side, the undisputed fact that, under the imperial rule of Rome, every subject nation practised its own creed undisturbed, so long as it did not incite

13

to civil disturbances. "The religious tenets of the Galileans, or Christians, were never made a subject of punishment, or even of inquiry" ("Decline and Fall," vol. ii., p. 215).

This view of the matter is thoroughly corroborated by Lardner: "The disciples of Jesus Christ were under the protection of the Roman law, since the God they worshipped and whose worship they recommended, was the God of the heavens and the earth, the same God whom the Jews worshipped, and the worship of whom was allowed of all over the Roman Empire, and established by special edicts and decrees in most, perhaps in all the places, in which we meet with St. Paul in his travels" ("Credibility," vol. i., pt. I, pp. 406, 407. Ed. 1727). He also quotes "a remarkable piece of justice done the Jews at Doris, in Syria, by Petronius, President of that province. The fact is this: Some rash young fellows of the place got in and set up a statue of the Emperor in the Jews' synagogue. Agrippa the Great made complaints to Petronius concerning this injury. Whereupon Petronius issued a very sharp precept to the magistrates of Doris. He terms this action an offence, not against the Jews only, but also against the Emperor; says, it is agreeable to the law of nature that every man should be master of his own places, according to the decree of the Emperor. I have, says he, given directions that they who have dared to do these things contrary to the edict of Augustus, be delivered to the centurion Vitellius Proculus, that they may be brought to me, and answer for their behaviour. And I require the chief men in the magistracy to discover the guilty to the centurion, unless they are willing to have it thought, that this injustice has been done with their consent; and that they see to it, that no sedition or tumult happen upon this occasion, which, I perceive, is what some are aiming at.... I do also require, that for the future, you seek no pretence for sedition or disturbance, but that all men worship [God] according to their own customs" (Ibid, pp. 382, 383). After giving some other facts, Lardner sums up: "These are authentic testimonies in behalf of the equity of the Roman Government in general, and of the impartial administration of justice by the Roman presidents—toward all the people of their provinces, how much soever they differed from each other in matters of religion" (Ibid, p. 401).

The evidence of persecution which consists in quotations from the Christian books ("Evidences," pages 33-52) cannot be admitted without evidence of the authenticity of the books quoted. The Acts and the Pauline epistles so grossly contradict each other that, having nothing outside themselves with which to compare them, they are mutually destructive. "The epistle to the Romans presents special difficulties to its acceptance as a genuine address to the Church of Rome in the era ascribed to it. The faith of this Church, at this early period, is said to be 'spoken of throughout the whole world'; and yet when Paul, according to the Acts, at a later time visited Rome, so little had this alleged Church influenced the neighbourhood, that the inquiring Jews of Rome are shown to be totally ignorant of what constituted Christianity, and to have looked to Paul to enlighten them" ("Portraiture and Mission of Jesus," p. 15). 2 Cor. is of very doubtful authenticity. The passage in James shows no fiery persecution. Hebrews is of later date. 2 Thess. again very doubtful. The "suffering" spoken of by Peter appears, from the context, to refer chiefly to reproaches, and a problematical "if any man suffer as a Christian." Had those he wrote to been then suffering, surely the apostle would have said: "When any man suffers ... let him not be ashamed." The whole question of the authenticity of the canonical books will be challenged later, and the weakness of this division of Paley's evidences will then be more fully apparent. Meanwhile we subjoin Lardner's view of these passages. He has been arguing that the Romans "protected the many rites of all their provinces;" and he proceeds: "There is, however, one difficulty which, I am aware, may be started by some persons. If the Roman Government, to which all the world was then subject, was so mild and gentle, and protected all men in the profession of their several religious tenets, and the practice of all their peculiar rites, whence comes it to pass that there are in the Epistles so many exhortations to the Christians to patience and constancy, and so many arguments of consolation suggested to them, as a suffering body of men? [Here follow some passages as in Paley.] To this I answer: 1. That the account St. Luke has given in the Acts of the Apostles of the behaviour of the Roman officers out of Judæa, and in it, is confirmed not only by the account I have given of the genius and nature of the Roman Government, but also by the testimony of the most ancient Christian writers. The Romans did afterwards depart from these moderate maxims; but it is certain that they were governed by them as long as the history of the Acts of the Apostles reaches. Tertullian and divers others do affirm that Nero was the first Emperor that persecuted the Christians; nor did he begin to disturb them till after Paul had left Rome the first time he was there (when he was sent thither by Festus), and, therefore, not until he was become an enemy to all mankind. And I think that, according to the account which Tacitus has given of Nero's inhumane treatment of the Christians at Rome, in the tenth year of his reign, what he did then was not owing to their having different principles in religion from the Romans, but proceeded from a desire he had to throw off from himself the odium of a vile action—namely, setting fire to the city—which he was generally charged with. And Sulpicius Severus, a Christian historian of the fourth century, says the same thing" ("Credibility of the Gospel History," vol. i., pages 416-420). Lardner, however, allows that the Jews persecuted the Christians where they could although they were unable to slay them. They probably persecuted them much in the same fashion that the Christians have persecuted Freethinkers during the present century.

But Paley adduces further the evidence of Clement, Hermas,

Polycarp, Ignatius, and a circular letter of the Church of Smyrna, to prove the sufferings of the eye-witnesses ("Evidences," pages 52-55). When we pass into writings of this description in later times, there is, indeed, plenty of evidence—in fact, a good deal too much, for they testify to such marvellous occurrences, that no trust is possible in anything which they say. Not only was St. Paul's head cut off, but the worthy Bishop of Rome, Linus, his contemporary (who is supposed to relate his martyrdom), tells us how, "instead of blood, nought but a stream of pure milk flowed from his veins;" and we are further instructed that his severed head took three jumps in "honour of the Trinity, and at each spot on which it jumped there instantly struck up a spring of living water, which retains at this day a plain and distinct taste of milk" ("Diegesis," pp. 256, 257). Against a mass of absurd stories of this kind, the only evidence of the persecution of Paley's eye-witnesses, we may set the remarks of Gibbon: "In the time of Tertullian and Clemens of Alexandria the glory of martyrdom was confined to St. Peter, St. Paul, and St. James. It was gradually bestowed on the rest of the Apostles by the more recent Greeks, who prudently selected for the theatre of their preaching and sufferings some remote country beyond the limits of the Roman Empire" ("Decline and Fall," vol. ii., p. 208, note). Later there was, indeed, more persecution; but even then the martyrdoms afford no evidence of the truth of Christianity. Martyrdom proves the sincerity, but not the truth, of the sufferer's belief; every creed has had its martyrs, and as the truth of one creed excludes the truth of every other, it follows that the vast majority have died for a delusion, and that, therefore, the number of martyrs it can reckon is no criterion of the truth of a creed, but only of the devotion it inspires. While we allow that the Christians underwent much persecution, there can be no doubt that the number of the sufferers has been grossly exaggerated. One can scarcely help suspecting that, as real martyrs were not forthcoming in as vast numbers as their supposed bones, martyrs were invented to fit the wealth-producing relics, as the relics did not fit the historical martyrs. "The total disregard of truth and probability in the representations of these primitive martyrdoms was occasioned by a very natural mistake. The ecclesiastical writers of the fourth and fifth centuries ascribed to the magistrates of Rome the same degree of implacable and unrelenting zeal which filled their own breasts against the heretics, or the idolaters of their own time.... But it is certain, and we may appeal to the grateful confessions of the first Christians, that the greatest part of those magistrates, who exercised in the provinces the authority of the Emperor, or of the Senate, and to whose hands alone the jurisdiction of life and death was entrusted, behaved like men of polished manners and liberal education, who respected the rules of justice, and who were conversant with the precepts of philosophy. They frequently declined the odious task of persecution, dismissed the charge with contempt, or suggested to the

16

accused Christian some legal evasion by which he might elude the severity of the laws. (Tertullian, in his epistle to the Governor of Africa, mentions several remarkable instances of lenity and forbearance which had happened within his own knowledge.)... The learned Origen, who, from his experience, as well as reading, was intimately acquainted with the history of the Christians, declares, in the most express terms, that the number of martyrs was very inconsiderable.... The general assertion of Origen may be explained and confirmed by the particular testimony of his friend Dionysius, who, in the immense city of Alexandria, and under the rigorous persecution of Decius, reckons only ten men and seven women who suffered for the profession of the Christian name" ("Decline and Fall," vol. ii., pp. 224-226. See throughout chap. xvi.). Gibbon calculates the whole number of martyrs of the Early Church at "somewhat less than two thousand persons;" and remarks caustically that the "Christians, in the course of their intestine dissensions, have inflicted far greater severities on each other than they had experienced from the zeal of infidels" (pp. 273, 274). Supposing, however, that the most exaggerated accounts of Church historians were correct, how would that support Paley's argument? His contention is that the "eye-witnesses" of miraculous events died in testimony of their belief in them; and myriads of martyrs in the second and third centuries are of no assistance to him. So we will retrace our steps to the eye-witnesses, and we find the position of Gibbon—as to the lives and labours of the Apostles being written later by men not confining themselves to facts—endorsed by Mosheim, who judiciously observes: "Many have undertaken to write this history of the Apostles, a history which we find loaded with fables, doubts, and difficulties, when we pursue it further than the books of the New Testament, and the most ancient writers in the Christian Church" ("Eccles. Hist.," p. 27, ed. 1847). What "ancient writers" Mosheim alludes to it is difficult to guess, as may be judged from his criticisms quoted below, on the "Apostolic Fathers," the most ancient of all; and in estimating the worth of his opinion, it is necessary to remember that he was himself an earnest Christian, although a learned and candid one, so that every admission he makes, which tells against Christianity, is of double weight, it being the admission of a friend and defender.

To the credit of Paley's apostolic evidences (Clement, Hermas, Polycarp, Ignatius, and letter from Smyrna), we may urge the following objections. Clement's writings are much disputed: "The accounts which remain of his life, actions, and death are, for the most part, uncertain. Two Epistles to the Corinthians, written in Greek, have been attributed to him, of which the second has been looked upon as spurious, and the first as genuine, by many learned writers. But even this latter seems to have been corrupted and interpolated by some ignorant and presumptuous author.... The learned are now unanimous in regarding the other writings which bear the name of Clemens (Clement) ... as

17

spurious productions ascribed by some impostor to this venerable prelate, in order to procure them a high degree of authority" (Ibid, pp. 31, 32).

"The first epistle, bearing the name of Clement, has been preserved to us in a single manuscript only. Though very frequently referred to by ancient Christian writers, it remained unknown to the scholars of Western Europe until happily discovered in the Alexandrian manuscript.... Who the Clement was, to whom these writings are ascribed, cannot with absolute certainty be determined. The general opinion is, that he is the same as the person of that name referred to by St. Paul (Phil. iv. 3). The writings themselves contain no statement as to their author.... Although, as has been said, positive certainty cannot be reached on the subject, we may with great probability conclude that we have in this epistle a composition of that Clement who is known to us from Scripture as having been an associate of the great apostle. The date of this epistle has been the subject of considerable controversy. It is clear from the writing itself that it was composed soon after some persecution (chapter I) which the Roman Church had endured; and the only question is, whether we are to fix upon the persecution under Nero or Domitian. If the former, the date will be about the year 68; if the latter, we must place it towards the close of the first century, or the beginning of the second. We possess no external aid to the settlement of this question. The lists of early Roman bishops are in hopeless confusion, some making Clement the immediate successor of St. Peter, others placing Linus, and others still Linus and Anacletus, between him and the apostle. The internal evidence, again, leaves the matter doubtful, though it has been strongly pressed on both sides. The probability seems, on the whole, to be in favour of the Domitian period, so that the epistle may be dated about A.D. 97" ("The Writings of the Apostolic Fathers." Translated by Rev. Dr. Roberts, Dr. Donaldson, and Rev. F. Crombie, pp. 3, 4. Ed. 1867). "Only a single-manuscript copy of the work is extant, at the end of the Alexandrian manuscript of the Scriptures. This copy is considerably mutilated. In some passages the text is manifestly corrupt, and other passages have been suspected of being interpolations" (Norton's "Genuineness of the Gospels," vol. i, p. 336. Ed. 1847).

The second epistle is rejected on all sides. "It is now generally regarded as one of the many writings which have been falsely ascribed to Clement.... The diversity of style clearly points to a different writer from that of the first epistle" ("Apostolic Fathers," page 53). "The second epistle ... is not mentioned at all by the earlier Fathers who refer to the first. Eusebius, who is the first writer who mentions it, expresses doubt regarding it, while Jerome and Photius state that it was rejected by the ancients. It is now universally regarded as spurious" ("Supernatural Religion," pp. 220, 221). "There is a second epistle ascribed to Clement, but we know not that this is as highly approved as the former, and know not that it has been in use with the ancients. There are also other writings reported to be his, verbose and of great length. Lately, and some time ago, those were produced that contain the dialogues of Peter and Apion, of which, however, not a syllable is recorded by the primitive Church" (Eusebius' "Eccles. Hist." bk. iii., chap. 38). "The first Greek Epistle alone can be confidently pronounced genuine" (Westcott on the "Canon of the New Testament," p. 24. Ed. 1875). The first epistle "is the only piece of Clement that can be relied on as genuine" ("Lardner's Credibility," pt. ii., vol. i., p. 62. Ed. 1734). "Besides the Epistle of Clement to the Corinthians there is a fragment of a piece, called his second epistle, which being doubtful, or rather plainly not Clement's, I don't quote as his." (Ibid, p. 106.)

This very dubious Clement (Paley quotes, be it said, from the first—or least doubtful—of his writings) only says that one of Paley's original witnesses was martyred, namely Peter; Paul, of course, was not an eye-witness of Christ's proceedings.

The Vision of Hermas is a simple rhapsody, unworthy of a moment's consideration, of which Mosheim justly remarks: "The discourse which he puts into the mouths of those celestial beings is more insipid and senseless than what we commonly hear among the meanest of the multitude" ("Eccles. Hist," p. 32). Its date is very doubtful; the Canon of Muratori puts it in the middle of the second century, saying that it was written by Hermas, brother to Pius, Bishop of Rome, who died A.D. 142. (See "Norton's Genuineness of the Gospels," vol. i., pp. 341, 342.) "The Epistle to the Philippians, which is ascribed to Polycarp, Bishop of Smyrna, who, in the middle of the second century, suffered martyrdom in a venerable and advanced age, is looked upon by some as genuine; by others as spurious; and it is no easy matter to determine this question" ("Eccles. Hist," p. 32). "Upon no internal ground can any part of this Epistle be pronounced genuine; there are potent reasons for considering it spurious, and there is no evidence of any value whatever supporting its authenticity" ("Sup. Rel.," p. 283).

The editors of the "Apostolic Fathers" dispute this assertion, and say: "It is abundantly established by external testimony, and is also supported by the internal evidence" (p. 67). But they add: "The epistle before us is not perfect in any of the Greek MSS. which contain it. But the chapters wanting in Greek are contained in an ancient Latin version. While there is no ground for supposing, as some have done, that the whole epistle is spurious, there seems considerable force in the arguments by which many others have sought to prove chap. xiii. to be an interpolation. The date of the epistle cannot be satisfactorily determined. It depends on the conclusion we reach as to some points, very difficult and obscure, connected with that account of the martyrdom of Polycarp which has come down to us. We shall not, however, be far wrong if we fix it about the middle of the second century" (Ibid, pp. 67, 68). Poor Paley! this weak evidence to the martyrdom of his eye-witnesses comes 150 years after Christ; and even then all that Polycarp may have said, if the epistle chance to be authentic, is that "they suffered," without any word of their martyrdom!

The authenticity of the letters of Ignatius has long been a matter of dispute. Mosheim, who accepts the seven epistles, says that, "Though I am willing to adopt this opinion as preferable to any other, yet I cannot help looking upon the authenticity of the epistle to Polycarp as extremely dubious, on account of the difference of style; and, indeed, the whole question relating to the epistles of St. Ignatius in general seems to me to labour under much obscurity, and to be embarrassed with many difficulties" ("Eccles. Hist.," p. 22).

"There are in all fifteen epistles which bear the name of Ignatius. These are the following: One to the Virgin Mary, two to the Apostle John, one to Mary of Cassobelæ, one to the Tarsians, one to the Antiochians, one to Hero (a deacon of Antioch), one to the Philippians, one to the Ephesians, one to the Magnesians, one to the Trallians, one to the Romans, one to the Philadelphians, one to the Smyrnians, and one to Polycarp. The first three exist only in Latin; all the rest are extant also in Greek. It is now the universal opinions of critics that the first eight of these professedly Ignatian letters are spurious. They bear in themselves indubitable proofs of being the production of a later age than that in which Ignatius lived. Neither Eusebius nor Jerome makes the least reference to them; and they are now, by common consent, set aside as forgeries, which were at various dates, and to serve special purposes, put forth under the name of the celebrated Bishop of Antioch. But, after the question has been thus simplified, it still remains sufficiently complex. Of the seven epistles which are acknowledged by Eusebius" ("Eccles. Hist," bk. iii., chap. 36), we possess two Greek recensions, a shorter and a longer. "It is plain that one or other of these exhibits a corrupt text; and scholars have, for the most part, agreed to accept the shorter form as representing the genuine letters of Ignatius.... But although the shorter form of the Ignatian letters had been generally accepted in preference to the longer, there was still a pretty prevalent opinion among scholars that even it could not be regarded as absolutely free from interpolations, or as of undoubted authenticity.... Upon the whole, however, the shorter recension was, until recently, accepted without much opposition ... as exhibiting the genuine form of the epistles of Ignatius. But a totally different aspect was given to the question by the discovery of a Syriac version of three of these epistles among the MSS. procured from the monastery of St. Mary Deipara, in the desert of Nitria, in Egypt [between 1838 and 1842].... On these being deposited in the British Museum, the late Dr. Cureton, who then had charge of the Syriac department, discovered among them, first, the epistle to Polycarp, and then again the same epistle, with those to the Ephesians and to the Romans, in two other volumes of manuscripts" ("Apostolic Fathers," pp. 139-142). Dr. Cureton gave it as his opinion that the Syriac letters are "the only true and genuine letters of the venerable Bishop of Antioch that have either come down to our times or were ever known in the earliest ages of the Christian Church" ("Corpus Ignatianum," ed. 1849, as quoted in the "Apostolic Fathers," p. 142).

"I have carefully compared the two editions, and am very well satisfied upon that comparison that the larger are an interpolation of the smaller, and not the smaller an epitome or abridgment of the larger. I desire no better evidence in a thing of this nature.... But whether the smaller themselves are the genuine writings of Ignatius, Bishop of Antioch, is a question that has been much disputed, and has employed the pens of the ablest critics. And whatever positiveness some may have shown on either side, I must own I have found it a very difficult question" ("Credibility," pt. 2, vol. ii., p. 153). The Syriac version was then, of course, unknown. Professor Norton, the learned Christian defender of the Gospels, says: "The seven shorter epistles, the genuineness of which is contended for, come to us in bad company.... There is, as it seems to me, no reasonable doubt that the seven shorter epistles ascribed to Ignatius are equally, with all the rest, fabrications of a date long subsequent to his time." "I doubt whether any book, in its general tone of sentiment and language, ever betrayed itself as a forgery more clearly than do these pretended epistles of Ignatius" ("Genuineness of the Gospels," vol. i., pp. 350 and 353, ed. 1847).

"What, then, is the position of the so-called Ignatian epistles? Towards the end of the second century Irenæus makes a very short quotation from a source unnamed, which Eusebius, in the fourth century, finds in an epistle attributed to Ignatius. Origen, in the third century, quotes a few words, which he ascribes to Ignatius, although without definite reference to any particular epistle; and, in the fourth century, Eusebius mentions seven epistles ascribed to Ignatius. There is no other evidence. There are, however, fifteen epistles extant, all of which are attributed to Ignatius, of all of which, with the exception of three, which are only known in a Latin version, we possess both Greek and Latin versions. Of seven of these epistles—and they are those mentioned by Eusebius—we have two Greek versions, one of which is very much shorter than the other; and, finally, we now possess a Syriac version of three epistles, only in a form still shorter than the shorter Greek version, in which are found all the quotations of the Fathers, without exception, up to the fourth century. Eight of the fifteen epistles are universally rejected as spurious (ante, p. 263). The longer Greek version of the remaining seven epistles is almost unanimously condemned as grossly interpolated; and the great majority of critics recognise that the shorter Greek version is also much interpolated; whilst the Syriac version, which, so far as MSS. are concerned, is by far the most ancient text of any letters which we possess, reduces their number to three, and their contents to a very small compass indeed. It is not surprising that the vast majority of critics have expressed doubt more or less strong regarding the authenticity of all these epistles, and that so large a number have repudiated them altogether. One thing is quite evident—that, amidst such a mass of falsification, interpolation, and fraud, the Ignatian epistles cannot, in any form, be considered evidence on any important point.... In fact, the whole of the Ignatian literature is a mass of falsification and fraud" ("Sup. Rel.," vol. i., pp. 270, 271, 274). The student may judge from this confusion, of fifteen reduced to seven long, and seven long reduced to seven short, and seven short reduced to three, and those three very doubtful, how thoroughly reliable must be Paley's arguments drawn from this "contemporary of Polycarp." Our editors of the "Fathers" very frankly remark: "As to the personal history of Ignatius, almost nothing is known" ("Apostolic Fathers," p. 143). Why, acknowledging this, they call him "celebrated," it is hard to say. Truly, the ways of Christian commentators are dark!

Paley's quotation is taken from the epistle to the Smyrnaeans (not one of the Syriac, be it noted), and is from the shorter Greek recension. It occurs in chap. iii., and only says that Peter, and those who were with him, saw Jesus after the resurrection, and believed: "for this cause also they despised death, and were found its conquerors." Men who believed in a resurrection might naturally despise death; but it is hard to see how this quotation—even were it authentic—shows that the apostles suffered for their belief. What strikes one as most remarkable—if Paley's contention of the sufferings of the witnesses be true, and these writings authentic—is that so very little mention is made of the apostles, of their labours, toils, and sufferings, and that these epistles are simply a kind of patchwork, chiefly of Old Testament materials, mixed up with exhortations about Christ.

The circular epistle of the Church of Smyrna is a curious document. Paley quotes a terrible account of the tortures inflicted, and one would imagine on reading it that many must have been put to death. We are surprised to learn, from the epistle itself, that Polycarp was only the twelfth martyr between the two towns of Smyrna and Philadelphia! The amount of dependence to be placed on the narrative may be judged by the following:—"As the flame blazed forth in great fury, we, to whom it was given to witness it, beheld a great miracle, and have been preserved that we might report to others what then took place. For the fire, shaping itself into the form of an arch, like the sail of a ship when filled with the wind, encompassed as by a circle the body of the martyr. And he appeared within, not like flesh which is burnt, but as bread that is baked, or as gold and silver glowing in a furnace. Moreover, we perceived such a sweet odour, as if frankincense or some such precious spices had been burning there. At length, when those men perceived that his body could not be consumed by the fire, they commanded an executioner to go near, and pierce him with a dagger. And on his doing this, there came forth a dove, and a great quantity of blood, so that the fire was extinguished" ("Apostolic Fathers," p. 92). What reliance can be placed on historians(?) who gravely relate that fire does not burn, and that when a man is pierced with a dagger a dove flies out, together with sufficient blood to quench a flaming pile? To make this precious epistle still more valuable, one of its transcribers adds to it:—"I again, Pionius, wrote them (these things) from the previously written copy, having carefully searched into them, and the blessed Polycarp having manifested them to me through a revelation[!] even as I shall show in what follows. I have collected these things, when they had almost faded away through the lapse of time" (Ibid, p. 96). If this is history, then any absurd dream may be taken as the basis of belief. We may add that this epistle does not mention the martyrdoms of the eye-witnesses, and it is hard to know why Paley drags it in, unless he wants to make us believe that his eye-witnesses suffered all the tortures he quotes; but even Paley cannot pretend that there is a scintilla of proof of their undergoing any such trials. Thus falls the whole argument based on the "twelve men, whose probity and good sense I had long known," dying for the persistent assertion of "a miracle wrought before their eyes," who are used as a parallel of the apostles, as an argument against Hume. For we have not yet proved that there were any eye-witnesses, or that they made any assertions, and we have entirely failed to prove that the eye-witnesses were martyred at all, or that the death of any one of them, save that of Peter, is even mentioned in the alleged documents, so that the "satisfactory evidences" of the "original witnesses of the Christian miracles" suffering and dying in attestation of those miracles amount to this, that in a disputed document Peter is said to have been martyred, and in another, still more doubtful, "the rest of the apostles" are said to have "suffered." Thus the first proposition of Paley falls entirely to the ground. The honest truth is that the history of the twelve apostles is utterly unknown, and that around their names gathers a mass of incredible and nonsensical myth and legend, similar in kind to other mythological fables, and entirely unworthy of credence by reasonable people.

Nor is proof less lacking of submission "from the same motives, to new rules of conduct." Nowhere is there a sign that Christian morality was enforced by appeal to the 2miracles of Christ; miracles were, in those days, too common an incident to attract much attention, and, indeed, if they could not win belief in the mission from those Jews before whom they were said to have been performed, what chance would they have had when the story of their working was only repeated by hearsay? Again, the rules of conduct were not "new;" the best parts of the Christian morality had been taught long before Christ (as we shall prove later on by quotations), and were familiar to the Greeks, Romans, and Egyptians, from the writings of their own philosophers. There would have been nothing remarkable in a new sect growing up among these peoples, accustomed as they were to the schools of the philosophers, with their various groups of disciples distinguished by special names. Why is there anything more wonderful in these Christian societies with a high moral code, than in the severe and stately morality inculcated and practised by the Stoics? For the submission of conduct to the "new rules," the less said the better. 1 Corinthians does not give us a very lofty idea of the morality current among the Christians there, and the angry reproaches of Jude imply much depravity; the messages to the seven Churches are generally reproving, not to dwell on many scattered passages of the same character. Outsiders, moreover, speak very harshly of the Christian societies. Tacitus—whose testimony must be allowed some weight, if he be quoted as a proof of the existence of the sect—says that they were held in abhorrence for their crimes, and were condemned for their "enmity to mankind" (the expression of Tacitus may either mean haters of mankind, or hated by mankind), expressions which show that the adherents of the higher and purer morality were, at least, singularly unfortunate in the impressions of it which they conveyed to their neighbours by their lives; and we find, further, the most scandalous crimes imputed to the Christians, necessitating the enforcement against them of edicts passed to put down the shameful Bacchanalian mysteries. And here, indeed, is the true cause of the persecution to which they were subjected under the just and merciful Roman sway, and this is a point that should not be lost sight of by the student.

About 186 B.C., according to Livy (lib. xxxix. c. 8-19), the Roman Government, discovering that certain "Bacchanalian mysteries" were habitually celebrated in Rome, issued stern edicts against the participants in them, and succeeding in, at least partially, suppressing them. The reason given by the Consul Postumius for these edicts was political, not religious. "Could they think," he asked, "that youths, initiated under such oaths as theirs, were fit to be made soldiers? That wretches brought out of the temple of obscenity could be trusted with arms? That those contaminated with the foul debaucheries of these meetings should be the champions for the chastity of the wives and children of the Roman people?" "Let us now closely examine how far the Eleusinian and Bacchanalian feasts resembled the Christian Agapae—whether the latter, modified and altered a little according to the change which would take place in the taste of the age, originated from the former, or were altogether from a different source. We have seen that the forementioned Pagan feasts were, throughout Italy, in a very flourishing state about 186 years before the Christian era. We have also seen that about this time they were, at least, partially suppressed in Italy, and those who were wont to take part in them dispersed over the world. Being zealously devoted to the religion of which these feasts were part, it is very natural to suppose that, wherever the votaries of this superstition settled, they soon established these feasts, which they were enabled to carry on secretly, and, therefore, for a considerable time, undetected.... Both Pagans and Christians, in ancient times, were particularly careful not to disclose their mysteries; to do so, in violation of their oaths, would cost their lives" ("The Prophet of Nazareth," by E.P. Meredith, notes, pp. 225, 226). Mr. Meredith then points out how in Rome, in Lyons, in Vienne, "the Christians were actually accused of murdering children and others—of committing adultery, incest, and other flagrant crimes in their secret lovefeasts. The question, therefore, arises—were they really guilty of the barbarous crimes with which they were so often formally charged, and for the commission of which they were almost as often legally condemned, and punished with death? Is it probable that persons at Rome, who had once belonged to these lovefeasts, should tell a deliberate falsehood that the Christians perpetrated these abominable vices, and that other persons in France, who had also been connected with these feasts, should falsely state that the Christians were guilty of the very same execrable crimes? There was no collusion or connection whatever between these parties, and in making their statements, they could have no self-interested motive. They lived in different countries, they did not make their statements within twenty years of the same time, and by making such statements they rendered themselves liable to be punished with death.... The same remark applies to the disclosures made, about 150 years after, by certain females in Damascus, far remote from either Lyons or Rome. These make precisely the same statement—that they had once been Christians, that they were privy to criminal acts among them, and that these Christians, in their very churches, committed licentious deeds. The Romans would never have so relentlessly persecuted the Christians had they not been guilty of some such atrocities as were laid to their charge. There are on record abundant proofs that the Romans, from the earliest account we have of them, tolerated all harmless religions— all such as were not directly calculated to endanger the public peace, or vitiate public morals, or render life and property unsafe.... So well known were those horrid vices to be carried on by all Christians in their nocturnal and secret assemblies, and so certain it was thought that every one who was a Christian participated in them, that for a person to be known to be a Christian was thought a strong presumptive proof that he was guilty of these offences. Hence, persons in their preliminary examinations, who, on being interrogated, answered that they were Christians, were thought proper subjects for committal to prison.... Pliny further indicates that while some brought before him, on information, refused to tell him anything as to the nature of their nocturnal meetings, others replied to his questions as far as their oath permitted them. They told him that it was their practice, as Christians,

25

to meet on a stated day, before daylight, to sing hymns; and to bind themselves by a solemn oath that they would do no wrong; that they would not steal, nor rob, nor commit any act of unchastity; that they would never violate a trust; and that they joined together in a common and innocent repast. While all these answers to the questions of the Proconsul are suggestive of the crimes with which the Christians were charged, still they are a denial of every one of them.... The whole tenor of historical facts is, however, against their testimony, and the Proconsul did not believe them; but, in order to get at the entire truth, put some of them to the torture, and ultimately adjourned their trial [see ante, pp. 203-205]. The manner in which Greek and Latin writers mention the Christians goes far to show that they were guilty of the atrocious crimes laid to their charge. Suetonius (in Nero) calls them, 'A race of men of new and villainous superstition' [see ante, p. 201]. The Emperor Adrian, in a letter to his brother-in-law, Servianus, in the year 134, as given by Vospicius, says: 'There is no presbyter of the Christians who is not either an astrologer, a soothsayer, or a minister of obscene pleasures.' Tacitus tells us that Nero inflicted exquisite punishment upon those people who, under the vulgar appellation of Christians, were held in abhorrence for their crimes. He also, in the same place, says they were 'odious to mankind;' and calls their religion a 'pernicious superstition' [see ante, p. 99]. Maximus, likewise, in his letter, calls them 'votaries of execrable vanity,' who had 'filled the world with infamy.' It would appear, however, that owing to the extreme measures taken against them by the Romans, both in Italy and in all the provinces, the Christians, by degrees, were forced to abandon entirely in their Agapae infant murders, together with every species of obscenity, retaining, nevertheless, some relics of them, such as the kiss of charity, and the bread and wine, which they contended was transubstantiated into real flesh and blood.... A very common way of repelling these charges was for one sect of Christians, which, of course, denounced all other sects as heretics, to urge that human sacrifices and incestuous festivals were not celebrated by that sect, but that they were practised by other sects; such, for example, as the Marcionites and the Capocratians. (Justin Mart., 'Apology,' i., 35; Iren., adv. Haer. i., 24; Clem. Alex., i., 3.) When Tertullian joined the Montanists, another sect of Christians, he divulged the criminal secrets of the Church which he had so zealously defended, by saying, in his 'Treatise on Fasting,' c. 17, that 'in the Agapae the young men lay with their sisters, and wallowed in wantonness and luxury'.... Remnants of these execrable customs remained for a long time, and vestiges of them exist to this very day, as well in certain words and phrases as in practice. The communion table to this very day is called the altar, the name of that upon which the ancients sacrificed their victims. The word sacrament has a meaning, as used by Pliny already cited, which carries us back to the solemn oath of the Agapaeists. The word mass carries us back still further, and

26

identifies the present mass with that of the Pagans.... Formerly the consecrated bread was called host, which word signifies a victim offered as sacrifice, anciently human very often.... Jerome and other Fathers called the communion bread—little body, and the communion table—mystical table; the latter, in allusion to the heathen and early Christian mysteries, and the former, in reference to the children sacrificed at the Agapae. The great doctrine of transubstantiation directly points to the abominable practice of eating human flesh at the Agapae.... Upon the whole, it is impossible, from the mass of evidence already adduced, to avoid the conclusion that the early Christians, in their Agapae, were really guilty of the execrable vices with which they were so often charged, and for which they were sentenced to death. This once admitted, a reasonable and adequate cause can be assigned for the severe persecutions of the Christians by the Roman Government—a Government which applied precisely the same laws and modes of persecution and punishment to them as to the votaries of the Bacchanalian and Eleusinian mysteries, well known to have been accustomed to offer human sacrifices, and indulge in the most obscene lasciviousness in their secret assemblies; and a Government which tolerated all kinds of religions, except those which encouraged practices dangerous to human life, or pernicious to the morals of subjects. Nor can the facts already advanced fail to show clearly that the Christian Agapae were of Pagan origin—were identically the same as those Pagan feasts which existed simultaneously with them" (Ibid, notes, pp. 227, 231).

There can be no doubt that the Christians suffered for these crimes whether or no they were guilty of them: "Three things are alleged against us: Atheism, Thyestean feasts, OEdipodean intercourse," says Athenagoras ("Apology," ch. iii). Justin Martyr refers to the same charges ("2nd Apology," ch. xii). "Monsters of wickedness, we are accused of observing a holy rite, in which we kill a little child and then eat it, in which after the feast we practise incest.... Come, plunge your knife into the babe, enemy of none, accused of none, child of all; or if that is another's work, simply take your place beside a human being dying before he has really lived, await the departure of the lately-given soul, receive the fresh young blood, saturate your bread with it, freely partake" ("Apology," Tertullian, secs. 7, 8). Tertullian pleads earnestly that these accusations were false: "if you cannot do it, you ought not to believe it of others. For a Christian is a man as well as you" (Ibid). Yet, when Tertullian became a Montanist, he declared that these very crimes were committed at the Agapae, so that he spoke falsely either in the one case or in the other. "It was sometimes faintly insinuated, and sometimes boldly asserted, that the same bloody sacrifices and the same incestuous festivals, which were so falsely ascribed to the orthodox believers, were in reality celebrated by the Marcionites, by the Carpocratians, and by several other sects of the

Gnostics.... Accusations of a similar kind were retorted upon the Church by the schismatics who had departed from its communion; and it was confessed on all sides that the most scandalous licentiousness of manners prevailed among great numbers of those who affected the name of Christians. A Pagan magistrate, who possessed neither leisure nor abilities to discern the almost imperceptible line which divides the orthodox faith from heretical depravity, might easily have imagined that their mutual animosity had extorted the discovery of their common guilt" ("Decline and Fall," Gibbon, vol. ii., pp. 204, 205). It was fortunate, the historian concludes, that some of the magistrates reported that they discovered no such criminality. It is, be it noted, simultaneously with the promulgation of these charges that the persecution of the Christians takes place; during the first century very little is heard of such, and there is very little persecution [see ante, pp. 209-213]. In the following century the charges are frequent, and so are the persecutions.

To these strong arguments may be added the acknowledgment in 1. Cor. xi., 17, 22, of disorder and drunkenness at these Agapae; the habit of speaking of the communion feast as "the Christian mysteries," a habit still kept up in the Anglican prayer-book; the fact that they took place at night, under cover of darkness, a custom for which there was not the smallest reason, unless the service were of a nature so objectionable as to bring it under the ban of the tolerant Roman law; and lastly, the use of the cross, and the sign of the cross, the central Christian emblem, and one that, especially in connection with the mysteries, is of no dubious signification. Thus, in the twilight in which they were veiled in those early days, the Christians appear to us as a sect of very different character to that bestowed upon them by Paley. A little later, when they emerge into historical light, their own writers give us sufficient evidence whereby we may judge them; and we find them superstitious, grossly ignorant, quarrelsome, cruel, divided into ascetics and profligates, between whom it is hard to award the palm for degradation and indecency.

Having "proved"—in the above fashion—that a number of people in the first century advanced "an extraordinary story," underwent persecution, and altered their manner of life, because of it, Paley thinks it "in the highest degree probable, that the story for which these persons voluntarily exposed themselves to the fatigues and hardships which they endured, was a miraculous story; I mean, that they pretended to miraculous evidence of some kind or other" ("Evidences," p. 64). That the Christians believed in a miraculous story may freely be acknowledged, but it is evidence of the truth of the story that we want, not evidence of their belief in it. Many ignorant people believe in witchcraft and in fortune-telling now-a-days, but their belief only proves their own ignorance, and not the truth of either superstition. The next step in the argument is that "the story which Christians have now" is "the story which Christians had then" and it is urged that there is in existence no trace of any story of Jesus Christ "substantially different from ours" ("Evidences," p. 69). It is hard to judge how much difference is covered by the word "substantially." All the apocryphal gospels differ very much from the canonical, insert sayings and doings of Christ not to be found in the received histories, and make his character the reverse of good or lovable to a far greater extent than "the four." That Christ was miraculously born, worked miracles, was crucified, buried, rose again, ascended, may be accepted as "substantial" parts of the story. Yet Mark and John knew nothing of the birth, while, if the Acts and the Epistles are to be trusted, the apostles were equally ignorant; thus the great doctrine of the Incarnation of God without natural generation, is thoroughly ignored by all save Matthew and Luke, and even these destroy their own story by giving genealogies of Jesus through Joseph, which are useless unless Joseph was his real father. The birth from a virgin, then has no claim to be part of Paley's miraculous story in the earliest times. The evidence of miracle-working by Christ to be found in the Epistles is chiefly conspicuous by its absence, but it figures largely in post-apostolic works. The crucifixion, resurrection, and ascension are generally acknowledged, and these three incidents compose the whole story for which a consensus of testimony can be claimed; it will, perhaps, be fair to concede also that Christ is recognised universally as a miracle-worker, in spite of the strange silence of the epistles. We need not refer to the testimony of Clement, Polycarp or Ignatius, having already shown what dependence may be placed on their writings. But we have now three new witnesses, Barnabas, Quadratus, and Justin Martyr. Paley says: "In an epistle, bearing the name of Barnabas, the companion of Paul, probably genuine, certainly belonging to that age, we have the sufferings of Christ," etc. (Evidences p. 75). "Probably genuine, certainly belonging to that age!" Is Paley joking with his readers, or only trading on their ignorance? "The letter itself bears no author's name, is not dated from any place, and is not addressed to any special community. Towards the end of the second century, however, tradition began to ascribe it to Barnabas, the companion of Paul. The first writer who mentions it is Clement of Alexandria [head of the Alexandrian School, A.D. 20who calls its author several times the 'Apostle Barnabas'.... We have already seen in the case of the Epistles ascribed to Clement of Rome, and, as we proceed, we shall become only too familiar with the fact, the singular facility with which, in the total absence of critical discrimination, spurious writings were ascribed by the Fathers to Apostles and their followers.... Credulous piety which attributed writings to every Apostle, and even to Jesus himself, soon found authors for each anonymous work of an edifying character.... In the earlier days of criticism, some writers, without much question, adopted the traditional view as to the authorship of the Epistles, but the great mass of critics are now agreed in asserting that the composition, which itself is perfectly anonymous, cannot be attributed to Barnabas the friend and fellow worker of Paul. Those who maintain the former opinion date the Epistle about A.D. 70-73, or even earlier, but this is scarcely the view of any living critic" ("Supernatural Religion," vol. i., pp. 237-239).

"From its contents it seems unlikely that it was written by a companion of Apostles and a Levite. In addition to this, it is probable that Barnabas died before A.D. 62; and the letter contains not only an allusion to the destruction of the Jewish temple, but also affirms the abnegation of the Sabbath, and the general celebration of the Lord's Day, which seems to show that it could not have been written before the beginning of the second century" ("Westcott on the Canon," p. 41). "Nothing certain is known as to the author of the following epistle. The writer's name is Barnabas; but scarcely any scholars now ascribe it to the illustrious friend and companion of St. Paul.... The internal evidence is now generally regarded as conclusive against this opinion.... The external evidence [ascribing it to Barnabas] is of itself weak, and should not make us hesitate for a moment in refusing to ascribe this writing to Barnabas, the apostle.... The general opinion is, that its date is not later than the middle of the second century, and that it cannot be placed earlier than some twenty or thirty years or so before. In point of style, both as respects thought and expression, a very low place must be assigned it. We know nothing certain of the region in which the author lived, or where the first readers were to be found" ("Apostolic Fathers," pp. 99, 100). The Epistle is not ascribed to Barnabas at all until the close of the second century. Eusebius marks it as "spurious" ("Eccles. Hist," bk. iii., chap. xxv). Lardner speaks of it as "probably Barnabas's, and certainly ancient" ("Credibility," pt. ii., vol. ii., p. 30). When we see the utter conflict of evidence as to the writings of all these "primitive" authors, we can scarcely wonder at the frank avowal of the Rev. Dr. Giles: "The writings of the Apostolical Fathers labour under a more heavy load of doubt and suspicion than any other ancient compositions, either sacred or profane" ("Christian Records," p. 53).

Paley, in quoting "Quadratus," does not tell us that the passage he quotes is the only writing of Quadratus extant, and is only preserved by Eusebius, who says that he takes it from an apology addressed by Quadratus to the Emperor Adrian. Adrian reigned from A.D. 117-138, and the apology must consequently have been presented between these dates. If the apology be genuine, Quadratus makes the extraordinary assertion that some of the people raised from the dead by Jesus were then living. Jesus is only recorded to have raised three people—a girl, a young man, and Lazarus; we will take their ages at ten, twenty, and thirty. "Some of" those raised cannot be less than two out of the three; we will say the two youngest. Then they were alive at the respectable ages of from 95-116, and from 105-126. The first may be taken as just within the limits of possibility; the second as beyond them; but

Quadratus talks in a wholesale fashion, which quite destroys his credibility, and we can lay but little stress on the carefulness or trustworthiness of a historian who speaks in such reckless words. Added to this, we find no trace of this passage until Eusebius writes it in the fourth century, and it is well known that Eusebius was not too particular in his quotations, thinking that his duty was only to make out the best case he could. He frankly says: "We are totally unable to find even the bare vestiges of those who may have travelled the way before us; unless, perhaps, what is only presented in the slight intimations, which some in different ways have transmitted to us in certain partial narratives of the times in which they lived.... Whatsoever, therefore, we deem likely to be advantageous to the proposed subject we shall endeavour to reduce to a compact body" ("Eccles. Hist.," bk. i., chap. i). Accordingly, he produces a full Church History out of materials which are only "slight intimations," and carefully draws out in detail a path of which not "even the bare vestiges" are left. Little wonder that he had to rely so much upon his imagination, when he had to build a church, and had no straws for his bricks.

Paley brings Justin Martyr (born about A.D. 103, died about A.D. 167) as his last authority—as after his time the story may be taken as established—and says: "From Justin's works, which are still extant, might be collected a tolerably complete account of Christ's life, in all points agreeing with that which is delivered in our Scriptures; taken, indeed, in a great measure, from those Scriptures, but still proving that this account, and no other, was the account known and extant in that age" ("Evidences," p. 77). If "no other" account was extant, Justin must have largely drawn on his own imagination when he pretends to be quoting. Jesus, according to Justin, is conceived "of the Word" ("Apol.," i. 33), not of the Holy Ghost, the third person, the Holy Ghost being said to be identical with the Word; and he is thus conceived by himself. He is born, not in Bethlehem in a stable, but in a "cave near the village," because Joseph could find no lodging in Bethlehem ("Dial." 78). The magi come, not from "the East," but from Arabia ("Dial." 77). Jesus works as a carpenter, making ploughs and yokes ("Dial." 88). The story of the baptism is very different ("Dial." 88). In the trial Jesus is set on the judgment seat, and tauntingly bidden to judge his accusers ("Apol.," i. 35). All the apostles deny him, and forsake him, after he is crucified ("Apol.," i. 50). These instances might be increased, and, as we shall see later, Justin manifestly quotes from accounts other than the canonical gospels. Yet Paley pretends that "no other" account was extant, and that in the very face of Luke i. 1, which declares that "many have taken in hand" the writing of such histories. If Paley had simply said that the story of a miracle-worker, named the Anointed Saviour, who was born of a virgin, was crucified, rose and ascended into heaven, was told with many variations among the Christians. from about 100 years after his supposed birth, he would have spoken truly; and had he added to this, that the very same story was told among Egyptians and Hindoos, many hundreds of years earlier, he would have treated his readers honestly, although he might not thereby have increased their belief in the "divine origin of Christianity."

Before we pass on to the last evidences offered by Paley, which necessitate a closer investigation into the value of the testimony borne by the patristic, to the canonical, writings, it will be well to put broadly the fact, that these Fathers are simply worthless as witnesses to any matter of fact, owing to the absurd and incredible stories which they relate with the most perfect faith. Of critical faculty they have none; the most childish nonsense is accepted by them, with the gravest face; no story is too silly, no falsehood too glaring, for them to believe and to retail, in fullest confidence of its truth. Gross ignorance is one of their characteristics; they are superstitious, credulous, illiterate, to an almost incredible extent. Clement considers that "the Lord continually proves to us that there shall be a future resurrection" by the following "fact," among others: "Let us consider that wonderful sign which takes place in Eastern lands—that is, in Arabia and the countries round about. There is a certain bird which is called a phoenix. This is the only one of its kind, and lives 500 years. And when the time of its dissolution draws near that it must die, it builds itself a nest of frankincense, and myrrh, and other spices, into which, when the time is fulfilled, it enters and dies. But, as the flesh decays, a certain kind of worm is produced, which, being nourished by the juices of the dead bird, brings forth feathers. Then, when it has acquired strength, it takes up that nest in which are the bones of its parent, and, bearing these, it passes from the land of Arabia into Egypt, to the city called Heliopolis. And in open day, flying in the sight of all men, it places them on the altar of the sun, and, having done this, hastens back to its former abode. The priests then inspect the registers of the dates, and find that it has returned exactly as the 500th year was completed" (1st Epistle of Clement, chap. xxv.). Surely the evidence here should satisfy Paley as to the truth of this story: "the open day," "flying in the sight of all men," the priests inspecting the registers, and all this vouched for by Clement himself! How reliable must be the testimony of the apostolic Clement! Tertullian, the Apostolic Constitutions, and Cyril of Jerusalem mention the same tale. We have already drawn attention to that which was seen by the writers of the circular letter of the Church of Smyrna. Barnabas loses himself in a maze of allegorical meanings, and gives us some delightful instruction in natural history; he is dealing with the directions of Moses as to clean and unclean animals: "'Thou shalt not,' he says, 'eat the hare.' Wherefore? 'Thou shalt not be a corrupter of boys, nor like unto such.' Because the hare multiplies, year by year, the places of its conception; for as many years as it lives, so many foramina it has. Moreover, 'Thou shalt not eat the hyaena.'... Wherefore? Because that animal annually changes its sex, and is at one time male, and at another female. Moreover, he has rightly detested the weasel ... For this animal conceives by the mouth.... Behold how well Moses legislated" (Epistle of Barnabas, chapter x.). "'And Abraham circumcised ten and eight and three hundred men of his household.' What, then, was the knowledge given to him in this? Learn the eighteen first, and then the three hundred. The ten and the eight are thus denoted—Ten by I, and Eight by H. You have Jesus. And because the cross was to express the grace by the letter T, he says also Three Hundred. He signifies, therefore, Jesus by two letters, and the cross by one.... No one has been admitted by me to a more excellent piece of knowledge than this, but I know that ye are worthy" (Ibid, chapter ix.). And this is Paley's companion of the Apostles! Ignatius tells us of the "star of Bethlehem." "A star shone forth in heaven above all other stars, and the light of which was inexpressible, while its novelty struck men with astonishment. And all the rest of the stars, with the sun and moon, formed a chorus to this star" (Epistle to the Ephesians, chap. xix.). Why should we accept Ignatius' testimony to the star, and reject his testimony to the sun and moon and stars singing to it? Or take Origen against Celsus: "I have this further to say to the Greeks, who will not believe that our Saviour was born of a virgin: that the Creator of the world, if he pleases, can make every animal bring forth its young in the same wonderful manner. As, for instance, the vultures propagate their kind in this uncommon way, as the best writers of natural history do acquaint us" (chap, xxxiii., as quoted in "Diegesis," p. 319). Or shall we turn to Irenæus, so invaluable a witness, since he knew Polycarp, who knew John, who knew Jesus? Listen, then, to the reminiscences of John, as reported by Irenæus: "John related the words of the Lord concerning the times of the kingdom of God: the days would come when vines would grow, each with 10,000 shoots, and to each shoot 10,000 branches, and to each branch 10,000 twigs, and to each twig 10,000 clusters, and to each cluster 10,000 grapes, and each grape which is crushed will yield twenty-five measures of wine. And when one of the saints will reach after one of these clusters, another will cry: 'I am a better cluster than it; take me, and praise the Lord because of me.' Likewise, a grain of wheat will produce 10,000 ears, each ear 10,000 grains, each grain ten pounds of fine white flour. Other fruits, and seeds, and herbs in proportion. The whole brute creation, feeding on such things as the earth brings forth, will become sociable and peaceable together, and subject to man with all humility" ("Iren. Haer.," v., 33, 3-4, as quoted in Keim's "Jesus of Nazara," p. 45). What trust can be placed in the truth of facts to which these men pretend to bear witness when we find St. Augustine preaching that "he himself, being at that time Bishop of Hippo Regius, had preached the Gospel of our Lord and Saviour Jesus Christ to a whole nation of men and women that had no heads, but had their eyes in their bosoms; and in countries still more southerly he preached to a nation among whom each individual had but one eye, and that situate in the middle of the forehead" ("Syntagma," p. 33, as quoted in "Diegesis," p. 257).

Eusebius tells us of a man, named Sanctus, who was tortured until his body "was one continued wound, mangled and shrivelled, that had entirely lost the form of man;" and, when the tormentors began again on the same day, he "recovered the former shape and habit of his limbs" ("Eccles. Hist," bk. v., chap. i.). He then was sent to the amphitheatre, passing down the lane of scourgers, was dragged about and lacerated by the wild beast, roasted in an iron chair, and after this was "at last dispatched!" Other accounts, such as that of a man scourged till his bones were "bared of the flesh," and then slowly tortured, are given as history, as though a man in that condition would not speedily bleed to death. But it is useless to give more of these foolish stories, which weary us as we toil through the writings of the early Church. Well may Mosheim say that the "Apostolic Fathers, and the other writers, who, in the infancy of the Church, employed their pens in the cause of Christianity, were neither remarkable for their learning nor their eloquence" ("Eccles. Hist," p. 32). Thoroughly unreliable as they are, they are useless as witnesses of supposed miraculous events; and, in relating ordinary occurrences, they should not be depended upon in any matter of importance, unless they be corroborated by more trustworthy historians.

The last point Paley urges in support of his proposition is, that the accounts contained in "the historical Books of the New Testament" are "deserving of credit as histories," and that such is "the situation of the authors to whom the four Gospels are ascribed that, if any one of the four be genuine, it is sufficient for our purpose." This brings us, indeed, to the crucial point of our investigation, for, as we can gain so little information from external sources, we are perforce driven to the Christian writings themselves. If they break down under criticism as completely as the external evidences have done, then Christianity becomes hopelessly discredited as to its historical basis, and must simply take rank with the other mythologies of the world. But before we can accept the writings as historical, we are bound to investigate their authenticity and credibility. Does the external evidence suffice to prove their authenticity? Do the contents of the books themselves commend them as credible to our intelligence? It is possible that, although the historical evidence authenticating them be somewhat defective, yet the thorough coherency and reasonableness of the books may induce us to consider them as reliable; or, if the latter points be lacking from the supernatural character of the occurrences related, yet the evidence of authenticity may be so overwhelming as to place the accuracy of the accounts beyond cavil. But if external evidence be wanting, and internal evidence be fatal to the truthfulness of the writings, then it will become our duty to remove them from the temple of history, and to place them in the fairy gardens of fancy and of myth, where they may amuse and instruct the student, without misleading him as to questions of fact.

The positions which we here lay down are:—

a. That forgeries bearing the names of Christ, and of the apostles, and of the early Fathers, were very common in the primitive Church.

b. That there is nothing to distinguish the canonical from the apocryphal writings.

c. That it is not known where, when, by whom, the canonical writings were selected.

d. That before about A.D. 180 there is no trace of four Gospels among the Christians.

e. That before that date Matthew, Mark, Luke, and John are not selected as the four evangelists.

f. That there is no evidence that the four Gospels mentioned about that date were the same as those we have now.

g. That there is evidence that two of them were not the same.

h. That there is evidence that the earlier records were not the Gospels now esteemed canonical.

i. That the books themselves show marks of their later origin.

j. That the language in which they are written is presumptive evidence against their authenticity.

k. That they are in themselves utterly unworthy of credit, from (1) the miracles with which they abound, (2) the numerous contradictions of each by the others, (3) the fact that the story of the hero, the doctrines, the miracles, were current long before the supposed dates of the Gospels; so that these Gospels are simply a patchwork composed of older materials.

Paley begins his argument by supposing that the first and fourth Gospels were written by the apostles Matthew and John, "from personal knowledge and recollection" ("Evidences," p. 87), and that they must therefore be either true, or wilfully false; the latter being most improbable, as they would then be "villains for no end but to teach honesty, and martyrs without the least prospect of honour or advantage" (Ibid, page 88). But supposing that Matthew and John wrote some Gospels, we should need proof that the Gospels which we have, supposing them to be copies of those thus written, have not been much altered since they left the apostles' hands. We should next ask how Matthew can report from "personal knowledge and recollection" all that comes in his Gospel before he was called from his tax-gathering, as well as many incidents at which he was not present? and whether his reliability as a witness is not terribly weakened by his making no distinction between what was fact within his own knowledge, and what was simple hearsay? Further, we remark that some of the teaching is the reverse of teaching "honesty," and that such instruction as Matt. v. 39-42 would, if accepted, exactly suit "villains;"

that the extreme glorification of the master would naturally be reflected upon "the twelve" who followed him, and the authority of the writers would thereby be much increased and confirmed; that pure moral teaching on some points is no guarantee of the morality of the teacher, for a tyrant, or an ambitious priest, would naturally wish to discourage crime of some kinds in those he desired to rule; that such tyrant or priest could find no better creed to serve his purpose than meek, submissive, non-resisting, heaven-seeking Christianity. Thus we find Mosheim saying of Constantine: "It is, indeed, probable that this prince perceived the admirable tendency of the Christian doctrine and precepts to promote the stability of government, by preserving the citizens in their obedience to the reigning powers, and in the practice of those virtues that render a State happy" ("Eccles. Hist," p. 87). We discover Charlemagne enforcing Christianity among the Saxons by sword and fire, hoping that it would, among other things, "induce them to submit more tamely to the government of the Franks" (Ibid, p. 170). And we see missionaries among the savages usurping "a despotic dominion over their obsequious proselytes" (Ibid, p. 157); and "St. Boniface," the "apostle of Germany," often employing "violence and terror, and sometimes artifice and fraud, in order to multiply the number of Christians" (Ibid, p. 169). Thus do "villains" very often "teach honesty." Nor is it true that these apostles were "martyrs [their martyrdom being unproved] without the least prospect of honour or advantage;" on the contrary, they desired to know what they would get by following Jesus. "What shall we have, therefore?... Ye which have followed me shall sit upon twelve thrones" (Matt. xix. 27-30); and, further, in Mark ix. 28-31, we are told that any one who forsakes anything for Jesus shall receive "an hundredfold now in this time," as well as eternal life in the world to come. Surely, then, there was "prospect" enough of "honour and advantage"? These remarks apply quite as strongly to Mark and Luke, neither of whom are pretended to be eye-witnesses. Of Mark we know nothing, except that it is said that there was a man named John, whose surname was Mark (Acts xii. 12 and 25), who ran away from his work (Acts xv. 38); and a man named Marcus, nephew of Barnabas (Col. iv. 10), who may, or may not, be the same, but is probably somebody else, as he is with Paul; and one of the same name is spoken of (2 Tim. ii.) as "profitable for the ministry," which John Mark was not, and who (Philemon 24) was a "fellow-labourer" with Paul in Rome, while John Mark was rejected in this capacity by Paul at Antioch. Why Mark, or John Mark, should write a Gospel, he not having been an eye-witness, or why Mark, or John Mark, should be identical with Mark the Evangelist, only writers of Christian evidences can hope to understand.

A. That forgeries, bearing the names of Christ, of the apostles, and of the early Fathers, were very common in the primitive Church.

"The opinions, or rather the conjectures, of the learned

concerning the time when the books of the New Testament were collected into one volume, as also about the authors of that collection, are extremely different. This important question is attended with great and almost insuperable difficulties to us in these latter times" (Mosheim's "Eccles. Hist.," p. 31). These difficulties arise, to a great extent, from the large number of forgeries, purporting to be writings of Christ, of the apostles, and of the apostolic Fathers, current in the early Church. "For, not long after Christ's ascension into heaven, several histories of his life and doctrines, full of pious frauds and fabulous wonders, were composed by persons whose intentions, perhaps, were not bad, but whose writings discovered the greatest superstition and ignorance. Nor was this all; productions appeared which were imposed upon the world by fraudulent men, as the writings of the holy apostles" (Ibid, p. 31). "Another erroneous practice was adopted by them, which, though it was not so universal as the other, was yet extremely pernicious, and proved a source of numberless evils to the Christian Church. The Platonists and Pythagoreans held it as a maxim, that it was not only lawful, but even praiseworthy, to deceive, and even to use the expedient of a lie, in order to advance the cause of truth and piety. The Jews, who lived in Egypt, had learned and received this maxim from them, before the coming of Christ, as appears incontestably from a multitude of ancient records; and the Christians were infected from both these sources with the same pernicious error, as appears from the number of books attributed falsely to great and venerable names, from the Sibylline verses, and several supposititious productions which were spread abroad in this and the following century. It does not, indeed, seem probable that all these pious frauds were chargeable upon the professors of real Christianity, upon those who entertained just and rational sentiments of the religion of Jesus. The greatest part of these fictitious writings undoubtedly flowed from the fertile invention of the Gnostic sects, though it cannot be affirmed that even true Christians were entirely innocent and irreproachable in this matter" (Ibid, p. 55). "This disingenuous and vicious method of surprising their adversaries by artifice, and striking them down, as it were, by lies and fiction, produced, among other disagreeable effects, a great number of books, which were falsely attributed to certain great men, in order to give these spurious productions more credit and weight" (Ibid, page 77). These forged writings being so widely circulated, it will be readily understood that "It is not so easy a matter as is commonly imagined rightly to settle the Canon of the New Testament. For my own part, I declare, with many learned men, that, in the whole compass of learning, I know no question involved with more intricacies and perplexing difficulties than this. There are, indeed, considerable difficulties relating to the Canon of the Old Testament, as appears by the large controversies between the Protestants and Papists on this head in the last, and latter end of the preceding, century; but these are solved with much more ease than those of the New.... In settling the old Testament collection, all that is requisite is to disprove the claim of a few obscure books, which have but the weakest pretences to be looked upon as Scripture; but, in the New, we have not only a few to disprove, but a vast number to exclude [from] the Canon, which seem to have much more right to admission than any of the apocryphal books of the Old Testament; and, besides, to evidence the genuineness of all those which we do receive, since, according to the sentiments of some who would be thought learned, there are none of them whose authority has not been controverted in the earliest ages of Christianity.... The number of books that claim admission [to the canon] is very considerable. Mr. Toland, in his celebrated catalogue, has presented us with the names of above eighty.... There are many more of the same sort which he has not mentioned" (J. Jones on "The Canon of the New Testament," vol. i., pp. 2-4. Ed. 1788).

The following list will give some idea of the number of the apocryphal writings from which the four Gospels, and other books of the New Testament, finally emerge as canonical:—

GOSPELS

1. Gospel according to the Hebrews.
2. Gospel written by Judas Iscariot.
3. Gospel of Truth, made use of by the Valentinians.
4. Gospel of Peter.
5. Gospel according to the Egyptians.
6. Gospel of Valentinus.
7. Gospel of Marcion.
8. Gospel according to the Twelve Apostles.
9. Gospel of Basilides.
10. Gospel of Thomas (extant).
11. Gospel of Matthias.
12. Gospel of Tatian.
13. Gospel of Scythianus.
14. Gospel of Bartholomew.
15. Gospel of Apelles.
16. Gospels published by Lucianus and Hesychius
17. Gospel of Perfection.
18. Gospel of Eve.
19. Gospel of Philip.
20. Gospel of the Nazarenes (qy. same as first)
21. Gospel of the Ebionites.
22. Gospel of Jude.
23. Gospel of Encratites.
24. Gospel of Cerinthus.
25. Gospel of Merinthus.

26. Gospel of Thaddaeus.

27. Gospel of Barnabas.

28. Gospel of Andrew.

29. Gospel of the Infancy (extant).

30. Gospel of Nicodemus, or Acts of Pilate and Descent of Christ to the Under World (extant).

31. Gospel of James, or Protevangelium (extant).

32. Gospel of the Nativity of Mary (extant).

33. Arabic Gospel of the Infancy (extant).

34. Syriac Gospel of the Boyhood of our Lord Jesus (extant).

MISCELLANEOUS

35. Letter to Agbarus by Christ (extant).

36. Letter to Leopas by Christ (extant).

37. Epistle to Peter and Paul by Christ.

38. Epistle by Christ produced by Manichees.

39. Hymn by Christ (extant).

40. Magical Book by Christ.

41. Prayer by Christ (extant).

42. Preaching of Peter.

43. Revelation of Peter.

44. Doctrine of Peter.

45. Acts of Peter.

46. Book of Judgment by Peter.

47. Book, under the name of Peter, forged by Lentius.

48. Preaching of Peter and Paul at Rome.

49. The Vision, or Acts of Paul and Thecla.

50. Acts of Paul.

51. Preaching of Paul.

52. Piece under name of Paul, forged by an "anonymous writer in Cyprian's time."

53. Epistle to the Laodiceans under name of Paul (extant).

54. Six letters to Seneca under name of Paul (extant).

55. Anabaticon or Revelation of Paul.

56. The traditions of Matthias.

57. Book of James.

58. Book, under name of James, forged by Ebionites.

59. Acts of Andrew, John, and Thomas.

60. Acts of John.

61. Book, under name of John, forged by Ebionites.

62. Book under name of John.

63. Book, under name of John, forged by Lentius.

64. Acts of Andrew.

65. Book under name of Andrew.

66. Book, under name of Andrew, by Naxochristes and Leonides.

67. Book under name of Thomas.

68. Acts of Thomas.

69. Revelation of Thomas.

70. Writings of Bartholomew.

71. Book, under name of Matthew, forged by Ebionites.

72. Acts of the Apostles by Leuthon, or Seleucus.

73. Acts of the Apostles used by Ebionites.

74. Acts of the Apostles by Lenticius.

75. Acts of the Apostles used by Manichees.

76. History of the Twelve Apostles by Abdias (extant).

77. Creed of the Apostles (extant).

78. Constitutions of the Apostles (extant).

79. Acts, under Apostles' names, by Leontius.

80. Acts, under Apostles' names, by Lenticius.

81. Catholic Epistle, in imitation of the Apostles of Themis, on the Montanists.

82. Revelation of Cerinthus, nominally apostolical.

83. Book of the Helkesaites which fell from Heaven.

84. Books of Lentitius.

85. Revelation of Stephen.

86. Works of Dionysius the Areopagite (extant).

87. History of Joseph the carpenter (extant).

88. Letter of Agbarus to Jesus (extant).

89. Letter of Lentulus (extant).

90. Story of Veronica (extant).

91. Letter of Pilate to Tiberius (extant).

92. Letters of Pilate to Herod (extant).

93. Epistle of Pilate to Cæsar (extant).

94. Report of Pilate the Governor (extant).

95. Trial and condemnation of Pilate (extant).

96. Death of Pilate (extant).

97. Story of Joseph of Arimathraea (extant).

98. Revenging of the Saviour (extant).

99. Epistle of Barnabas.

100. Epistle of Polycarp.

101-15. Fifteen epistles of Ignatius (see above, pages 217-220.)

116. Shepherd of Hermas.

117. First Epistle to the Corinthians of Clement (possibly partly authentic).

118. Second Epistle to the Corinthians of Clement.

119. Apostolic Canons of Clement.

120. Recognitions of Clement and Clementina.

121-122. Two Epistles of St. Clement of Rome (written in Syriac).

123-128. Six books of Justin Martyr.

129-132. Four books of Justin Martyr.

The above are collected from Jones' On the Canon, Supernatural Religion, Eusebius, Mosheim's Ecclesiastical History, Cowper's Apocryphal Gospels, Dr. Giles' Christian Records, and the Apostolic Fathers.

After reading this list, the student will be able to appreciate the value of Paley's argument, that, "if it had been an easy thing in the early times of the institution to have forged Christian writings, and to have obtained currency and reception to the forgeries, we should have had many appearing in the name of Christ himself" ("Evidences," p. 106). Paley acknowledges "one attempt of this sort, deserving of the smallest notice;" and, in a note, adds three more of those mentioned above. Let us see what the evidence is of the genuineness of the letter to Agbarus, the "one attempt" in question, as given by Eusebius. Agbarus, the prince of Edessa, reigning "over the nations beyond the Euphrates with great glory," was afflicted with an incurable disease, and, hearing of Jesus, sent to him to entreat deliverance. The letter of Agbarus is carried to Jesus, "at Jerusalem, by Ananias, the courier," and the answer of Jesus, also written, is returned by the same hands. The letter of Jesus runs as follows, and is written in Syriac: "Blessed art thou, O Agbarus, who, without seeing me, hast believed in me! For it is written concerning me, that they who have seen me will not believe, that they who have not seen me may believe and live. But in regard to what thou hast written, that I should come to thee, it is necessary that I should fulfil all things here, for which I have been sent. And, after this fulfilment, thus to be received again by Him that sent me. And after I have been received up, I will send to thee a certain one of my disciples, that he may heal thy affliction, and give life to thee, and to those who are with thee." After the ascension of Jesus, Thaddaeus, one of the seventy, is sent to Edessa, and lodges in the house of Tobias, the son of Tobias, and heals Agbarus and many others. "These things were done in the 340th year" (Eusebius does not state what he reckons from). The proof given by Eusebius for the truth of the account is as follows: "Of this also we have the evidence, in a written answer, taken from the public records of the city of Edessa, then under the government of the king. For, in the public registers there, which embrace the ancient history and the transactions of Agbarus, these circumstances respecting him are found still preserved down to the present day. There is nothing, however, like hearing the epistles themselves, taken by us from the archives, and the style of it, as it has been literally translated by us, from the Syriac language" ("Eccles. Hist.," bk. i., chap. xiii.). And Paley calls this an attempt at forgery, "deserving of the smallest notice," and dismisses it in a few lines. It would be interesting to know for what other "Scripture," canonical or uncanonical, there is evidence of authenticity so strong as for this; exactness of detail in names; absence of any exaggeration more than is implied in recounting any miracle; the transaction recorded in the public archives; seen there by Eusebius

41

himself; copied down and translated by him; such evidence for any one of the Gospels would make belief far easier than it is at present. The assertion of Eusebius was easily verifiable at the time (to use the favourite argument of Christians for the truth of any account); and if Eusebius here wrote falsely, of what value is his evidence on any other point? A Freethinker may fairly urge that Eusebius is not trustworthy, and that this assertion of his about the archives is as likely to be false as true; but the Christian can scarcely admit this, when so much depends, for him, on the reliability of the great Church historian, all whose evidence would become worthless if he be once allowed to have deliberately fabricated that which did not exist.

We have already noticed the writings of the Apostolic Fathers, and pointed out the numerous forgeries circulated under their names, and the consequent haze hanging over all the early Christian writers, until we reach the time of Justin Martyr. Thus we entirely destroy the whole basis of Paley's argument, that "the historical books of the New Testament ... are quoted, or alluded to, by a series of Christian writers, beginning with those who were contemporary with the Apostles, or who immediately followed them" ("Evidences," page 111;) for we have no certain writings of any such contemporaries. In dealing with the positions f. and h., we shall seek to prove that in the writings of the Apostolic Fathers—taking them as genuine—as well as in Justin Martyr, and in other Christian works up to about A.D. 180, the quotations said to be from the canonical Gospels conclusively show that other Gospels were used, and not our present ones; but no further evidence than the long list of apocryphal writings, given on pp. 240-243 is needed in order to prove our first proposition, that forgeries, bearing the name of Christ, of the apostles, and of the early fathers, were very common in the primitive Church.

B. "That there is nothing to distinguish the canonical from the apocryphal writings." "Their pretences are specious and plausible, for the most part going under the name of our Saviour himself, his apostles, their companions, or immediate successors. They are generally thought to be cited by the first Christian writers with the same authority (at least, many of them) as the sacred books we receive. This Mr. Toland labours hard to persuade us; but, what is more to be regarded, men of greater merit and probity have unwarily dropped expressions of the like nature. Everybody knows (says the learned Casaubon against Cardinal Baronius) that Justin Martyr, Clemens Alexandrinus, Tertullian, and the rest of the primitive writers, were wont to approve and cite books which now all men know to be apocryphal. Clemens Alexandrinus (says his learned annotator, Sylburgius) was too much pleased with apocryphal writings. Mr. Dodwell (in his learned dissertation on Irenæus) tells us that, till Trajan, or, perhaps, Adrian's time, no canon was fixed; the supposititious pieces of the heretics were received by the faithful, the

42

apostles' writings bound up with theirs, and indifferently used in the churches. To mention no more, the learned Mr. Spanheim observes, that Clemens Alexandrinus and Origen very often cite apocryphal books under the express name of Scripture.... How much Mr. Whiston has enlarged the Canon of the New Testament, is sufficiently known to the learned among us. For the sake of those who have not perused his truly valuable books I would observe, that he imagines the 'Constitutions of the Apostles' to be inspired, and of greater authority than the occasional writings of single Apostles and Evangelists. That the two Epistles of Clemens, the Doctrine of the Apostles, the Epistle of Barnabas, the Shepherd of Hermas, the second book of Esdras, the Epistles of Ignatius, and the Epistle of Polycarp, are to be reckoned among the sacred authentic books of the New Testament; as also that the Acts of Paul, the Revelation, Preaching, Gospel and Acts of Peter, were sacred books, and, if they were extant, should be of the same authority as any of the rest" (J. Jones, on the "Canon," p. 4-6). This same learned writer further says: "That many, or most of the books of the New Testament, have been rejected by heretics in the first ages, is also certain. Faustus Manichæus and his followers are said to have rejected all the New Testament, as not written by the Apostles. Marcion rejected all, except St. Luke's Gospel. The Manichees disputed much against the authority of St. Matthew's Gospel. The Alogians rejected the Gospel of St. John as not his, but made by Cerinthus. The Acts of the Apostles were rejected by Severus, and the sect of his name. The same rejected all Paul's Epistles, as also did the Ebionites, and the Helkesaites. Others, who did not reject all, rejected some particular epistles.... Several of the books of the New Testament were not universally received, even among them who were not heretics, in the first ages.... Several of them have had their authority disputed by learned men in later times" (Ibid, pp. 8, 9).

If recognition by the early writers be taken as a proof of the authenticity of the works quoted, many apocryphal documents must stand high. Eusebius, who ranks together the Acts of Paul, the Shepherd of Hermas, the Revelation of Peter, the Epistle of Barnabas, the Institutions of the Apostles, and the Revelation of John (now accounted canonical) says that these were not embodied in the Canon (in his time) "notwithstanding that they are recognised by most ecclesiastical writers" ("Eccles. Hist.," bk. iii., chap. xxv.). The Canon, in his time, was almost the same as at present, but the canonicity of the epistles of James and Jude, the 2nd of Peter, the 2nd and 3rd of John, and the Revelation, was disputed even as late as when he wrote. Irenæus ranks the Pastor of Hermas as Scripture; "he not only knew, but also admitted the book called Pastor" (Ibid, bk. v., chap. viii.). "The Pastor of Hermas is another work which very nearly secured permanent canonical rank with the writings of the New Testament. It was quoted as Holy Scripture by the Fathers, and held to be divinely inspired, and it was publicly read in the churches. It has place with the Epistle of Barnabas in the Sinaitic Codex, after the canonical books" ("Supernatural Religion," vol. i., p. 261).

The two Epistles of Clement are only "preserved to us in the Codex Alexandrinus, a MS. assigned by the most competent judges to the second half of the fifth, or beginning of the sixth century, in which these Epistles follow the books of the New Testament. The second Epistle ... thus shares with the first the honour of a canonical position in one of the most ancient codices of the New Testament" ("Sup. Rel.," vol. i., p. 220). These epistles are, also, amongst those mentioned in the Apostolic Canons. "Until a comparatively late date this [the first of Clement] Epistle was quoted as Holy Scripture" (Ibid, p. 222). Origen quotes the Epistle of Barnabas as Scripture, and calls it a "Catholic Epistle" (Ibid, p. 237), and this same Father regards the Shepherd of Hermas as also divinely inspired. (Norton's "Genuineness of the Gospels," vol. i., p. 341). Gospels, other than the four canonical, are quoted as authentic by the earliest Christian writers, as we shall see in establishing position h; thus destroying Paley's contention ("Evidences," p. 187) that there are no quotations from apocryphal writings in the Apostolical Fathers, the fact being that such quotations are sown throughout their supposed writings.

It is often urged that the expression, "it is written," is enough to prove that the quotation following it is of canonical authority.

"Now with regard to the value of the expression, 'it is written,' it may be remarked that in no case could its use, in the Epistle of Barnabas, indicate more than individual opinion, and it could not, for reasons to be presently given, be considered to represent the opinion of the Church. In the very same chapter in which the formula is used in connection with the passage we are considering, it is also employed to introduce a quotation from the Book of Enoch, [Greek: peri hou gegraptai hos Henoch legei], and elsewhere (c. xii.) he quotes from another apocryphal book as one of the prophets.... He also quotes (c. vi.) the apocryphal book of Wisdom as Holy Scripture, and in like manner several unknown works. When it is remembered that the Epistle of Clement to the Corinthians, the Pastor of Hermas, the Epistle of Barnabas itself, and many other apocryphal works have been quoted by the Fathers as Holy Scripture, the distinctive value of such an expression may be understood" (Ibid, pp. 242, 243). "The first Christian writers ... quote ecclesiastical books from time to time as if they were canonical" (Westcott on "The Canon," p. 9). "In regard to the use of the word [Greek: gegraptai], introducing the quotation, the same writer [Hilgenfeld] urges reasonably enough that it cannot surprise us at a time when we learn from Justin Martyr that the Gospels were read regularly at public worship [or rather, that the memorials of the Apostles were so read]; it ought not, however, to be pressed too far as involving a claim to special divine inspiration, as the same word is used in the epistle in regard to the apocryphal book of Enoch; and it is clear, also, from Justin, that the Canon of the Gospels was not yet formed, but only forming" ("Gospels in the Second Century," Rev. W. Sanday, p. 73. Ed. 1876). Yet, in spite of all this, Paley says, "The phrase, 'it is written,' was the very form in which the Jews quoted their Scriptures. It is not probable, therefore, that he would have used this phrase, and without qualification, of any books but what had acquired a kind of Scriptural authority" ("Evidences," p. 113). Tischendorf argues on Paley's lines and says that "it was natural, therefore, to apply this form of expression to the Apostles' writings, as soon as they had been placed in the Canon with the books of the Old Testament. When we find, therefore, in ancient ecclesiastical writings, quotations from the Gospels introduced with this formula, 'it is written,' we must infer that, at the time when the expression was used, the Gospels were certainly treated as of equal authority with the books of the Old Testament" ("When Were Our Gospels Written?" p. 89. Eng. Ed., 1867). Dr. Tischendorf, if he believe in his own argument, must greatly enlarge his Canon of the New Testament.

Paley's further plea that "these apocryphal writings were not read in the churches of Christians" ("Evidences," p. 187) is thoroughly false. Eusebius tells us of the Pastor of Hermas: "We know that it has been already in public use in our churches" ("Eccles. Hist.," bk. iii., ch. 3). Clement's Epistle "was publicly read in the churches at the Sunday meetings of Christians" ("Sup. Rel," vol. i., p. 222). Dionysius of Corinth mentions this same early habit of reading any valued writing in the churches: "In this same letter he mentions that of Clement to the Corinthians, showing that it was the practice to read in the churches, even from the earliest times. 'To-day,' says he, 'we have passed the Lord's holy-day, in which we have read your epistle, in reading which we shall always have our minds stored with admonition, as we shall, also, from that written to us before by Clement'" (Eusebius' "Eccles. Hist.," bk. iv., ch. 23). So far is "reading in the churches" to be accepted as a proof, even of canonicity, much less of genuineness, that Eusebius remarks that "the disputed writings" were "publicly used by many in most of the churches" (Ibid, bk. iii., ch. 31). Paley then takes as a further mark of distinction, between canonical and uncanonical, that the latter "were not admitted into their volume" and "do not appear in their catalogues," but we have already seen that the only MS. copy of Clement's first Epistle is in the Codex Alexandrinus (see ante p. 246), while the Epistle of Barnabas and the Pastor of Hermas find their place in the Sinaitic Codex (see ante p. 246); the second Epistle of Clement is also in the Codex Alexandrinus, and both epistles are in the Apostolic constitutions (see ante p. 247). The Canon of Muratori—worthless as it is, it is used as evidence by Christians—brackets the Apocalypse of John and of Peter ("Sup. Rel.," vol. ii., p. 241). Canon Westcott says: "'Apocryphal' writings were added to manuscripts of the New

Testament, and read in churches; and the practice thus begun continued for a long time. The Epistle of Barnabas was still read among the 'apocryphal Scriptures' in the time of Jerome; a translation of the Shepherd of Hermas is found in a MS. of the Latin Bible as late as the fifteenth century. The spurious Epistle to the Laodicenes is found very commonly in English copies of the Vulgate from the ninth century downwards, and an important catalogue of the Apocrypha of the New Testament is added to the Canon of Scripture subjoined to the Chronographia of Nicephorus, published in the ninth century" ("On the Canon," pp. 8, 9). Paley's fifth distinction, that they "were not noticed by their [heretical] adversaries" is as untrue as the preceding ones, for even the fragments of "the adversaries" preserved in Christian documents bear traces of reference to the apocryphal writings, although, owing to the orthodox custom of destroying unorthodox books, references of any sort by heretics are difficult to find. Again, Paley should have known, when he asserted that the uncanonical writings were not alleged as of authority, that the heretics did appeal to gospels other than the canonical. Marcion, for instance, maintained a Gospel varying from the recognised one, while the Ebionites contended that their Hebrew Gospel was the only true one. Eusebius further tells us of books "adduced by the heretics under the name of the Apostles, such, viz., as compose the Gospels of Peter, Thomas, and Matthew, and others beside them, or such as contain the Acts of the Apostles, by Andrew and John, and others" ("Eccles. Hist," bk. iii., ch. 25. See also ante p. 246). It is hard to believe that Paley was so grossly ignorant as to know nothing of these facts; did he then deliberately state what he knew to be utterly untrue? His last "mark" does not touch our position, as the commentaries, etc., are too late to be valuable as evidence for the alleged superiority of the canonical writings during the first two centuries. The other section of Paley's argument, that "when the Scriptures [a very vague word] are quoted, or alluded to, they are quoted with peculiar respect, as books sui generis" is met by the details given above as to the fashion in which the Fathers referred to the writings now called uncanonical, and by the evidence adduced in this section we may fairly claim to have proved that, so far as external testimony goes, there is nothing to distinguish the canonical from the apocryphal writings.

But there is another class of evidence relied upon by Christians, wherewith they seek to build up an impassable barrier between their sacred books and the dangerous uncanonical Scriptures, namely, the intrinsic difference between them, the dignity of the one, and the puerility of the other. Of the uncanonical Gospels Dr. Ellicott writes: "Their real demerits, their mendacities, their absurdities, their coarseness, the barbarities of their style, and the inconsequence of their narratives, have never been excused or condoned" ("Cambridge Essays," for 1856, p. 153, as quoted in introduction of "The Apocryphal

Gospels," by B.H. Cowper, p. x. Ed. 1867). "We know before we read them that they are weak, silly, and profitless—that they are despicable monuments even of religious fiction" (Ibid, p. xlvii). How far are such harsh expressions consonant with fact? It is true that many of the tales related are absurd, but are they more absurd than the tales related in the canonical Gospels? One story, repeated with variations, runs as follows: "This child Jesus, being five years old, was playing at the crossing of a stream, and he collected the running waters into pools, and immediately made them pure, and by his word alone he commanded them. And having made some soft clay, he fashioned out of it twelve sparrows; and it was the Sabbath when he did these things. And there were also many other children playing with him. And a certain Jew, seeing what Jesus did, playing on the Sabbath, went immediately and said to Joseph, his father, Behold, thy child is at the water-course, and hath taken clay and formed twelve birds, and hath profaned the Sabbath. And Joseph came to the place, and when he saw him, he cried unto him, saying, Why art thou doing these things on the Sabbath, which it is not lawful to do? And Jesus clapped his hands, and cried unto the sparrows, and said to them, Go away; and the sparrows flew up and departed, making a noise. And the Jews who saw it were astonished, and went and told their leaders what they had seen Jesus do" ("Gospel of Thomas: Apocryphal Gospels," B.H. Cowper, pp. 130, 131). Making the water pure by a word is no more absurd than turning water into wine (John ii. 1-11); or than sending an angel to trouble it, and thereby making it health-giving (John v. 2-4); or than casting a tree into bitter waters, and making them sweet (Ex. xv. 25). The fashioning of twelve sparrows out of soft clay is not stranger than making a woman out of a man's rib (Gen. ii. 21); neither is it more, or nearly so, curious as making clay with spittle, and plastering it on a blind man's eyes in order to make him see (John ix. 6); nay, arguing à la F.D. Maurice, a very strong reason might be made out for this proceeding. Thus, Jesus came to reveal the Father to men, and his miracles were specially arranged to show how God works in the world; by turning the water into wine, and by multiplying the loaves, he reminds men that it is God whose hand feeds them by all the ordinary processes of nature. In this instructive miracle of the clay formed into sparrows, which fly away at his bidding, Jesus reveals his unity with the Father, as the Word by whom all things were originally made; for "out of the ground, the Lord God formed every beast of the field and every fowl of the air" (Gen. ii. 19) at the creation, and when the Son was revealed to bring about the new creation, what more appropriate miracle could he perform than this reminiscence of paradise, clearly suggesting to the Jews that the Jehovah, who, of old, formed the fowls of the air out of the ground, was present among them in the incarnate Word, performing the same mighty work? Exactly in this fashion do Maurice, Robertson, and others of their school, deal with the miracles

47

of Christ recorded in the canonical gospels (see Maurice on the Miracles, Sermon IV., in "What is Revelation?"). The number, twelve, is also significant, being that of the tribes of Israel, and the local colouring—the complaining Jews and the violated Sabbath—is in perfect harmony with the other gospels. The action of Jesus, vindicating the conduct complained of by the performance of a miracle, is in the fullest accord with similar instances related in the received stories. It is, however, urged that some of the miracles of Jesus, as given in the apocrypha, are dishonouring to him, because of their destructive character; the son of Annas, the scribe, spills the water the child Jesus has collected, and Jesus gets angry and says, "Thou also shalt wither like a tree;" and "suddenly the boy withered altogether" (Ap. Gos., p. 131). This seems in thorough unity with the spirit Jesus showed in later life, when he cursed the fig-tree, because it did not bear fruit in the wrong season, and "presently the fig-tree withered away" (Matt. xxi. 19). Or a child, running against him purposely, falls dead; or a master lifting his hand against him, has the arm withered which essays to strike. Later, of Judas, who betrays him, we read that, "falling headlong, he burst asunder in the midst, and all his bowels gushed out" (Acts i. 18); while, in the Old Testament, which speaks of Christ, we are told, in figures, we learn that, when Jeroboam tried to seize a prophet, "his hand, which he put forth against him, dried up, so that he could not pull it in again to him" (1 Kings xiii. 4). If destructiveness be thought injurious when related of Jesus, what shall we say to the wanton destruction of the herd of swine which Jesus filled with devils, and sent racing into the sea? (Matt. viii. 28-34.) The miracle the child works to rectify a mistake of his father's in his carpenter's business, taking hold of some wood which has been cut too short and lengthening it, is certainly not more silly than the miracle worked by the man when money is short, and he (Matt. xvii. 24-27) sends Peter to catch a fish with money in its mouth (why not, by the way, have fished directly for the coin? it would be quite as possible for a coin to transfix itself on a hook, as for a fish, with a piece of money in its mouth, to swallow a hook). Other miracles recorded in the apocryphal gospels, of healing and of raising the dead, are identical in spirit with those told of him in the canonical. We may also remark that, unless there were some received traditions of miracles worked by Jesus in his household, there is no reason for the evident expectation of some help which is said to have been shown by Mary when the guests want wine at the wedding (John ii. 3-5). That verse 11 states that this was his first miracle is only one of the many inconsistencies of the gospel stories. Passing from these gospels of the infancy to those which tell of the sufferings of Jesus, we shall find in the "Gospel of Nicodemus, or Acts of Pilate," much that shows their full accordance with the received writings of the New Testament. This point is so important, as equalising the canonical and uncanonical gospels, that no excuse is needed for proving it by somewhat extensive extracts. The gospel opens as follows: "I, Ananias, a provincial warden, being a disciple of the law, from the divine Scriptures recognised our Lord Jesus Christ, and came to him by faith; and was also accounted worthy of holy baptism. Now, when searching the records of what was wrought in the time of our Lord Jesus Christ, which the Jews laid up under Pontius Pilate, I found that these Acts were written in Hebrew, and by the good pleasure of God I translated them into Greek for the information of all who call on the name of our Lord Jesus Christ, under the government of our Lord Flavius Theodosius, the 17th year, and in the 6th consulate of Flavius Valentinianus, in the 9th indiction." It may here be noted for what it is worth that Justin Martyr (1st Apology, chap, xxxv.) refers the Romans to the Acts of Pilate as public documents open to them, which is testimony far stronger than he gives to any canonical gospel. "In the 15th year of the government of Tiberius Cæsar, King of the Romans, and of Herod, King of Galilee, the 9th year of his reign, on the 8th before the calends of April, which is the 25th of March; in the consulship of Rufus and Rubellio; in the 4th year of the 202nd Olympiad, when Joseph Caiaphas was high priest of the Jews. Whatsoever, after the cross and passion of our Lord Jesus Christ, the Saviour God, Nicodemus recorded and wrote in Hebrew, and left to posterity, is after this fashion" ("Apocryphal Gospels," B.H. Cowper, pp. 229, 230). In the first chapter we learn how the Jews came to Pilate, and accuse Jesus, "that he saith he is the son of God and a king; moreover, he profaneth the Sabbaths, and wisheth to abolish the law of our fathers." After some conversation, Jesus is brought, and in chap. 2 we read the message from Pilate's wife, and "Pilate, having called the Jews, said to them, Ye know that my wife is religious, and inclined to practise Judaism with you. They said unto him, Yea, we know it. Pilate saith to them, Behold my wife hath sent to me, saying, Have nothing to do with this just man, for I have suffered very much because of him in the night. But the Jews answered, and said to Pilate, Did we not tell thee that he is a magician? Behold, he hath sent a dream to thy wife." The trial goes on, and Pilate declares the innocence of Jesus, and then confers with him as in John xviii. 33-37. Then comes the question (chaps, iii. and iv.): "Pilate saith unto him, What is truth? Jesus saith to him, Truth is from heaven. Pilate saith, Is truth not upon earth? Jesus saith to Pilate, Thou seest how they who say the truth are judged by those who have power upon earth. And, leaving Jesus within the prætorium, Pilate went out to the Jews, and saith unto them, I find no fault in him." The conversation between Pilate and the Jews is then related more fully than in the canonical accounts, and after this follows a scene of much pathos, which is far more in accord with the rest of the tale than the accepted story, wherein the multitude are represented as crying with one voice for his death. Nicodemus (chap. v.) first rises and speaks for Jesus: "Release him, and wish no evil against him. If the

49

miracles which he doth are of God, they will stand; but, if of men, they will come to nought... Now, therefore, release this man, for he is not deserving of death." Then (chaps. vi., vii., and viii.): "One of the Jews, starting up, asked the governor that he might say a word. The governor saith, If thou wilt speak, speak. And the Jew said, I lay thirty-eight years on my bed in pain and affliction. And when Jesus came, many demoniacs, and persons suffering various diseases, were healed by him; and some young men had pity on me, and carried me with my bed, and took me to him; and when Jesus saw me, he had compassion, and said the word to me, Take up thy bed, and walk; and I took up my bed and walked. The Jews said to Pilate, Ask him what day it was when he was healed. He that was healed said, On the Sabbath. The Jews said, Did we not tell thee so? that on the Sabbath he healeth and casteth out demons? And another Jew, starting up, said, I was born blind; I heard a voice, but saw no person; and as Jesus passed by, I cried with a loud voice, Have pity on me, Son of David, and he had pity on me, and placed his hands upon my eyes, and immediately I saw. And another Jew, leaping up, said, I was a cripple, and he made me straight with a word. And another said, I was a leper, and he healed me with a word. And a certain woman cried out from a distance, and said, I had an issue of blood, and I touched the hem of his garment, and my issue of blood, which had been for twelve years, was stayed. The Jews said, We have a law not to admit a woman to witness. And others, a multitude, both of men and of women, cried and said, This man is a prophet, and demons are subject unto him. Pilate said to those who said that demons were subject to him, Why were your teachers not also subject to him? They say unto Pilate, We know not. And others said, That he raised up Lazarus from the sepulchre, when he had been dead four days. And the governor, becoming afraid, said to all the multitude of the Jews, Why will ye shed innocent blood?" The story proceeds much as in the gospels, the names of the malefactors being given; and when Pilate remarks the three hours' darkness to the Jews, they answer, "An eclipse of the sun has happened in the usual manner" (chap. xi.). Chap. xiii. gives a full account of the conversation between the Jews and the Roman soldiers alluded to in Matt. xxviii. 11-15. The remaining chapters relate the proceedings of the Jews after the resurrection, and are of no special interest. There is a second Gospel of Nicodemus, varying on some points from the one quoted above, which assumes to be "compiled by a Jew, named Aeneas; translated from the Hebrew tongue into the Greek, by Nicodemus, a Roman Toparch." Then we find a second part of the Gospel of Nicodemus, or "The Descent of Christ to the Under World," which relates how Jesus descended into Hades, and how he ordered Satan to be bound, and then he "blessed Adam on the forehead with the sign of the cross; and he did this also to the patriarchs, and the prophets, and martyrs, and forefathers, and took them up, and sprang up out of Hades." This story manifestly runs side by side with the tradition in 1. Pet. iii. 19, 20, wherein it is stated that Jesus "went and preached unto the spirits in prison," and that preaching is placed between his death (v. 18) and his resurrection (v. 21). The saving by baptism (v. 21) is also alluded to in this connection in Nicodemus, wherein (chap. xi.) the dead are baptised. The Latin versions of the Gospels of Nicodemus vary in details from the Greek, but not more than do the four canonical. In these, as in all the apocryphal writings, there is nothing specially to distinguish them from the accepted Scriptures; improbabilities and contradictions abound in all; miracles render them all alike incredible; myriad chains of similarity bind them all to each other, necessitating either the rejection of all as fabulous, or the acceptance of all as historical. Whether we regard external or internal evidence, we come to the same conclusion, that there is nothing to distinguish the canonical from the uncanonical writings.

C. That it is not known where, when, by whom, the canonical writings were selected. Tremendously damaging to the authenticity of the New Testament as this statement is, it is yet practically undisputed by Christian scholars. Canon Westcott says frankly: "It cannot be denied that the Canon was formed gradually. The condition of society and the internal relations of the Church presented obstacles to the immediate and absolute determination of the question, which are disregarded now, only because they have ceased to exist. The tradition which represents St. John as fixing the contents of the New Testament, betrays the spirit of a later age" (Westcott "On the Canon," p. 4). "The track, however, which we have to follow is often obscure and broken. The evidence of the earliest Christian writers is not only uncritical and casual, but is also fragmentary" (Ibid, p. 11). "From the close of the second century, the history of the Canon is simple, and its proof clear... Before that time there is more or less difficulty in making out the details of the question.... Here, however, we are again beset with peculiar difficulties. The proof of the Canon is embarrassed both by the general characteristics of the age in which it was fixed, and by the particular form of the evidence on which it first depends. The spirit of the ancient world was essentially uncritical" (Ibid, pp. 6-8). In dealing with "the early versions of the New Testament," Westcott admits that "it is not easy to over-rate the difficulties which beset any inquiry into the early versions of the New Testament" ("On the Canon," p. 231). He speaks of the "comparatively scanty materials and vague or conflicting traditions" (Ibid). The "original versions of the East and West" are carefully examined by him; the oldest is the "Peshito," in Syriac—i.e., Aramæan, or Syro-Chaldaic. This must, of course, be only a translation of the Testament, if it be true that the original books were written in Greek. The time when this version was formed is unknown, and Westcott argues that "the very obscurity which hangs over its origin is a proof of its venerable age" (Ibid, p. 240); and he refers it to "the first

51

half of the second century," while acknowledging that he does so "without conclusive authority" (Ibid). The Peshito omits the second and third epistles of John, second of Peter, that of Jude, and the Apocalypse. The origin of the Western version, in Latin, is quite as obscure as that of the Syriac; and it is also incomplete, compared with the present Canon, omitting the epistle of James and the second of Peter (Ibid, p. 254). All the evidence so laboriously gathered together by the learned Canon proves our proposition to demonstration. But, it is admitted on all hands, that "it is impossible to assign any certain time when a collection of these books, either by the Apostles, or by any council of inspired or learned men, near their time, was made.... The matter is too certain to need much to be said of it" (Jones "On the Canon," vol. i, p. 7). Jones adds that he hopes to confute "these specious objections ... in the fourth part of this book," in which he endeavours to prove the Gospels and Acts to be genuine, so that it does not much matter when they were collected together. In the time of Eusebius the Canon was still unsettled, as he ranks among the disputed and spurious works, the epistles of James and Jude, second of Peter, second and third of John, and the Apocalypse ("Eccles. Hist.," bk. iii., chap. 25). It is not necessary to offer any further proof in support of our position, that it is not known where, when, by whom, the canonical writings were selected.

D. That before about A.D. 180 there is no trace of FOUR gospels among the Christians. The first step we take in attacking the four canonical gospels, apart from the writings of the New Testament as a whole, is to show that there was no "sacred quaternion" spoken of before about A.D. 180, i.e., the supposed time of Irenæus. Irenæus is said to have been a bishop of Lyons towards the close of the second century; we find him mentioned in the letter sent by the Churches of Vienne and Lyons to "brethren in Asia and Phrygia," as "our brother and companion Irenæus," and as a presbyter much esteemed by them ("Eccles. Hist." bk. v., chs. 1, 4). This letter relates a persecution which occurred in "the 17th year of the reign of the Emperor Antoninus Verus," i.e., A.D. 177. Paley dates the letter about A.D. 170, but as it relates the persecution of A.D. 177, it is difficult to see how it could be written about seven years before the persecution took place. In that persecution Pothinus, bishop of Lyons, is said to have been slain; he was succeeded by Irenæus (Ibid bk. v., ch. 5), who, therefore, could not possibly have been bishop before A.D. 177, while he ought probably to be put a year or two later, since time is needed, after the persecution, to send the account of it to Asia by the hands of Irenæus, and he must be supposed to have returned and to have settled down in Lyons before he wrote his voluminous works; A.D. 180 is, therefore, an almost impossibly early date, but it is, at any rate, the very earliest that can be pretended for the testimony now to be examined. The works against heresies were probably written, the first three about A.D. 190, and the remainder about A.D. 198. Irenæus is the first Christian writer who mentions four Gospels; he says:—"Matthew produced his Gospel, written among the Hebrews, in their own dialect, whilst Peter and Paul proclaimed the Gospel and founded the church at Rome. After the departure of these, Mark, the disciple and interpreter of Peter, also transmitted to us in writing what had been preached by him. And Luke, the companion of Paul, committed to writing the Gospel preached by him. Afterwards John, the disciple of our Lord, the same that lay upon his bosom, also published the Gospel, whilst he was yet at Ephesus in Asia" (Quoted by Eusebius, bk. v., ch. 8, from 3rd bk. of "Refutation and Overthrow of False Doctrine," by Irenæus).

The reasons which compelled Irenæus to believe that there must be neither less nor more than four Gospels in the Church are so convincing that they deserve to be here put on record. "It is not possible that the Gospels can be either more or fewer in number than they are. For, since there are four zones [sometimes translated "corners" or "quarters"] of the world in which we live, and four Catholic spirits, while the Church is scattered throughout all the world, and the pillar and grounding of the Church is the Gospel and the spirit of life; it is fitting she should have four pillars, breathing out immortality on every side, and vivifying men afresh. From which fact it is evident that the Word, the Artificer of all, He that sitteth upon the Cherubim, and contains all things, He who was manifested to men, has given us the Gospel under four aspects, but bound together by one Spirit.... For the Cherubim too were four-faced, and their faces were images of the dispensation of the Son of God.... And, therefore, the Gospels are in accord with these things, among which Christ Jesus is seated" ("Irenæus," bk. iii., chap. xi., sec. 8). The Rev. Dr. Giles, writing on Justin Martyr, the great Christian apologist, candidly says: "The very names of the Evangelists Matthew, Mark, Luke, and John, are never mentioned by him—do not occur once in all his works. It is, therefore, childish to say that he has quoted from our existing Gospels, and so proves their existence, as they now are, in his own time.... He has nowhere remarked, like those Fathers of the Church who lived several ages after him, that there are four Gospels of higher importance and estimation than any others.... All this was the creation of a later age, but it is wanting in Justin Martyr, and the defect leads us to the conclusion that our four Gospels had not then emerged from obscurity, but were still, if in being, confounded with a larger mass of Christian traditions which, about this very time, were beginning to be set down in writing" ("Christian Records," pp. 71, 72).

Had these four Gospels emerged before A.D. 180, we should most certainly find some mention of them in the Mishna. "The Mishna, a collection of Jewish traditions compiled about the year 180, takes no notice of Christianity, though it contains a chapter headed 'De Cultu Peregrino, of strange worship.' This omission is thought by Dr. Paley to prove nothing, for, says he, 'it cannot be disputed but that Christianity was perfectly well known to the world at this time.' It cannot, certainly, be disputed that Christianity was beginning to be known to the world, but whether it had yet emerged from the lower classes of persons among whom it originated, may well be doubted. It is a prevailing error, in biblical criticism, to suppose that the whole world was feelingly alive to what was going on in small and obscure parts of it. The existence of Christians was probably known to the compilers of the Mishna in 180, even though they did not deign to notice them, but they could not have had any knowledge of the New Testament, or they would undoubtedly have noticed it; if, at least, we are right in ascribing to it so high a character, attracting (as we know it does) the admiration of every one in every country to which it is carried" (Ibid, p. 35).

There is, however, one alleged proof of the existence of four, and only four, Gospels, put forward by Paley:—Tatian, a follower of Justin Martyr, and who flourished about the year 170, composed a harmony or collection of the Gospels, which he called Diatessaron, of the Four. This title, as well as the work, is remarkable, because it shows, that then, as now, there were four and only four, Gospels in general use with Christians ("Evidences," pp. 154, 155). Paley does not state, until later, that the "follower of Justin Martyr" turned heretic and joined the Encratites, an ascetic and mystic sect who taught abstinence from marriage, and from meat, etc.; nor does he tell us how doubtful it is what the Diatessaron—now lost—really contained. He blandly assures us that it is a harmony of the four Gospels, although all the evidence is against him. Irenæus, as quoted by Eusebius, says of Tatian that "having apostatised from the Church, and being elated with the conceit of a teacher, and vainly puffed up as if he surpassed all others," he invented some new doctrines, and Eusebius further tells us: "Their chief and founder, Tatianus, having formed a certain body and collection of Gospels, I know not how, has given this the title Diatessaron, that is the Gospel by the four, or the Gospel formed of the four" ("Eccles. Hist," bk. iv., ch. 29). Could Eusebius have written that Tatian formed this, I know not how, if it had been a harmony of the Gospels recognised by the Church when he wrote? and how is it that Paley knows all about it, though Eusebius did not? And still further, after mentioning the Diatessaron, Eusebius says of another of Tatian's books: "This book, indeed, appears to be the most elegant and profitable of all his works" (Ibid). More profitable than a harmony of the four Gospels! So far as the name goes, as given by Eusebius, it would seem to imply one Gospel written by four authors. Epiphanius states: "Tatian is said to have composed the Gospel by four, which is called by some, the Gospel according to the Hebrews" ("Sup. Rel.," vol. ii., p. 155). Here we get the Diatessaron identified with the widely-spread and popular early Gospel of the Hebrews. Theodoret (circa A.D. 457) says that he found more than 200 such books in use in Syria, the

Christians not perceiving "the evil design of the composition;" and this is Paley's harmony of the Gospels! Theodoret states that he took these books away, "and instead introduced the Gospels of the four Evangelists;" how strange an action in dealing with so useful a work as a harmony of the Gospels, to confiscate it entirely and call it an evil design! To complete the value of this work as evidence to "four, and only four, Gospels," we are told by Victor of Capua, that it was also called Diapente, i.e., "by five" ("Sup. Rel.," vol. ii., p. 153). In fact, there is no possible reason for calling the work—whose contents ate utterly unknown—a harmony of the Gospels at all; the notion that it is a harmony is the purest of assumptions. There is some slight evidence in favour of the identity of the Diatessaron with the Gospel of the Hebrews. "Those, however, who called the Gospel used by Tatian the Gospel according to the Hebrews, must have read the work, and all that we know confirms their conclusion. The work was, in point of fact, found in wide circulation precisely in the places in which, earlier, the Gospel according to the Hebrews was more particularly current. The singular fact that the earliest reference to Tatian's 'harmony' is made a century and a half after its supposed composition, that no writer before the 5th century had seen the work itself, indeed, that only two writers before that period mention it at all, receives its natural explanation in the conclusion that Tatian did not actually compose any harmony at all, but simply made use of the same Gospel as his master Justin Martyr, namely, the Gospel according to the Hebrews, by which name his Gospel had been called by those best informed" ("Sup. Rel.," vol. ii., pp. 158, 159). As it is not pretended by any that there is any mention of four Gospels before the time of Irenæus, excepting this "harmony," pleaded by some as dated about A.D. 170, and by others as between 170 and 180, it would be sheer waste of time and space to prove further a point admitted on all hands. This step of our argument is, then, on solid and unassailable ground—that before about A.D. 180 there is no trace of FOUR Gospels among the Christians.

E. That, before that date, Matthew, Mark, Luke, and John, are not selected as the four evangelists. This position necessarily follows from the preceding one, since four evangelists could not be selected until four Gospels were recognised. Here, again, Dr. Giles supports the argument we are building up. He says: "Justin Martyr never once mentions by name the evangelists Matthew, Mark, Luke, and John. This circumstance is of great importance; for those who assert that our four canonical Gospels are contemporary records of our Saviour's ministry, ascribe them to Matthew, Mark, Luke, and John, and to no other writers. In this they are, in a certain sense, consistent; for contemporary writings [? histories] are very rarely anonymous. If so, how could they be proved to be contemporary? Justin Martyr, it must be remembered, wrote in 150; but neither he, nor any writer before him, has alluded, in the most remote degree, to four specific Gospels, bearing the names of Matthew, Mark, Luke, and John. Let those who think differently produce the passages in which such mention is to be found" ("Christian Records," Rev. Dr. Giles, p. 73). Two of these names had, however, emerged a little earlier, being mentioned as evangelists by Papias, of Hierapolis. His testimony will be fully considered below in establishing position g.

F. That there is no evidence that the four Gospels mentioned about that date were the same as those we have now. This brings us to a most important point in our examination; for we now attack the very key of the Christian position—viz., that, although the Gospels be not mentioned by name previous to Irenæus, their existence can yet be conclusively proved by quotations from them, to be found in the writings of the Fathers who lived before Irenæus. Paley says: "The historical books of the New Testament—meaning thereby the four Gospels and the Acts of the Apostles—are quoted, or alluded to, by a series of Christian writers, beginning with those who were contemporary with the Apostles or who immediately followed them, and proceeding in close and regular succession from their time to the present." And he urges that "the medium of proof stated in this proposition is, of all others, the most unquestionable, the least liable to any practices of fraud, and is not diminished by the lapse of ages" ("Evidences," pp. 111, 112). The writers brought in evidence are: Barnabas, Clement, Hermas, Ignatius, Polycarp, Papias, Justin Martyr, Hegesippus, and the epistle from Lyons and Vienne. Before examining the supposed quotations in as great detail as our space will allow, two or three preliminary remarks are needed on the value of this offered evidence as a whole.

In the first place, the greater part of the works brought forward as witnesses are themselves challenged, and their own dates are unknown; their now accepted writings are only the residuum of a mass of forgeries, and Dr. Giles justly says: "The process of elimination, which gradually reduced the so-called writings of the first century from two folio volumes to fifty slender pages, would, in the case of any other profane works, have prepared the inquirer for casting from him, with disgust, the small remnant, even if not fully convicted of spuriousness; for there is no other case in record of so wide a disproportion between what is genuine and what is spurious" ("Christian Records," p. 67). Their testimony is absolutely worthless until they are themselves substantiated; and from the account given of them above (pp 214-221, and 232-235), the student is in a position to judge of the value of evidence depending on the Apostolic Fathers. Professor Norton remarks: "When we endeavour to strengthen this evidence by appealing to the writings ascribed to Apostolical Fathers, we, in fact, weaken its force. At the very extremity of the chain of evidence, where it ought to be strongest, we are attaching defective links, which will bear no weight" ("Genuineness of the Gospels," vol. i., p. 357). Again, supposing that we admit these witnesses, their repetition of sayings of Christ, or references to his life, do not—in the absence of quotations specified by them as taken from Gospels written by Matthew, Mark, Luke, and John—prove that, because similar sayings or actions are recorded in the present canonical Gospels, therefore, these latter existed in their days, and were in their hands. Lardner says on this point: "Here is, however, one difficulty, and 'tis a difficulty which may frequently occur, whilst we are considering these very early writers, who were conversant with the Apostles, and others who had seen or heard our Lord; and were, in a manner, as well acquainted with our Saviour's doctrine and history as the Evangelists themselves, unless their quotations or allusions are very express and clear. The question, then, here is, whether Clement in these places refers to words of Christ, written and recorded, or whether he reminds the Corinthians of words of Christ, which he and they might have heard from the Apostles, or other eye-and-ear-witnesses of our Lord. Le Clerc, in his dissertation on the four Gospels, is of opinion that Clement refers to written words of our Lord, which were in the hands of the Corinthians, and well known to them. On the other hand, I find, Bishop Pearson thought, that Clement speaks of words which he had heard from the Apostles themselves, or their disciples. I certainly make no question but the three first Gospels were writ before this time. And I am well satisfied that Clement might refer to our written Gospels, though he does not exactly agree with them in expression. But whether he does refer to them is not easy to determine concerning a man who, very probably, knew these things before they were committed to writing; and, even after they were so, might continue to speak of them, in the same manner he had been wont to do, as things he was well informed of, without appealing to the Scriptures themselves" ("Credibility," pt. II., vol. i., pp. 68-70). Canon Westcott, after arguing that the Apostolic Fathers are much influenced by the Pauline Epistles, goes on to remark: "Nothing has been said hitherto of the coincidences between the Apostolic Fathers and the Canonical Gospels. From the nature of the case, casual coincidences of language cannot be brought forward in the same manner to prove the use of a history as of a letter. The same facts and words, especially if they be recent and striking, may be preserved in several narratives. References in the sub-apostolic age to the discourses or actions of our Lord, as we find them recorded in the Gospels, show, as far as they go, that what the Gospels relate was then held to be true; but it does not necessarily follow that they were already in use, and were the actual source of the passages in question. On the contrary, the mode in which Clement refers to our Lord's teaching—'the Lord said,' not 'saith'—seems to imply that he was indebted to tradition, and not to any written accounts, for words most closely resembling those which are still found in our Gospels. The main testimony of the Apostolic Fathers is, therefore, to the substance, and

57

not to the authenticity, of the Gospels" ("On the Canon," pp. 51, 52). An examination of the Apostolic Fathers gives us little testimony as to "the substance of the Gospels;" but the whole passage is here given to show how much Canon Westcott, writing in defence of the Canon, finds himself obliged to give up of the position occupied by earlier apologists. Dr. Giles agrees with the justice of these remarks of Lardner and Westcott. He writes: "The sayings of Christ were, no doubt, treasured up like household jewels by his disciples and followers. Why, then, may we not refer the quotation of Christ's words, occurring in the Apostolical Fathers, to an origin of this kind? If we examine a few of those quotations, the supposition, just stated, will expand into reality.... The same may be said of every single sentence found in any of the Apostolical Fathers, which, on first sight, might be thought to be a decided quotation from one of the Gospels according to Matthew, Mark, Luke, or John. It is impossible to deny the truth of this observation; for we see it confirmed by the fact that the Apostolical Fathers do actually quote Moses, and other old Testament writers, by name—'Moses hath said,' 'but Moses says,' etc.—in numerous passages. But we nowhere meet with the words, 'Matthew hath said in his Gospel,' 'John hath said,' etc. They always quote, not the words of the Evangelists, but the words of Christ himself directly, which furnishes the strongest presumption that, though the sayings of Christ were in general vogue, yet the evangelical histories, into which they were afterwards embodied, were not then in being. But the converse of this view of the case leads us to the same conclusion. The Apostolical Fathers quote sayings of Christ which are not found in our Gospels.... There is no proof that our New Testament was in existence during the lives of the Apostolical Fathers, who, therefore, could not make citations out of books which they had never seen" ("Christian Records," pp. 51-53). "There is no evidence that they [the four Gospels] existed earlier than the middle of the second century, for they are not named by any writer who lived before that time" (Ibid, p. 56). In searching for evidence of the existence of the Gospels during the earlier period of the Church's history, Christian apologists have hitherto been content to seize upon a phrase here and there somewhat resembling a phrase in the canonical Gospels, and to put that forward as a proof that the Gospels then were the same as those we have now. This rough-and-ready plan must now be given up, since the most learned Christian writers now agree, with the Freethinkers, that such a method is thoroughly unsatisfactory.

Yet, again, admitting these writers as witnesses, and allowing that they quote from the same Gospels, their quotations only prove that the isolated phrases they use were in the Gospels of their day, and are also in the present ones; and many such cases might occur in spite of great variations in the remainder of the respective Gospels, and would by no means prove that the Gospels they used were identical with ours.

If Josephus, for instance, had ever quoted some sentences of Socrates recorded by Plato, that quotation, supposing that Josephus were reliable, would prove that Plato and Socrates both lived before Josephus, and that Plato wrote down some of the sayings of Socrates; but it would not prove that a version of Plato in our hands to-day was identical with that used by Josephus. The scattered and isolated passages woven in by the Fathers in their works would fail to prove the identity of the Gospels of the second century with those of the nineteenth, even were they as like parallel passages in the canonical Gospels as they are unlike them.

It is "important," says the able anonymous writer of "Supernatural Religion," "that we should constantly bear in mind that a great number of Gospels existed in the early Church which are no longer extant, and of most of which even the names are lost. We will not here do more than refer, in corroboration of this fact, to the preliminary statement of the author of the third Gospel: 'Forasmuch as many ([Greek: polloi]) have taken in hand to set forth a declaration of those things which are surely believed among us, etc.' It is, therefore, evident that before our third synoptic was written, many similar works were already in circulation. Looking at the close similarity of the large portions of the three synoptics, it is almost certain that many of the [Greek: polloi] here mentioned bore a close analogy to each other, and to our Gospels; and this is known to have been the case, for instance, amongst the various forms of the 'Gospel according to the Hebrews,' distinct mention of which we meet with long before we hear anything of our Gospels. When, therefore, in early writings, we meet with quotations closely resembling, or, we may add, even identical with passages which are found in our Gospels—the source of which, however, is not mentioned, nor is any author's name indicated—the similarity, or even identity, cannot by any means be admitted as evidence that the quotation is necessarily from our Gospels, and not from some other similar work now no longer extant; and more especially not when, in the same writings, there are other quotations from apocryphal sources different from our Gospels. Whether regarded as historical records or as writings embodying the mere tradition of the early Christians, our Gospels cannot for a moment be recognised as the exclusive depositaries of the genuine sayings and doings of Jesus; and so far from the common possession by many works in early times of such words of Jesus, in closely similar form, being either strange or improbable, the really remarkable phenomena is that such material variation in the report of the more important historical teaching should exist amongst them. But whilst similarity to our Gospels in passages quoted by early writers from unnamed sources cannot prove the use of our Gospels, variation from them would suggest or prove a different origin; and, at least, it is obvious that quotations which do not agree with our Gospels cannot, in any case, indicate their existence" ("Sup. Rel.," vol. i., pp. 217-219).

We will now turn to the witness of Paley's Apostolic Fathers, bearing always in mind the utter worthlessness of their testimony; worthless as it is, however, it is the only evidence Christians have to bring forward to prove the identity of their Gospels with those [supposed to have been] written in the first century. Let us listen to the opinion given by Bishop Marsh: "From the Epistle of Barnabas, no inference can be deduced that he had read any part of the New Testament. From the genuine epistle, as it is called, of Clement of Rome, it may be inferred that Clement had read the first Epistle to the Corinthians. From the Shepherd of Hermas no inference whatsoever can be drawn. From the Epistles of Ignatius, it may be concluded that he had read St. Paul's Epistle to the Ephesians, and that there existed in his time evangelical writings, though it cannot be shown that he has quoted from them. From Polycarp's Epistle to the Philippians, it appears that he had heard of St. Paul's Epistle to that community, and he quotes a passage which is in the first Epistle to the Corinthians, and another which is in the Epistle to the Ephesians; but no positive conclusion can be drawn with respect to any other epistle, or any of the four Gospels" (Marsh's "Michaelis," vol. i., p. 354, as quoted in Norton's "Genuineness of the Gospels," vol. i., p. 3). Very heavily does this tell against the authenticity of these records, for "if the four Gospels and other books were written by those who had been eye-witnesses of Christ's miracles, and the five Apostolic Fathers had conversed with the Apostles, it is not to be conceived that they would not have named the actual books themselves which possessed so high authority, and would be looked up to with so much respect by all the Christians. This is the only way in which their evidence could be of use to support the authenticity of the New Testament as being the work of the Apostles; but this is a testimony which the five Apostolical Fathers fail to supply. There is not a single sentence, in all their remaining works, in which a clear allusion to the New Testament is to be found" ("Christian Records," Rev. Dr. Giles, p. 50).

Westcott, while claiming in the Apostolic Fathers a knowledge of most of the epistles, writes very doubtfully as to their knowledge of the Gospels (see above p. 264), and after giving careful citations of all possible quotations, he sums up thus: "1. No evangelic reference in the Apostolic Fathers can be referred certainly to a written record. 2. It appears most probable from the form of the quotations that they were derived from oral tradition. 3. No quotation contains any element which is not substantially preserved in our Gospels. 4. When the text given differs from the text of our Gospels it represents a later form of the evangelic tradition. 5. The text of St. Matthew corresponds more nearly than the other synoptic texts with the quotations and references as a whole" ("On the Canon," p. 62). There appears to be no proof whatever of conclusions 3 and 4, but we give them all as they stand. But we will take these Apostolic Fathers one by one, in the order used by Paley.

BARNABAS. We have already quoted Bishop Marsh and Dr. Giles as regards him. There is "nothing in this epistle worthy of the name of evidence even of the existence of our Gospels" ("Sup. Rel.," vol. i., p. 260). The quotation sometimes urged, "There are many called, few chosen," is spoken of by Westcott as a "proverbial phrase," and phrases similar in meaning and manner may be found in iv. Ezra, viii. 3, ix. 15 ("Sup. Rel.," vol. i., p. 245); in the latter work the words occur in a relation similar to that in which we find them in Barnabas; in both the judgment is described, and in both the moral drawn is that there are many lost and few saved; it is the more likely that the quotation is taken from the apocryphal work, since many other quotations are drawn from it throughout the epistle. The quotation "Give to every one that asketh thee," is not found in the supposed oldest MS., the Codex Sinaiticus, and is a later interpolation, clearly written in by some transcriber as appropriate to the passage in Barnabas. The last supposed quotation, that Christ chose men of bad character to be his disciples, that "he might show that he came not to call the righteous, but sinners," is another clearly later interpolation, for it jars with the reasoning of Barnabas, and when Origen quotes the passage he omits the phrase. In a work which "has been written at the request, and is published at the cost of the Christian Evidence Society," and which may fairly, therefore, be taken as the opinion of learned, yet most orthodox, Christian opinion, the Rev. Mr. Sanday writes: "The general result of our examination of the Epistle of Barnabas may, perhaps, be stated thus, that while not supplying by itself certain and conclusive proof of the use of our Gospels, still the phenomena accord better with the hypothesis of such a use. This epistle stands in the second line of the Evidence, and as a witness is rather confirmatory than principal" ("Gospels in the Second Century," p. 76. Ed. 1876). And this is all that the most modern apologetic criticism can draw from an epistle of which Paley makes a great display, saying that "if the passage remarked in this ancient writing had been found in one of St. Paul's Epistles, it would have been esteemed by every one a high testimony to St. Matthew's Gospel" ("Evidences," p. 113).

CLEMENT OF ROME.—"Tischendorf, who is ever ready to claim the slightest resemblance in language as a reference to new Testament writings, admits that although this Epistle is rich in quotations from the Old Testament, and here and there that Clement also makes use of passages from Pauline Epistles, he nowhere refers to the Gospels" ("Sup. Rel.," vol. i. pp. 227, 228). The Christian Evidence Society, through Mr. Sanday, thus criticises Clement: "Now what is the bearing of the Epistle of Clement upon the question of the currency and authority of the Synoptic Gospels? There are two passages of some length which are, without doubt, evangelical quotations, though whether they are derived from the Canonical Gospels or not may be doubted" ("Gospels in the Second Century," page 61). After balancing the arguments for and against the first of these passages, Mr. Sanday concludes: "Looking at the arguments on both sides, so far as we can give them, I incline, on the whole, to the opinion that Clement is not quoting from our Gospels; but I am quite aware of the insecure ground on which this opinion rests. It is a nice balance of probabilities, and the element of ignorance is so large that the conclusion, whatever it is, must be purely provisional. Anything like confident dogmatism on the subject seems to me entirely out of place. Very much the same is to be said of the second passage" (Ibid, p. 66).

The quotations in Clement, apparently from some other evangelic work, will be noted under head h, and these are those cited in Paley.

HERMAS.—Tischendorf relinquishes this work also as evidence for the Gospels. Lardner writes: "In Hermas are no express citations of any books of the New Testament" ("Credibility," vol. i. pt. 2, p. 116). He thinks, however, that he can trace "allusions to" "words of Scripture." Westcott says that "The Shepherd contains no definite quotation from either Old or New Testament" ("On the Canon," p. 197); but he also thinks that Hermas was "familiar with" some records of "Christ's teaching." Westcott, however, does not admit Hermas as an Apostolic Father at all, but places him in the middle of the second century. "As regards the direct historical evidence for the genuineness of the Gospels, it is of no importance. No book is cited in it by name. There are no evident quotations from the Gospels" (Norton's "Genuineness of the Gospels," vol. i, pp. 342, 343).

IGNATIUS.—It would be wasted time to trouble about Ignatius at all, after knowing the vicissitudes through which his supposed works have passed (see ante pp. 217-220); and Paley's references are such vague "quotations" that they may safely be left to the judgment of the reader. Tischendorf, claiming two and three phrases in it, says somewhat confusedly: "Though we do not wish to give to these references a decisive value, and though they do not exclude all doubt as to their applicability to our Gospels, and more particularly to that of St. John, they nevertheless undoubtedly bear traces of such a reference" ("When were our Gospels Written," p. 61, Eng. ed.). This conclusion refers, in Tischendorf, to Polycarp, as well as to Ignatius. In these Ignatian Epistles, Mr. Sanday only treats the Curetonian Epistles (see ante, p. 218) as genuine, and in these he finds scarcely any coincidences with the Gospels. The parallel to Matthew x. 16, "Be ye, therefore, wise as serpents and harmless as doves," is doubtful, as it is possible "that Ignatius may be quoting, not directly from our Gospel, but from one of the original documents (such as Ewald's hypothetical 'Spruch-Sammlung'), out of which our Gospel was composed" ("Gospels in the Second Century," p. 78). An allusion to the "star" of Bethlehem may have, "as it appears to have, reference to the narrative of Matt, ii... [but see, ante, p. 233, where the account given of the star is widely different from the evangelic notice]. These are (so far as I am aware) the only coincidences to be found in the Curetonian version" (Ibid, pp. 78, 79).

POLYCARP.—This epistle lies under a heavy weight of suspicion, and has besides little worth analysing as possible quotations from the Gospels. Paley quotes, "beseeching the all-seeing God not to lead us into temptation." Why not finish the passage? Because, if he had done so, the context would have shown that it was not a quotation from a gospel identical with our own—"beseeching the all-seeing God not to lead us into temptation, as the Lord hath said, The spirit, indeed, is willing, but the flesh is weak." If this be a quotation at all, it is from some lost gospel, as these words are nowhere found thus conjoined in the Synoptics.

Thus briefly may these Apostolic Fathers be dismissed, since their testimony fades away as soon as it is examined, as a mist evaporates before the rays of the rising sun. We will call up Paley's other witnesses.

PAPIAS.—In the fragment preserved by Eusebius there is no quotation of any kind; the testimony of Papias is to the names of the authors of two of the Gospels, and will be considered under g.

JUSTIN MARTYR.—We now come to the most important of the supposed witnesses, and, although students must study the details of the controversy in larger works, we will endeavour to put briefly before them the main reasons why Freethinkers reject Justin Martyr as bearing evidence to the authenticity of the present Gospels, and in this résumé we begin by condensing chapter iii. of "Supernatural Religion", vol. i., pp. 288-433, so far as it bears on our present position. Justin Martyr is supposed to have died about A.D. 166, having been put to death in the reign of Marcus Aurelius; he was by descent a Greek, but became a convert to Christianity, strongly tinged with Judaism. The longer Apology, and the Dialogue with Trypho, are the works chiefly relied upon to prove the authenticity. The date of the first Apology is probably about A.D. 147; the Dialogue was written later, perhaps between A.D. 150 and 160. In these writings Justin quotes very copiously from the Old Testament, and he also very frequently refers to facts of Christian history, and to sayings of Jesus. Of these references, for instance, some fifty occur in the first Apology, and upwards of seventy in the Dialogue with Trypho; a goodly number, it will be admitted, by means of which to identify the source from which he quotes. Justin himself frequently and distinctly says that his information and quotations are derived from the "Memoirs of the Apostles," but, except upon one occasion, which we shall hereafter consider, when he indicates Peter, he never mentions an author's name. Upon examination it is found that, with only one or two brief exceptions, the numerous quotations from these "Memoirs" differ more or less widely from parallel passages in our Synoptic Gospels, and in many cases differ in the same respects as similar quotations found in other writings of the second century, the writers of which are known to have made use of uncanonical Gospels; and further, that these passages are quoted several times, at intervals, by Justin, with the same variations. Moreover, sayings of Jesus are quoted from the "Memoirs" which are not found in our Gospels at all, and facts in the life of Jesus, and circumstances of Christian history, derived from the same source, not only are not found in our Gospels, but are in contradiction with them. Various theories have been put forward by Christian apologists to lessen the force of these objections. It has been suggested that Justin quoted from memory, condensed or combined to suit his immediate purpose; that the "Memoirs" were a harmony of the Gospels, with additions from some apocryphal work; that along with our Gospels Justin used apocryphal Gospels; that he made use of our Gospels, preferring, however, to rely chiefly on an apocryphal one. Results so diverse show how dubious must be the value of the witness of Justin Martyr. Competent critics almost universally admit that Justin had no idea of ranking the "Memoirs of the Apostles" among canonical writings. The word translated "Memoirs" would be more correctly rendered "Recollections," or "Memorabilia," and none of these three terms is an appropriate title for works ranking as canonical Gospels. Great numbers of spurious writings, under the names of apostles, were current in the early Church, and Justin names no authors for the "Recollections" he quotes from, only saying that they were composed "by his Apostles and their followers," clearly indicating that he was using some collective recollections of the Apostles and those who followed them. The word "Gospels," in the plural, is only once applied to these "Recollections;" "For the Apostles, in the 'Memoirs' composed by them, which are called Gospels." "The last expression [Greek: kaleitai euaggelai], as many scholars have declared, is a manifest interpolation. It is, in all probability, a gloss on the margin of some old MS. which some copyist afterwards inserted in the text. If Justin really stated that the 'Memoirs' were called Gospels, it seems incomprehensible that he should never call them so himself. In no other place in his writings does he apply the plural to them, but, on the contrary, we find Trypho referring to the 'so-called Gospel,' which he states that he had carefully read, and which, of course, can only be Justin's 'Memoirs,' and again, in another part of the same dialogue, Justin quotes passages which are written 'in the Gospel.' The term 'Gospel' is nowhere else used by Justin in reference to a written record." The public reading of the Recollections, mentioned by Justin, proves nothing, since many works, now acknowledged as spurious, were thus read (see ante, pp. 248, 249). Justin does not regard the Recollections as inspired, attributing inspiration only to prophetic writings, and he accepts them as authentic solely because the events

64

they narrate are prophesied of in the Old Testament. The omission of any author's name is remarkable, since, in quoting from the Old Testament, he constantly refers to the author by name, or to the book used; but in the very numerous quotations, supposed to be from the Gospels, he never does this, save in one single instance, mentioned below, when he quotes Peter. On the theory that he had our four Gospels before him, this is the more singular, since he would naturally have distinguished one from the other. The only writing in the New Testament referred to by name is the Apocalypse, by "a certain man whose name was John, one of the apostles of Christ," and it is impossible that John should be thus mentioned, if Justin had already been quoting from a Gospel bearing his name under the general title of Recollections. Justin clearly quotes from a written source and excludes oral tradition, saying that in the Recollections is recorded "everything that concerns our Saviour Christ." (The proofs that Justin quotes from records other than the Gospels will be classed under position h, and are here omitted.) Justin knows nothing of the shepherds of the plain, and the angelic appearance to them, nor of the star guiding the wise men to the place where Jesus was, although he relates the story of the birth, and the visit of the wise men. Two short passages in Justin are identical with parallel passages in Matthew, but "it cannot be too often repeated, that the mere coincidence of short historical sayings in two works by no means warrants the conclusion that the one is dependent on the other." In the first Apology, chaps, xv., xvi., and xvii. are composed almost entirely of examples of Christ's teaching, and with the exception of these two brief passages, not one quotation agrees verbally with the canonical Gospels. We have referred to one instance wherein the name of Peter is mentioned in connection with the Recollections. Justin says: "The statement also that he (Jesus) changed the name of Peter, one of the Apostles, and that this is also written in his 'Memoirs,'" etc. This refers the "Memoirs" to Peter, and it is suggested that it is, therefore, a reference to the Gospel of Mark, Mark having been supposed to have written his Gospel under the direction of Peter. There was a "Gospel according to Peter" current in the early Church, probably a variation from the Gospel of the Hebrews, so highly respected and so widely used by the primitive writers. It is very probable that this is the work to which Justin so often refers, and that it originally bore the simple title of "The Gospel," or the "Recollections of Peter." A version of this Gospel was also known as the "Gospel According to the Apostles," a title singularly like the "Recollections of the Apostles" by Justin. Seeing that in Justin's works his quotations, although so copious, do not agree with parallel passages in our Gospels, we may reasonably conclude that "there is no evidence that he made use of any of our Gospels, and he cannot, therefore, even be cited to prove their very existence, and much less the authenticity and character of records whose authors he does not once name." Passing from this case, ably worked out by this learned

65

and clever writer (and we earnestly recommend our readers, if possible, to study his careful analysis for themselves, since he makes the whole question thoroughly intelligible to English readers, and gives them evidence whereby they can form their own judgments, instead of accepting ready-made conclusions), we will examine Canon Westcott's contention. He admits that the difficulties perplexing the evidence of Justin are "great;" that there are "additions to the received narrative, and remarkable variations from its text, which, in some cases, are both repeated by Justin and found also in other writings" ("On the Canon," p. 98). We regret to say that Dr. Westcott, in laying the case before his readers, somewhat misleads them, although, doubtless, unintentionally. He speaks of Justin telling us that "Christ was descended from Abraham through Jacob, Judah, Phares, Jesse, and David," and omits the fact that Justin traces the descent to Mary alone, and knows nothing as to a descent traced to Joseph, as in both Matthew and Luke (see below, under h). He speaks of Justin mentioning wise men "guided by a star," forgetting that Justin says nothing of the guidance, but only writes: "That he should arise like a star from the seed of Abraham, Moses showed beforehand.... Accordingly, when a star rose in heaven at the time of his birth, as is recorded in the 'Memoirs' of his Apostles, the Magi from Arabia, recognising the sign by this, came and worshipped him" ("Dial.," ch. cvi.). He speaks of Justin recording "the singing of the Psalm afterwards" (after the last supper), omitting that Justin only says generally ("Dial.," ch. cvi., to which Dr. Westcott refers us) that "when living with them (Christ) sang praises to God." But as we hereafter deal with these discrepancies, we need not dwell on them now, only warning our readers that since even such a man as Dr. Westcott thus misrepresents facts, it will be well never to accept any inferences drawn from such references as these without comparing them with the original. One of the chief difficulties to the English reader is to get a reliable translation. To give but a single instance. In the version of Justin here used (that published by T. Clark, Edinburgh), we find in the "Dialogue," ch. ciii., the following passage: "His sweat fell down like drops of blood while he was praying." And this is referred to by Canon Westcott (p. 104) as a record of the "bloody sweat." Yet, in the original, there is no word analogous to "of blood;" the passage runs: "sweat as drops fell down," and it is recorded by Justin as a proof that the prophecy, "my bones are poured out like water" was fulfilled in Christ. The clumsy endeavour to create a likeness to Luke xxii. 44 destroys Justin's argument. Further on (p. 113) Dr. Westcott admits that the words "of blood" are not found in Justin; but it is surely misleading, under these circumstances, to say that Justin mentions "the bloody sweat." Westcott only maintains seven passages in the whole of Justin's writings, wherein he distinctly quotes from the "Memoirs;" i.e., only seven that can be maintained as quotations from the canonical

66

Gospels—the contention being that the "Memoirs" are the Gospels. He says truly, if naively, "The result of a first view of these passages is striking." Very striking, indeed; for, "of the seven, five agree verbally with the text of St. Matthew or St. Luke, exhibiting, indeed, three slight various readings not elsewhere found, but such as are easily explicable. The sixth is a condensed summary of words related by St. Matthew; the seventh alone presents an important variation in the text of a verse, which is, however, otherwise very uncertain" (pp. 130, 131. The italics are our own). That is, there are only seven distinct quotations, and all of these, save two, are different from our Gospels. The whole of Dr. Westcott's analysis of these passages is severely criticised in "Supernatural Religion," and in the edition of 1875 of Dr. Westcott's book, from which we quote, some of the expressions he previously used are a little modified. The author of "Supernatural Religion" justly says: "The striking result, to summarise Canon Westcott's own words, is this. Out of seven professed quotations from the 'Memoirs,' in which he admits we may expect to find the exact language preserved, five present three variations; one is a compressed summary, and does not agree verbally at all; and the seventh presents an important variation" (vol. i., p. 394).

Dr. Giles speaks very strongly against Paley's distortion of Justin Martyr's testimony, complaining: "The works of Justin Martyr do not fall in the way of one in a hundred thousand of our countrymen. How is it, then, to be deprecated that erroneous statements should be current about him! How is it to be censured that his testimony should be changed, and he should be made to speak a falsehood!" ("Christian Records," p. 71). Dr. Giles then argues that Justin would have certainly named the books and their authors had they been current and reverenced in his time; that there were numberless Gospels current at that date; that Justin mentions occurrences that are only found related in such apocryphal Gospels. He then compares seventeen passages in Justin Martyr with parallel passages in the Gospels, and concludes that Justin "gives us Christ's sayings in their traditionary forms, and not in the words which are found in our four Gospels." We will select two, to show his method of criticising, translating the Greek, instead of giving it, as he does, in the original. In the Apology, ch. xv., Justin writes: "If thy right eye offend thee, cut it out, for it is profitable for thee to enter into the kingdom of heaven with one eye, than having two to be thrust into the everlasting fire." "This passage is very like Matt. v. 29: 'If thy right eye offend thee, pluck it out, and cast it from thee; for it is profitable for thee that one of thy members should perish, and not that thy whole body should be cast into hell.' But it is also like Matt, xviii. 9: 'And if thine eye offend thee, pluck it out and cast it from thee; it is better for thee to enter into life with one eye, rather than having two eyes to be cast into hell-fire.' And it bears an equal likeness to Mark ix. 47: 'And if thine eye offend thee, pluck it out; it is better for thee to enter into the kingdom of God with one eye than, having two eyes, to be cast into hell-fire.' Yet, strange to say, it is not identical in words with either of the three" (pp. 83, 84). "I came not to call the righteous but sinners to repentance." "In this only instance is there a perfect agreement between the words of Justin and the canonical Gospels, three of which, Matthew, Mark, and Luke, give the same saying of Christ in the same words. A variety of thoughts here rush upon the mind. Are these three Gospels based upon a common document? If so, is not Justin Martyr's citation drawn from the same anonymous document, rather than from the three Gospels, seeing he does not name them? If, on the other hand, Justin has cited them accurately in this instance, why has he failed to do so in the others? For no other reason than that traditionary sayings are generally thus irregularly exact or inexact, and Justin, citing from them, has been as irregularly exact as they were" (Ibid, p. 85). "The result to which a perusal of his works will lead is of the gravest character. He will be found to quote nearly two hundred sentiments or sayings of Christ; but makes hardly a single clear allusion to all those circumstances of time or place which give so much interest to Christ's teaching, as recorded in the four Gospels. The inference is that he quotes Christ's sayings as delivered by tradition or taken down in writing before the four Gospels were compiled" (Ibid, pp. 89, 90). Paley and Lardner both deal with Justin somewhat briefly, calling every passage in his works resembling slightly any passage in the Gospels a "quotation;" in both cases only ignorance of Justin's writings can lead any reader to assent to the inferences they draw.

HEGESIPPUS was a Jewish Christian, who, according to Eusebius, flourished about A.D. 166. Soter is said to have succeeded Anicetus in the bishopric of Rome in that year, and Hegesippus appears to have been in Rome during the episcopacy of both. He travelled about from place to place, and his testimony to the Gospels is that "in every city the doctrine prevails according to what is declared by the law, and the prophets, and the Lord" ("Eccles. Hist," bk. iv., ch. 22). Further, Eusebius quotes the story of the death of James, the Apostle, written by Hegesippus, and in this James is reported to have said to the Jews: "Why do ye now ask me respecting Jesus, the Son of Man? He is now sitting in the heavens, on the right hand of great power, and is about to come on the clouds of heaven." And when he is being murdered, he prays, "O Lord God and Father forgive them, for they know not what they do" (see "Eccles. Hist.," bk. ii., ch. 23). The full absurdity of regarding this as a testimony to the Gospels will be seen when it is remembered that it is implied thereby that James, the brother and apostle of Christ, knew nothing of his words until he read them in the Gospels, and that he was murdered before the Gospel of Luke, from which alone he could quote the prayer of Jesus, is thought, by most Christians, to have been written. One other fragment of Hegesippus is preserved by Stephanus Gobarus, wherein Hegesippus, speaking against Paul's assertion "that eye hath not seen, nor ear heard," opposes to it the saying of the Lord, "Blessed are your eyes, for they see, and your ears that hear." This is paralleled by Matt. xiii. 16 and Luke x. 23. "We need not point out that the saying referred to by Hegesippus, whilst conveying the same sense as that in the two Gospels, differs as materially from them as they do from each other, and as we might expect a quotation taken from a different, though kindred, source, like the Gospel according to the Hebrews, to do" ("Sup. Rel.," vol. i., p. 447). Why does not Paley tell us that Eusebius writes of him, not that he quoted from the Gospels, but that "he also states some particulars from the Gospel of the Hebrews and from the Syriac, and particularly from the Hebrew language, showing that he himself was a convert from the Hebrews. Other matters he also records as taken from the unwritten tradition of the Jews" ("Eccles. Hist.," bk. iv., ch 22). Here, then, we have the source of the quotations in Hegesippus, and yet Paley conceals this, and deliberately speaks of him as referring to our Gospel of Matthew!

EPISTLE OF THE CHURCHES OF LYONS AND VIENNE.—Paley quietly dates this A.D. 170, although the persecution it describes occurred in A.D. 177 (see ante, pp. 257, 258). The "exact references to the Gospels of Luke and John and to the Acts of the Apostles," spoken of by Paley ("Evidences," p. 125), are not easy to find. Westcott says: "It contains no reference by name to any book of the New Testament, but its coincidences of language with the Gospels of St. Luke and St. John, with the Acts of the Apostles, with the Epistles of St. Paul to the Romans, Corinthians (?), Ephesians, Philippians, and the First to Timothy, with the first Catholic Epistles of St. Peter and St. John, and with the Apocalypse, are indisputable" ("On the Canon," p. 336). Unfortunately, neither Paley nor Dr. Westcott refer us to the passages in question, Paley quoting only one. We will, therefore, give one of these at full length, leaving our readers to judge of it as an "exact reference:" "Vattius Epagathus, one of the brethren who abounded in the fulness of the love of God and man, and whose walk and conversation had been so unexceptionable, though he was only young, shared in the same testimony with the elder Zacharias. He walked in all the commandments and righteousness of the Lord blameless, full of love to God and his neighbour" ("Eusebius," bk. v., chap. i). This is, it appears, an "exact reference" to Luke i. 6, and we own we should not have known it unless it had been noted in "Supernatural Religion." Tischendorf, on the other hand, refers the allusion to Zacharias to the Protevangelium of James ("Sup. Rel.," vol. ii., p. 202).

The second "exact reference" is, that Vattius had "the Spirit more abundantly than Zacharias;" "such an unnecessary and insidious comparison would scarcely have been made had the writer known our Gospel and regarded it as inspired Scripture" ("Sup. Rel.," vol. ii., p.

204). The quotation "that the day would come when everyone that slayeth you will think he is doing God a service," is one of those isolated sayings referred to Christ which might be found in any account of his works, or might have been handed down by tradition. This epistle is the last witness called by Paley, prior to Irenæus, and might, indeed, fairly be regarded as contemporary with him.

Although Paley does not allude to the "Clementines," books falsely ascribed to Clement of Rome, these are sometimes brought to prove the existence of the Gospels in the second century. But they are useless as witnesses, from the fact that the date at which they were themselves written is a matter of dispute. "Critics variously date the composition of the original Recognitions from about the middle of the second century to the end of the third, though the majority are agreed in placing them, at least, in the latter century" ("Sup. Rel.," vol. ii., p. 5). "It is unfortunate that there are not sufficient materials for determining the date of the Clementine Homilies" ("Gospels in the Second Century," Rev. W. Sanday, p. 161). Part of the Clementines, called the "Recognitions," is useless as a basis for argument, for these "are only extant in a Latin translation by Rufinus, in which the quotations from the Gospels have evidently been assimilated to the canonical text which Rufinus himself uses" (Ibid). Of the rest, "we are struck at once by the small amount of exact coincidence, which is considerably less than that which is found in the quotations from the Old Testament" (Ibid, p. 168). "In the Homilies there are very numerous quotations of expressions of Jesus, and of Gospel History, which are generally placed in the mouth of Peter, or introduced with such formula as 'The teacher said,' 'Jesus said,' 'He said,' 'The prophet said,' but in no case does the author name the source from which these sayings and quotations are derived.... De Wette says, 'The quotations of evangelical works and histories in the pseudo-Clementine writings, from their free and unsatisfactory nature, permit only uncertain conclusions as to their written source.' Critics have maintained very free and conflicting views regarding that source. Apologists, of course, assert that the quotations in the Homilies are taken from our Gospels only. Others ascribe them to our Gospels, with a supplementary apocryphal work, the Gospel according to the Hebrews, or the Gospel according to Peter. Some, whilst admitting a subsidiary use of some of our Gospels, assert that the author of the Homilies employs, in preference, the Gospel according to Peter; whilst others, recognising also the similarity of the phenomena presented by these quotations with those of Justin's, conclude that the author does not quote our Gospels at all, but makes use of the Gospel according to Peter, or the Gospel according to the Hebrews. Evidence permitting of such divergent conclusions manifestly cannot be of a decided character" ("Sup. Rel.," vol. ii., pp. 6, 7).

On Basilides (teaching c. A.D. 135) and Valentinus (A.D. 140), two of the early Gnostic teachers, we need not delay, for there is scarcely anything left of their writings, and all we know of them is drawn from the writings of their antagonists; it is claimed that they knew and made use of the canonical Gospels, and Canon Westcott urges this view of Basilides, but the writer of "Supernatural Religion" characterises this plea "as unworthy of a scholar, and only calculated to mislead readers who must generally be ignorant of the actual facts of the case" (vol. ii., p. 42). Basilides says that he received his doctrine from Glaucias, the "interpreter of Peter," and "it is apparent, however, that Basilides, in basing his doctrines on these apocryphal books as inspired, and upon tradition, and in having a special Gospel called after his own name, which, therefore, he clearly adopts as the exponent of his ideas of Christian truth, absolutely ignores the canonical Gospels altogether, and not only does not offer any evidence for their existence, but proves that he did not recognise any such works as of authority. Therefore, there is no ground whatever for Tischendorf's assumption that the Commentary of Basilides 'On the Gospel' was written upon our Gospels, but that idea is, on the contrary, negatived in the strongest way by all the facts of the case" ("Sup. Rel.," vol. ii., pp. 45, 46). Both with this ancient heretic, as with Valentinus, it is impossible to distinguish what is ascribed to him from what is ascribed to his followers, and thus evidence drawn from either of them is weaker even than usual.

Marcion, the greatest heretic of the second century, ought to prove a useful witness to the Christians if the present Gospels had been accepted in his time as canonical. He was the son of the Christian Bishop of Sinope, in Pontus, and taught in Rome for some twenty years, dating from about A.D. 140. Only one Gospel was acknowledged by him, and fierce has been the controversy as to what this Gospel was. It is only known to us through his antagonists, who generally assert that the Gospel used by him was the third Synoptic, changed and adapted to suit his heretical views. Paley says, "This rash and wild controversialist published a recension or chastised edition of St. Luke's Gospel" ("Evidences," p. 167), but does not condescend to give us the smallest reason for so broad an assertion. This question has, however, been thoroughly debated among German critics, the one side maintaining that Marcion mutilated Luke's Gospel, the other that Marcion's Gospel was earlier than Luke's, and that Luke's was made from it; while some, again, maintained that both were versions of an older original. From this controversy we may conclude that there was a strong likeness between Marcion's Gospel and the third Synoptic, and that it is impossible to know which is the earlier of the two. The resolution of the question is made hopeless by the fact that "the principal sources of our information regarding Marcion's Gospel are the works of his most bitter denouncers Tertullian and Epiphanius" ("Sup. Rel.," vol. ii., p. 88). "At the very best, even if the hypothesis that

71

Marcion's Gospel was a mutilated Luke were established, Marcion affords no evidence in favour of the authenticity or trustworthy character of our third Synoptic. His Gospel was nameless, and his followers repudiated the idea of its having been written by Luke; and regarded even as the earliest testimony for the existence of Luke's Gospel, that testimony is not in confirmation of its genuineness and reliability, but, on the contrary, condemns it as garbled and interpolated" (Ibid, pp. 146, 147).

It is scarcely worth while to refer to the supposed evidence of the "Canon of Muratori," since the date of this fragment is utterly unknown. In the year 1740 Muratori published this document in a collection of Italian antiquities, stating that he had found it in the Ambrosian library at Milan, and that he believed that the MS. from which he took it had been in existence about 1000 years. It is not known by whom the original was written, and it bears no date: it is but a fragment, commencing: "at which, nevertheless, he was present, and thus he placed it. Third book of the Gospel according to Luke." Further on it speaks of "the fourth of the Gospels of John." The value of the evidence of an anonymous fragment of unknown date is simply nil. "It is by some affirmed to be a complete treatise on the books received by the Church, from which fragments have been lost; while others consider it a mere fragment itself. It is written in Latin, which by some is represented as most corrupt, whilst others uphold it as most correct. The text is further rendered almost unintelligible by every possible inaccuracy of orthography and grammar, which is ascribed diversely to the transcriber, to the translator, and to both. Indeed, such is the elastic condition of the text, resulting from errors and obscurity of every imaginable description, that, by means of ingenious conjectures, critics are able to find in it almost any sense they desire. Considerable difference of opinion exists as to the original language of the fragment, the greater number of critics maintaining that the composition is a translation from the Greek, while others assert it to have been originally written in Latin. Its composition is variously attributed to the Church of Africa, and to a member of the Church in Rome" ("Sup. Rel.," vol. ii., pp. 238, 239). On a disputable scrap of this kind no argument can be based; there is no evidence even to show that the thing was in existence at all until Muratori published it; it is never referred to by any early writer, nor is there a scintilla of evidence that it was known to the early Church.

After a full and searching analysis of all the documents, orthodox and heretical, supposed to have been written in the first two centuries after Christ, the author of "Supernatural Religion" thus sums up:— "After having exhausted the literature and the testimony bearing on the point, we have not found a single distinct trace of any one of those Gospels during the first century and a half after the death of Jesus.... Any argument for the mere existence of our Synoptics based upon their

72

supposed rejection by heretical leaders and sects has the inevitable disadvantage, that the very testimony which would show their existence would oppose their authenticity. There is no evidence of their use by heretical leaders, however, and no direct reference to them by any writer, heretical or orthodox, whom we have examined" (vol. ii., pp, 248, 249). Nor is the fact of this blank absence of evidence of identity all that can be brought to bear in support of our proposition, for there is another fact that tells very heavily against the identity of the now accepted Gospels with those that were current in earlier days, namely, the noteworthy charge brought against the Christians that they changed and altered their sacred books; the orthodox accused the unorthodox of varying the Scriptures, and the heretics retorted the charge with equal pertinacity. The Ebionites maintained that the Hebrew Gospel of Matthew was the only authentic Gospel, and regarded the four Greek Gospels as unreliable. The Marcionites admitted only the Gospel resembling that of Luke, and were accused by the orthodox of having altered that to suit themselves. Celsus, writing against Christianity, formulates the charge: "Some believers, like men driven by drunkenness to commit violence on themselves, have altered the Gospel history, since its first composition, three times, four times, and oftener, and have re-fashioned it, so as to be able to deny the objections made against it" ("Origen Cont. Celsus," bk. ii., chap. 27, as quoted by Norton, p. 63). Origen admits "that there are those who have altered the Gospels," but pleads that it has been done by heretics, and that this "is no reproach against true Christianity" (Ibid). Only, most reverend Father of the Church, if heretics accuse orthodox, and orthodox accuse heretics, of altering the Gospels, how are we to be sure that they have come down unaltered to us? Clement of Alexandria notes alterations that had been made. Dionysius, of Corinth, complaining of the changes made in his own writings, bears witness to this same fact: "It is not, therefore, matter of wonder if some have also attempted to adulterate the sacred writings of the Lord, since they have attempted the same in other works that are not to be compared with these" ("Eusebius," bk. iv., ch. 23). Faustus, the Manichæan, the great opponent of Augustine, writes: "For many things have been inserted by your ancestors in the speeches of our Lord, which, though put forth under his name, agree not with his faith; especially since—as already it has been often proved by us—that these things were not written by Christ, nor his Apostles, but a long while after their assumption, by I know not what sort of half Jews, not even agreeing with themselves, who made up their tale out of report and opinions merely; and yet, fathering the whole upon the names of the Apostles of the Lord, or on those who were supposed to have followed the Apostles; they mendaciously pretended that they had written their lies and conceits according to them" (Lib. 33, ch. 3, as quoted and translated in "Diegesis," pp. 61, 62).

The truth is, that in those days, when books were only written, the widest door was opened to alterations, additions, and omissions; incidents or remarks written, perhaps, in the margin of the text by one transcriber, were transferred into the text itself by the next copyist, and were thereafter indistinguishable from the original matter. In this way the celebrated text of the three witnesses (1 John, v. 7) is supposed to have crept into the text. Dealing with this, in reference to the New Testament, Eichhorn points out that it was easy to alter a manuscript in transcribing it, and that, as manuscripts were written for individual use, such alterations were considered allowable, and that the altered manuscript, being copied in its turn, such changes passed into circulation unnoticed. Owners of manuscripts added to them incidents of the life of Christ, or any of his sayings, which they had heard of, and which were not recorded in their own copies, and thus the story grew and grew, and additional legends were incorporated with it, until the historical basis became overlaid with myth. The vast number of readings in the New Testament, no less—according to Dr. Angus, one of the present Revision Committee—than 100,000, prove the facility with which variations were introduced into MSS. by those who had charge of them. In heated and angry controversy between different schools of monks appeals were naturally made to the authority of the Scriptures, and what more likely—indeed more certain—than that these monks should introduce variations into their MS. copies favouring the positions for which they were severally contending?

The most likely way in which the Gospels grew into their present forms is, that the various traditions relating to Christ were written down in different places for the instruction of catechumens, and that these, passing from hand to hand, and mouth to mouth, grew into a large mass of disjointed stories, common to many churches. This mass was gradually sifted, arranged, moulded into historical shape, which should fit into the preconceived notions of the Messiah, and thus the four Gospels gradually grew into their present form, and were accepted on all hands as the legacy of the apostolic age. No careful reader can avoid noticing the many coincidences of expression between the three synoptics, and deducing from these coincidences the conclusion that one narrative formed the basis of the three histories. Ewald supposes the existence of a Spruchsammlung—collected sayings of Christ—but such a collection is not enough to explain the phenomena we refer to. Dr. Davidson says: "The rudiments of an original oral Gospel were formed in Jerusalem, in the bosom of the first Christian Church; and the language of it must have been Aramæan, since the members consisted of Galileans, to whom that tongue was vernacular. It is natural to suppose that they were accustomed to converse with one another on the life, actions, and doctrines of their departed Lord, dwelling on the particulars that interested them most, and rectifying the accounts given by one another, where such accounts were

74

erroneous, or seriously defective. The Apostles, who were eye-witnesses of the public life of Christ, could impart correctness to the narratives, giving them a fixed character in regard to authenticity and form. In this manner an original oral Gospel in Aramæan was formed. We must not, however, conceive of it as put into the shape of any of our present Gospels, or as being of like extent; but as consisting of leading particulars in the life of Christ, probably the most striking and the most affecting, such as would leave the best impression on the minds of the disciples. The incidents and sayings connected with their Divine Master naturally assumed a particular shape from repetition, though it was simply a rudimental one. They were not compactly linked in regular or systematic sequence. They were the oral germ and essence of a Gospel, rather than a proper Gospel itself, at least, according to our modern ideas of it. But the Aramæan language was soon laid aside. When Hellenists evinced a disposition to receive Christianity, and associated themselves with the small number of Palestinian converts, Greek was necessarily adopted. As the Greek-speaking members far out-numbered the Aramæan-speaking brethren, the oral Gospel was put into Greek. Henceforward Greek, the language of the Hellenists, became the medium of instruction. The truths and facts, before repeated in Hebrew, were now generally promulgated in Greek by the apostles and their converts. The historical cyclus, which had been forming in the Church at Jerusalem, assumed a determinate character in the Greek tongue" ("Introduction to the New Testament," by S. Davidson, LL.D., p. 405. Ed. 1848). Thus we find learned Christians obliged to admit an uninspired collection as the basis of the inspired Gospel, and laying down a theory which is entirely incompatible with the idea that the Synoptic Gospels were written by Matthew, Mark, and Luke. Our Gospels are degraded into versions of an older Gospel, instead of being the inspired record of contemporaries, speaking "that we do know."

Canon Westcott writes of the three Synoptic Gospels, that "they represent, as is shown by their structure, a common basis, common materials, treated in special ways. They evidently contain only a very small selection from the words and works of Christ, and yet their contents are included broadly in one outline. Their substance is evidently much older than their form.... The only explanation of the narrow and definite limit within which the evangelic history (exclusive of St. John's Gospel) is confined, seems to be that a collection of representative words and works was made by an authoritative body, such as the Twelve, at a very early date, and that this, which formed the basis of popular teaching, gained exclusive currency, receiving only subordinate additions and modifications. This Apostolic Gospel—the oral basis, as I have endeavoured to show elsewhere, of the Synoptic narratives—dates unquestionably from the very beginning of the Christian society" ("On the Canon," preface, pp. xxxviii., xxxix). Mr.

75

Sanday speaks of the "original documents out of which our Gospel was composed" ("Gospels in the Second Century," page 78), and he writes: "Doubtless light would be thrown upon the question if we only knew what was the common original of the two Synoptic texts" (Ibid, p. 65). "The first three Gospels of our Canon are remarkably alike, their writers agree in relating the same thing, not only in the same manner, but likewise in the very words, as must be evident to every common reader who has paid the slightest attention to the subject.... [Here follow a number of parallel passages from the three synoptics.] The agreement between the three evangelists in these extracts is remarkable, and leads to the question how such coincidences could arise between works which, from the first years of Christianity until the beginning of the seventeenth century, were understood to be perfectly independent, and to have had each a separate and independent origin. The answer to this question may at last, after more than a hundred years of discussion, be given with tolerable certainty, if we are allowed to judge of this subject according to the rules of reason and common sense, by which all other such difficulties are resolved. 'The most eminent critics'—we quote from 'Marsh's Michaelis,' vol. iii., part 2, page 170—'are at present decidedly of opinion that one of the two suppositions must necessarily be adopted—either that the three evangelists copied from each other, or that all the three drew from a common source, and that the notion of an absolute independence, in respect to the composition of our three first Gospels, is no longer tenable'.... The alternative between a common source and copying from each other, is now no longer in the same position as in the days of Michaelis or Bishop Marsh. To decide between the two is no longer difficult. No one will now admit that either of the four evangelists has copied from the other three, 1. Because in neither of the four is there the slightest notice of the others. 2. Because, if either of the evangelists may be thought, from the remarkable similarity of any particular part of his narrative, to have copied out of either of the other Gospels, we immediately light upon so many other passages, wholly inconsistent with what the other three have related on the same subject, that we immediately ask why he has not copied from the others on those points also. It only remains, therefore, for us to infer that there was a common source, first traditional and then written—the [Greek: Apomnemoneumata], in short, or 'Memorials,' etc., of Justin Martyr, and that from this source the four canonical Gospels, together with thirty or forty others, many of which are still in existence, were, at various periods of early Christianity, compiled by various writers" ("Christian Records," Dr. Giles, pp. 266, 270, 271). Dean Alford puts forward a somewhat similar theory; he considers that the oral teaching of the apostles to catechumens and others, the simple narrative of facts relating to Christ, gradually grew into form and was written down, and that this accounts for the marked similarity of some passages in the different Gospels. He says:—"I believe, then, that the Apostles, in virtue not merely of their having been eye-and-ear witnesses of the Evangelic history, but especially of their office, gave to the various Churches their testimony in a narrative of facts, such narrative being modified in each case by the individual mind of the Apostle himself, and his sense of what was requisite for the particular community to which he was ministering.... It would be easy and interesting to follow the probable origin and growth of this cycle of narratives of the words and deeds of our Lord in the Church at Jerusalem, for both the Jews and the Hellenists—the latter under such teachers as Philip and Stephen—commissioned and authenticated by the Apostles. In the course of such a process some portions would naturally be written down by private believers for their own use, or that of friends. And as the Church spread to Samaria, Caesarea, and Antioch, the want would be felt in each of those places of similar cycles of oral teaching, which, when supplied, would thenceforward belong to, and be current in, those respective Churches. And these portions of the Evangelic history, oral or partially documentary, would be adopted under the sanction of the Apostles, who were as in all things, so especially in this, the appointed and divinely-guided overseers of the whole Church. This common substratum of Apostolic teachings—never formally adopted by all, but subject to all the varieties of diction and arrangement, addition and omission, incident to transmission through many individual minds, and into many different localities—I believe to have been the original source of the common part of our three Gospels" ("Greek Test.," Dean Alford, vol. i., Prolegomena, ch. i., sec. 3, par. 6; ed. 1859. The italics are Dean Alford's).

Eichhorn's theory of the growth of the Gospels is one very generally accepted; he considers that the present Gospels were not in common circulation before the end of the second century, and that before that time other Gospels were in common use, differing considerably from each other, but resting on a common foundation of historical fact; all these, he thinks, were versions of an "original Gospel," a kind of rough outline of Christ's life and discourses, put together without method or plan, and one of these would be the "Memoirs of the Apostles," of which Justin Martyr speaks. The Gospels, as we have them, are careful compilations made from these earlier histories, and we notice that, at the end of the second, and the beginning of the third, centuries, the leaders of the Church endeavour to establish the authority of the four more methodically arranged Gospels, so as to check the reception of other Gospels, which were relied upon by heretics in their controversies.

Strauss gives a careful resume of the various theories of the formation of the Gospels held by learned men, and shows how the mythic theory was gradually developed and strengthened; "according to George, mythus is the creation of a fact out of an idea" ("Life of

77

Jesus," Strauss, vol. i., p. 42; ed. 1846), and the mythic theory supposes that the ideas of the Messiah were already in existence, and that the story of the Gospels grew up by the translation of these ideas into facts: "Many of the legends respecting him [Jesus] had not to be newly invented; they already existed in the popular hope of the Messiah, having been mostly derived, with various modifications, from the Old Testament, and had merely to be transferred to Jesus, and accommodated to his character and doctrines. In no case could it be easier for the person who first added any new feature to the description of Jesus, to believe himself its genuineness, since his argument would be: Such and such things must have happened to the Messiah; Jesus was the Messiah; therefore, such and such things happened to him" (Ibid, pp. 81, 82). "It is not, however, to be imagined that any one individual seated himself at his table to invent them out of his own head, and write them down as he would a poem; on the contrary, these narratives, like all other legends, were fashioned by degrees, by steps which can no longer be traced; gradually acquired consistency, and at length received a fixed form in our written Gospels" (Ibid, p. 35). From the considerations here adduced—the lack of quotations from our Gospels in the earliest Christian writers, both orthodox and heretical; the accusations against each made by the other of introducing chants and modifications in the Gospels; the facility with which MSS. were altered before the introduction of printing; the coincidences between the Gospels, showing that they are drawn from a common source; from all these facts we finally conclude that there is no evidence that the Four Gospels mentioned about that date (A.D. 180) were the same as those we have now.

G. That there is evidence that two of them were not the same. "The testimony of Papias is of great interest and importance in connection with our inquiry, inasmuch as he is the first ecclesiastical writer who mentions the tradition that Matthew and Mark composed written records of the life and teaching of Jesus; but no question has been more continuously contested than that of the identity of the works to which he refers with our actual Canonical Gospels. Papias was Bishop of Hierapolis, in Phrygia, in the first half of the second century, and is said to have suffered martyrdom under Marcus Aurelius about A.D. 164-167. About the middle of the second century he wrote a work in five books, entitled 'Exposition of the Lord's Oracles,' which, with the exception of a few fragments preserved to us chiefly by Eusebius and Irenæus, is unfortunately no longer extant. This work was less based on written records of the teaching of Jesus than on that which Papias had been able to collect from tradition, which he considered more authentic, for, like his contemporary, Hegesippus, Papias avowedly prefers tradition to any written works with which he was acquainted" ("Sup. Rel.," vol. i., pp. 449, 450). Before giving the testimony attributed to Papias, we must remark two or three points which will influence our judgment concerning him. Paley speaks of him, on the authority of Irenæus, as "a hearer of John, and companion of Polycarp" ("Evidences," p. 121); but Paley omits to tell us that Eusebius points out that Irenæus was mistaken in this statement, and that Papias "by no means asserts that he was a hearer and an eye-witness of the holy Apostles, but informs us that he received the doctrines of faith from their intimate friends" ("Eccles. Hist.", bk. iii., ch. 39). Eusebius subjoins the passage from Papias, which states that "if I met with any one who had been a follower of the elders anywhere, I made it a point to inquire what were the declarations of the elders: what was said by Andrew, Peter, or Philip; what by Thomas, James, John, Matthew, or any other of the disciples of our Lord; what was said by Aristion, and the Presbyter John, disciples of the Lord" (Ibid). Seeing that Papias died between A.D. 164 and 167, and that the disciples of Jesus were Jesus' own contemporaries, any disciple that Papias heard, when a boy, would have reached a portentous age, and, between the age of the disciple and the youth of Papias, the reminiscences would probably be of a somewhat hazy character. It is to Papias that we owe the wonderful account of the vines (ante, p. 234) of the kingdom of God, given by Irenæus, who states that "these things are borne witness to in writing by Papias, the hearer of John, and a companion of Polycarp.... And he says, in addition, 'Now these things are credible to believers.' And he says that 'when the traitor, Judas, did not give credit to them, and put the question, How then can things about to bring forth so abundantly be wrought by the Lord? the Lord declared, They who shall come to these (times) shall see'" ("Irenæus Against Heresies," bk. v., ch. 33, sec. 4). The recollections of Papias scarcely seem valuable as to quality. Next we note that Papias could scarcely put a very high value on the Apostolic writings, since he states that "I do not think that I derived so much benefit from books as from the living voice of those that are still surviving" ("Eccles. Hist," bk. iii., ch. 39), i.e., of those who had been followers of the Apostles. How this remark of Papias tallies with the supposed respect shown to the Canonical Gospels by primitive writers, it is for Christian apologists to explain. We then mark that we have no writing of Papias to refer to that pretends to be original. We have only passages, said to be taken from his writings, preserved in the works of Irenæus and Eusebius, and neither of these ecclesiastical penmen inspire the student with full confidence; even Eusebius mentions him in doubtful fashion; "there are said to be five books of Papias;" he gives "certain strange parables of our Lord and of his doctrine, and some other matters rather too fabulous;" "he was very limited in his comprehension, as is evident from his discourses" ("Eccles. Hist.," bk. iii., ch. 39). We thus see that the evidence of Papias is discredited at the very outset, perhaps to the advantage of the Christians, however, for his testimony is fatal to the Canonical Gospels. Papias is said to have written: "And John the Presbyter also said this: Mark being the interpreter of Peter, whatsoever he recorded he wrote with great accuracy, but not, however, in the order in which it was spoken or done by our Lord, but as before said, he was in company with Peter, who gave him such instruction as was necessary, but not to give a history of our Lord's discourses; wherefore Mark has not erred in anything, by writing some things as he has recorded them; for he was carefully attentive to one thing, not to pass by anything that he heard, or to state anything falsely in these accounts" ("Eccles. Hist.," bk iii., ch. 39). How far does this account apply to the Gospel now known as "according to St. Mark?" Far from showing traces of Petrine influence, such traces are conspicuous by their absence. "Not only are some of the most important episodes in which Peter is represented by the other Gospels as a principal actor altogether omitted, but throughout the Gospel there is the total absence of anything which is specially characteristic of Petrine influence and teaching. The argument that these omissions are due to the modesty of Peter is quite untenable, for not only does Irenæus, the most ancient authority on the point, state that this Gospel was only written after the death of Peter, but also there is no modesty in omitting passages of importance in the history of Jesus, simply because Peter himself was in some way concerned in them, or, for instance, in decreasing his penitence for such a denial of his master, which could not but have filled a sad place in the Apostle's memory. On the other hand, there is no adequate record of special matter which the intimate knowledge of the doings and sayings of Jesus possessed by Peter might have supplied to counterbalance the singular omissions. There is infinitely more of the spirit of Peter in the first Gospel than there is in the second. The whole internal evidence, therefore, shows that this part of the tradition of the Presbyter John transmitted by Papias does not apply to our Gospel" ("Sup. Rel.," vol. i., pp. 459, 460). But a far stronger objection to the identity of the work spoken of by Papias with the present Gospel of Mark, is drawn from the description of the document as given by him. "The discrepancy, however, is still more marked when we compare with our actual second Gospel the account of the work of Mark, which Papias received from the Presbyter. Mark wrote down from memory some parts [Greek: enia] of the teaching of Peter regarding the life of Jesus, but as Peter adapted his instructions to the actual circumstances [Greek: pros tas chreias] and did not give a consecutive report [Greek: suntaxis] of the discourses or doings of Jesus, Mark was only careful to be accurate, and did not trouble himself to arrange in historical order [Greek: taxis] his narrative of the things which were said or done by Jesus, but merely wrote down facts as he remembered them. This description would lead us to expect a work composed of fragmentary reminiscences of the teaching of Peter, without orderly sequence or connection. The absence of orderly arrangement is the most prominent feature in the description, and forms the burden of the whole. Mark writes 'what he remembered;' 'he did not arrange in order the things that were either said or done by Christ;' and then follow the apologetic expressions of explanation—he was not himself a hearer or follower of the Lord, but derived his information from the occasional preaching of Peter, who did not attempt to give a consecutive narrative, and, therefore, Mark was not wrong in merely writing things without order as he happened to hear or remember them. Now it is impossible in the work of Mark here described to recognise our present second Gospel, which does not depart in any important degree from the order of the other two Synoptics, and which, throughout, has the most evident character of orderly arrangement.... The great majority of critics, therefore, are agreed in concluding that the account of the Presbyter John recorded by Papias does not apply to our second Canonical Gospel at all" ("Sup. Rel.," vol. 1, pp. 460, 461). "This document, also, is mentioned by Papias, as quoted by Eusebius; the account which they give of it is not applicable to the work which we now have. For the 'Gospel according to St. Mark' professes to give a continuous history of Christ's life, as regularly as the other three Gospels, but the work noticed by Papias is expressly stated to have been memoranda, taken down from time to time as Peter delivered them, and it is not said that Mark ever reduced these notes into the form of a more perfect history" ("Christian Records," Rev. Dr. Giles, pp. 94, 95). "It is difficult to see in what respects Mark's Gospel is more loose and disjointed than those of Matthew and Luke.... We are inclined to agree with those who consider the expression [Greek: ou taxei] unsuitable to the present Gospel of Mark. As far as we are able to understand the entire fragment, it is most natural to consider John the Presbyter or Papias assigning a sense to [Greek: ou taxei] which does not agree with the character of the canonical document" ("Introduction to the New Testament," Dr. Davidson, p. 158). This Christian commentator is so disgusted with the conviction he honestly expresses as to the unsuitability of the phrase in question as applied to Mark, that he exclaims: "We presume that John the Presbyter was not infallible.... In the present instance, he appears to have been mistaken in his opinion. His power of perception was feeble, else he would have seen that the Gospel which he describes as being written [Greek: ou taxei], does not differ materially in arrangement from that of Luke. Like Papias, the Presbyter was apparently destitute of critical ability and good judgment, else he could not have entertained an idea so much at variance with fact" (Ibid, p. 159). We may add, for what it is worth, that "according to the unanimous belief of the early Church this Gospel was written at Rome. Hence the conclusion was drawn that it must have been composed in the language of the Romans; that is, Latin. Even in the old Syriac version, a remark is annexed, stating that the writer preached the Gospel in Roman (Latin) at Rome; and the Philoxenian version has a marginal annotation to the same effect. The Syrian Churches seem to have entertained this opinion

81

generally, as may be inferred not only from these versions, but from some of their most distinguished ecclesiastical writers, such as Ebedjesu. Many Greek Manuscripts, too, have a similar remark regarding the language of our Gospel, originally taken, perhaps from the Syriac" (Ibid, pp. 154, 155). We conclude, then, that the document alluded to by the Presbyter John, as reported by Papias through Eusebius, cannot be identical with the present canonical Gospel of Mark. Nor is the testimony regarding Matthew less conclusive: "Of Matthew he has stated as follows: 'Matthew composed his history in the Hebrew dialect, and every one translated it as he was able'" ("Eccles. Hist," Eusebius, bk. iii., ch. 39). The word here translated "history" is [Greek: ta logia] and would be more correctly rendered by "oracles" or "discourses," and much controversy has arisen over this term, it being contended that [Greek: logia] could not rightly be extended so as to include any records of the life of Christ: "It is impossible upon any but arbitrary grounds, and from a foregone conclusion, to maintain that a work commencing with a detailed history of the birth and infancy of Jesus, his genealogy, and the preaching of John the Baptist, and concluding with an equally minute history of his betrayal, trial, crucifixion, and resurrection, and which relates all the miracles, and has for its evident aim throughout the demonstration that Messianic prophecy was fulfilled in Jesus, could be entitled [Greek: ta logia] the oracles or discourses of the Lord. For these and other reasons ... the majority of critics deny that the work described by Papias can be the same as the Gospel in our Canon bearing the name of Matthew" ("Sup. Rel.," vol. i., pp. 471, 472). But the fact which puts the difference between the present "Matthew" and that spoken of by Papias beyond dispute is that Matthew, according to Papias, "wrote in the Hebrew dialect," i.e., the Syro-Chaldaic, or Aramæan, while the canonical Matthew is written in Greek. "There is no point, however, on which the testimony of the Fathers is more invariable and complete than that the work of Matthew was written in Hebrew or Aramaic" ("Sup. Rel.," vol. i., p. 475). This industrious author quotes Papias, Irenæus, Pantænus in Eusebius, Eusebius, Origen, Cyril of Jerusalem, Epiphanius, Jerome, in support of his assertion, and remarks that "the same tradition is repeated by Chrysostom, Augustine and others" (Ibid, pp. 475-477). "We believe that Matthew wrote his Gospel in Hebrew, meaning by that term the common language of the Jews of his time, because such is the uniform statement of all ancient writers who advert to the subject. To pass over others whose authority is of less weight, he is affirmed to have written in Hebrew by Papias, Irenæus, Origen, Eusebius, and Jerome. Nor does any ancient author advance a contrary opinion" ("Genuineness of the Gospels," Norton, vol. i., pp. 196, 197). "Ancient historical testimony is unanimous in declaring that Matthew wrote his Gospel in Hebrew, i.e., in the Aramæan or Syro-Chaldaic language, at that time the vernacular

82

tongue of the Jews in Palestine" (Davidson's "Introduction to the New Testament," p. 3). After a most elaborate presentation of the evidences, the learned doctor says: "Let us now pause to consider this account of the original Gospel of Matthew. It runs through all antiquity. None doubted of its truth, as far as we can judge from their writings. There is not the least trace of an opposite tradition" (Ibid, p. 37). The difficulty of Christian apologists is, then, to prove that the Gospel written by Matthew in Hebrew is the same as the Gospel according to Matthew in Greek, and sore have been the shifts to which they have been driven in the effort. Dean Alford, unable to deny that all the testimony which could be relied upon to prove that Matthew wrote at all, also proved that he wrote in Hebrew, and aware that an unauthorised translation, which could not be identified with the original, could never claim canonicity, fell back on the remarkable notion that he himself translated his Hebrew Gospel into Greek; in the edition of his Greek Testament published in 1859, however, he gives up this notion in favour of the idea that the original Gospel of Matthew was written in Greek.

Of his earlier theory of translation by Matthew, Davidson justly says: "It is easy to perceive its gratuitous character. It is a clumsy expedient, devised for the purpose of uniting two conflicting opinions— for saving the credit of ancient testimony, which is on the side of a Hebrew original, and of meeting, at the same time, the difficulties supposed to arise from the early circulation of the Greek.... The advocates of the double hypothesis go in the face of ancient testimony. Besides, they believe that Matthew wrote in Hebrew, for the use of Jewish converts. Do they also suppose his Greek Gospel to have been intended for the same class? If so, the latter was plainly unnecessary: one Gospel was sufficient for the same persons. Or do they believe that the second edition of it was designed for Gentile Christians? if so, the notion is contradicted by internal evidence, which proves that it was written specially for Jews. In short, the hypothesis is wholly untenable, and we are surprised that it should have found so many advocates" ("Introduction to the New Testament," p. 52). The fact is, that no one knows who was the translator—or, rather, the writer—of the Greek Gospel. Jerome honestly says that it is not known who translated it into Greek. Dr. Davidson has the following strange remarks: "The author indeed must ever remain unknown; but whether he were an apostle or not, he must have had the highest sanction in his proceeding. His work was performed with the cognisance, and under the eye of Apostolic men. The reception it met with proved the general belief of his calling, and competency to the task. Divine superintendence was exercised over him" (Ibid, pp. 72, 73). It is difficult to understand how Dr. Davidson knows that divine superintendence was exercised over an unknown individual. Dr. Giles argues against the hypothesis that our Greek Gospel is a translation: "If St. Matthew wrote his Gospel in Hebrew, why has the original perished? The existing Greek text is either a translation of the Hebrew, or it is a separate work. But it cannot be a translation, for many reasons, 1. Because there is not the slightest evidence on record of its being a translation. 2. Because it is unreasonable to believe that an authentic work—written by inspiration—would perish, or be superseded by, an unauthenticated translation—for all translations are less authentic than their originals. 3. Because there are many features in our present Gospel according to St. Matthew, which are common to the Gospels of St. Mark and St. Luke; which would lead to the inference that the latter are translations also. Besides, there is nothing in the Gospel of St. Matthew, as regards its style or construction, that would lead to the inference of its being a translation, any more than all the other books contained in the New Testament. For these reasons we conclude that the 'Hebrew Gospel of St. Matthew,' which perhaps no one has seen since Pantænus, who brought it from India, and the 'Greek Gospel according to St. Matthew,' are separate and independent works" ("Christian Records." Rev. Dr. Giles, pp. 93, 94). It must not be forgotten that there was in existence in the early Church a Hebrew Gospel which was widely spread, and much used. It was regarded by the Ebionites, or Jewish Christians, later known as Nazarenes, as the only authentic Gospel, and Epiphanius, writing in the fourth century, says: "They have the Gospel of Matthew very complete; for it is well known that this is preserved among them as it was first written in Hebrew" ("Opp.," i. 124, as quoted by Norton). But this Gospel, known as the "Gospel according to the Hebrews," was not the same as the Greek "Gospel according to St. Matthew." If it had been the same, Jerome would not have thought it worth while to translate it; the quotations that he makes from it are enough to prove to demonstration that the present Gospel of Matthew is not that spoken of in the earliest days. "The following positions are deducible from St. Jerome's writings: 1. The authentic Gospel of Matthew was written in Hebrew. 2. The Gospel according to the Hebrews was used by the Nazarenes and Ebionites. 3. This Gospel was identical with the Aramæan original of Matthew" (Davidson's "Introduction to the New Testament," p. 12). To these arguments may be added the significant fact that the quotations in Matthew from the Old Testament are taken from the Septuagint, and not from the Hebrew version. The original Hebrew Gospel of Matthew would surely not have contained quotations from the Greek translation, rather than from the Hebrew original, of the Jewish Scriptures. If our present Gospel is an accurate translation of the original Matthew, we must believe that the Jewish Matthew, writing for Jews, did not use the Hebrew Scriptures, with which his readers would be familiar, but went out of his way to find the hated Septuagint, and re-translated it into Hebrew. Thus we find that the boasted testimony said to be recorded by Papias to the effect that Matthew and Mark wrote our two first

84

synoptical Gospels breaks down completely under examination, and that instead of proving the authenticity of the present Gospels, it proves directly the reverse, since the description there given of the writings ascribed to Matthew and Mark is not applicable to the writings that now bear their names, so that we find that in Papias there is evidence that two of the Gospels were not the same.

H. That there is evidence that the earlier records were not the Gospels now esteemed Canonical. This position is based on the undisputed fact that the "Evangelical quotations" in early Christian writings differ very widely from sentences of somewhat similar character in the Canonical Gospels, and also from the circumstance that quotations not to be found in the Canonical Gospels are found in the writings referred to. Various theories are put forward, as we have already seen, to account for the differences of expression and arrangement: the Fathers are said to have quoted loosely, to have quoted from memory, to have combined, expanded, condensed, at pleasure. To prove this general laxity of quotation, Christian apologists rely much on what they assert is a similar laxity shown in quoting from the Old Testament; and Mr. Sanday has used this argument with considerable skill. But it does not follow that variations in quotations from the Old Testament spring from laxity and carelessness; they are generally quite as likely to spring from multiplicity of versions, for we find Mr. Sanday himself saying that "most of the quotations that we meet with are taken from the LXX. Version; and the text of that version was, at this particular time especially, uncertain and fluctuating. There is evidence to show that it must have existed in several forms, which differed more or less from that of the extant MSS. It would be rash, therefore, to conclude at once, because we find a quotation differing from the present text of the LXX., that it differed from that which was used by the writer making the quotation" ("Gospels in the Second Century," pp. 16, 17). Besides, it must not be forgotten that the variation is sometimes too persistent to spring from looseness of quotation, and that the same variation is not always confined to one author. The position for which we contend will be most clearly appreciated by giving, at full length, one of the passages most relied upon by Christian apologists; and we will take, as an example of supposed quotation, the long passage in Clement, chap. xiii.:—

MATTHEW	CLEMENT	LUKE
v. 7. Blessed are the pitiful, for they shall be pitied. vi. 14. For if ye	Especially remembering the word of the Lord Jesus when he spake, teaching gentleness and long-suffering.	vi. 36. Be ye, therefore, merciful, as your Father also is merciful.

forgive men their trespasses, your heavenly Father will also forgive you. vii. 12. All things, therefore, whatsoever ye would that men should do unto you, even so do ye unto them.	For thus he said:	vi. 37. Acquit, and ye shall be acquitted.
	Pity ye, that ye may be pitied: forgive, that it may be forgiven unto you. As ye do, so shall it be done unto you; as ye give, so shall it be given unto you; as ye judge, so shall it be judged unto you; as ye are kind, so shall kindness be shown unto you:	vi. 31. And as ye would that they should do unto you, do ye also unto them likewise. vi. 18. Give, and it shall be given unto you.
vii. 2. For with what judgment ye judge, ye shall be judged, and with what measure ye mete it shall be measured unto you.	with that measure ye mete, with it shall it be measured unto you.	vi. 37. And judge not, and ye shall not be judged. For with what measure ye mete, it shall be measured unto you again.

The English, as here given, represents as closely as possible both the resemblances and the differences of the Greek text. What reader, in reading this, can believe that Clement picked out a bit here and a bit there from the Canonical Gospels, and then wove them into one connected whole, which he forthwith represented as said thus by Christ? To the unprejudiced student the hypothesis will, at once, suggest itself—there must have been some other document current in Clement's time, which contained the sayings of Christ, from which this quotation was made. Only the exigencies of Christian apologetic work forbid the general adoption of so simple and so natural a solution of the question. Mr. Sanday says: "Doubtless light would be thrown upon the question if we only knew what was the common original of the two Synoptic texts ... The differences in these extra-Canonical quotations do not exceed the differences between the Synoptic Gospels themselves; yet by far the larger proportion of critics regard the resemblances in the Synoptics as due to a common written source used either by all three or by two of them" ("Gospels in the Second Century," p. 65). It is clear that Jesus could not have said these passages in the words given by Matthew, Clement, and Luke, repeating himself in three different forms, now connectedly, now in fragments; two, at least, out of the three must give an imperfect report. Mr. Sanday, by speaking of "the common original of the two Synoptic texts," clearly shows that he does not regard the Synoptic version as original, and thereby helps to buttress our contention, that the Gospels we have now are not the only ones that were current in the early Church, and that they had no exclusive authority—in fact, that they were not "Canonical." Further on, Mr. Sanday, referring to Polycarp, says: "I cannot but think that there has been somewhere a written version different from our Gospels to which he and Clement have had access ... It will be observed that all the quotations refer either to the double or treble Synoptics, where we have already proof of the existence of the saying in question in more than a single form, and not to those portions that are peculiar to the individual Evangelists. The author of 'Supernatural Religion' is, therefore, not without reason when he says that they may be derived from other collections than our actual Gospels. The possibility cannot be excluded" ("Gospels in the Second Century," pp. 86, 87). The other passage from Clement is yet more unlike anything in the Canonical Gospels: in chap. xlvi. we read:—

MATTHEW	CLEMENT	LUKE	MARK
xxvi. 24. Woe to that man by whom the Son of man is delivered up; well for him if that man had not been born.	He said: Woe to that man; well for him that he had not been born than that he should offend one of my elect; better for him a millstone should be attached (to him), and he should be drowned in the sea, than that he should offend one of my little ones.	xvii. 1. Woe through whom they (offences) come. 2.It were advantageous for him that a great millstone were hanged around his neck, and he cast in the sea, than that he should offend one of these little ones.	xiv. 21. Woe to that man by whom the Son of man is delivered up, well for him if that man had not been born.
xviii. 6. But whoso shall offend one of these little ones which believe in me, it were profitable for him that a great millstone were suspended upon his neck, and that he were drowned in the depth of the sea.			ix. 42. And whosoever shall offend one of these little ones which believe in me, it is well for him rather that a great millstone were hanged about his neck, and he thrown in the sea.

"This quotation is clearly not from our Gospels, but is derived from a different written source.... The slightest comparison of the passage with our Gospels is sufficient to convince any unprejudiced mind that it is neither a combination of texts, nor a quotation from memory. The language throughout is markedly different, and, to present even a superficial parallel, it is necessary to take a fragment of the discourse of Jesus at the Last Supper, regarding the traitor who should deliver him up (Matt. xxvi. 24), and join it to a fragment of his remarks in connection with the little child whom he set in the midst (xviii. 6)" ("Sup. Rel.," vol. i., pp. 233, 234).

In Polycarp a passage is found much resembling that given from Clement, chap, xiii., but not exactly reproducing it, which is open to the same criticism as that passed on Clement.

If we desire to prove that Gospels other than the Canonical were in use, the proof lies ready to our hands. In chap. xlvi. of Clement we read: "It is written, cleave to the holy, for they who cleave to them shall be made holy." In chap. xliv.: "And our Apostles knew, through our Lord Jesus Christ, that there would be contention regarding the office of the episcopate." The author of "Supernatural Religion" gives us passages somewhat resembling this. He said: "There shall be schisms and heresies," from Justin Martyr ("Trypho," chap. xxxv): "There shall be, as the Lord said, false apostles, false prophets, heresies, desires for supremacy," from the "Clementine Homilies": "From these came the false Christs, false prophets, false apostles, who divided the unity of the Church," from Hegesippus (vol. i. p. 236).

In Barnabas we read, chap. vi.: "The Lord saith, He maketh a new creation in the last times. The Lord saith, Behold I make the first as the last." Chap. vii.: Jesus says: "Those who desire to behold me, and to enter into my kingdom, must, through tribulation and suffering, lay hold upon me."

In Ignatius we find: Ep. Phil., chap, vii.: "But the Spirit proclaimed, saying these words: Do ye nothing without the Bishop." "There is, however, one quotation, introduced as such, in this same Epistle, the source of which Eusebius did not know, but which Origen refers to 'the Preaching of Peter,' and Jerome seems to have found in the Nazarene version of the 'Gospel according to the Hebrews.' This phrase is attributed to our Lord when he appeared 'to those about Peter and said to them, Handle me, and see that I am not an incorporeal spirit.' But for the statement of Origen, that these words occurred in the 'Preaching of Peter,' they might have been referred without much difficulty to Luke xxiv. 39" ("Gospels in the Second Century," p. 81). And they most certainly would have been so referred, and dire would have been Christian wrath against those who refused to admit these words as a proof of the canonicity of Luke's Gospel in the time of Ignatius.

If, turning to Justin Martyr, we take one or two passages resembling other passages to be found in the Canonical, we shall then see the same type of differences as we have already remarked in

88

Clement. In the fifteenth and sixteenth chapters of the first "Apology" we find a collection of the sayings of Christ, most of which are to be read in the Sermon on the Mount; in giving these Justin mentions no written work from which he quotes. He says: "We consider it right, before giving you the promised explanation, to cite a few precepts given by Christ himself" ("Apology," chap. xiv). If these had been taken from Gospels written by Apostles, is it conceivable that Justin would not have used their authority to support himself?

MATTHEW	JUSTIN
v. 46. For if ye should love them which love you, what reward have ye? do not even the publicans the same?	And of our love to all, he taught thus: If ye love them that love ye, what new things do ye? for even fornicators do this; but I say unto you: Pray for your enemies, and love them which hate you, and bless them which curse you, and offer prayer for them which despitefully use you.
v. 44. But I say unto you, love your enemies, bless them which curse you, do good to them which hate you, and pray for them which despitefully use you and persecute you.	

The corresponding passage in Luke is still further from Justin (Luke vi. 32-35). "It will be observed that here again Justin's Gospel reverses the order in which the parallel passage is found in our synoptics. It does so indeed, with a clearness of design which, even without the actual peculiarities of diction and construction, would indicate a special and different source. The passage varies throughout from our Gospels, but Justin repeats the same phrases in the same order elsewhere" ("Sup. Rel," v. i. p. 353, note 2).

MATTHEW	JUSTIN
v. 42. Give thou to him that asketh thee, and from him that would borrow of thee turn not thou away.	He said: Give ye to every one that asketh, and from him that desireth to borrow turn not ye away: for if ye lend to them from whom ye hope to receive, what new thing do ye? for even the publicans do this.
Luke vi. 34. And if you lend to them from whom ye hope to receive, what thank have ye; for sinners also lend to sinners to receive as much again.	
Matt. vi. 19, 20. Lay not up for	But ye, lay not up for yourselves upon the earth, where moth and rust doth corrupt, and robbers break through, but lay up for yourselves in the heavens, where neither moth nor

yourselves treasures upon earth, where moth and rust doth corrupt, and where thieves break through and steal. But lay up for yourselves treasures in heaven, where neither moth nor rust doth corrupt, and where thieves do not break through nor steal.

xvi. 26. For what shall a man be profited if he shall gain the whole world, but lose his soul? or what shall a man give in exchange for his soul?

rust doth corrupt.

For what is a man profited, if he shall gain the whole world, but destroy his soul? or what shall he give in exchange for it? Lay up, therefore, in the heavens, where neither moth nor rust doth corrupt.

This passage is clearly unbroken in Justin, and forms one connected whole; to parallel it from the Synoptics we must go from Matthew v., 42, to Luke vi., 34, then to Matthew vi., 19, 20, off to Matthew xvi. 26, and back again to Matthew vi. 19; is such a method of quotation likely, especially when we notice that Justin, in quoting passages on a given subject (as at the beginning of chap. xv. on chastity), separates the quotations by an emphatic "And," marking the quotation taken from another place? These passages will show the student how necessary it is that he should not accept a few words as proof of a quotation from a synoptic, without reading the whole passage in which they occur. The coincidence of half a dozen words is no quotation when the context is different, and there is no break between the context and the words relied upon. "It is absurd and most arbitrary to dissect a passage, quoted by Justin as a consecutive and harmonious whole, and finding parallels more or less approximate to its various phrases scattered up and down distant parts of our Gospels, scarcely one of which is not materially different from the reading of Justin, to assert that he is quoting these Gospels freely from memory, altering, excising, combining, and inter-weaving texts, and introverting their order, but nevertheless making use of them and not of others. It is perfectly obvious that such an assertion is nothing but the merest assumption" ("Sup. Rel.," vol. i., p. 364). Mr. Sanday's conclusion as to Justin is: "The à priori probabilities of the case, as well as the actual phenomena of Justin's Gospel, alike tend to show that he did make use either mediately or immediately of our Gospels, but that he did not assign to them an exclusive authority, and that he probably made use along with them of other documents no longer extant" ("Gospels in the Second Century," p. 117). It is needless to multiply analyses of quotations, as the system applied to the two given above can be carried out for himself by the student in other cases. But a far weightier proof

90

remains that Justin's "Memoirs of the Apostles" were not the Canonical Gospels; and that is, that Justin used expressions, and mentions incidents which are not to be found in our Gospels, and some of which are to be found in Apocryphal Gospels. For instance, in the first "Apology," chap. xiii., we read: "We have been taught that the only honour that is worthy of him is not to consume by fire what he has brought into being for our sustenance, but to use it for ourselves and those who need, and with gratitude to him to offer thanks by invocations and hymns for our creation, and for all the means of health, and for the various qualities of the different kinds of things, and for the changes of the seasons; and to present before him petitions for our existing again in incorruption through faith in him. Our teacher of these things is Jesus Christ, who also was born for this purpose." "He has exhorted us to lead all men, by patience and gentleness, from shame and the love of evil" (Ibid, chap. xvi.). "For the foal of an ass stood bound to a vine" (Ibid, chap. xxxii.). "The angel said to the Virgin, Thou shalt call his name Jesus, for he shall save his people from their sins" (chap. xxxiii.). "They tormented him, and set him on the judgment seat, and said, Judge us" (chap. xxxv.). "Our Lord Jesus Christ said, In whatsoever things I shall take you, in these I shall judge you" ("Trypho," chapter xlviii.). These are only some out of the many passages of which no resemblance is to be found in the Canonical Gospels.

The best way to show the truth of Paley's contention—that "from Justin's works, which are still extant, might be collected a tolerably complete account of Christ's life, in all points agreeing with that which is delivered in our Scriptures; taken indeed, in a great measure, from those Scriptures, but still proving that this account and no other, was the account known and extant in that age" ("Evidences," p. 77)—will be to give the story from Justin, mentioning every notice of Christ in his works, which gives anything of his supposed life, only omitting passages relating solely to his teaching, such as those given above. The large majority of these are taken from the "Dialogue with Trypho," a wearisome production, in which Justin endeavours to convince a Jew that Christ is the Messiah, by quotations from the Jewish Scriptures (which, by the way, include Esdras, thus placing that book on a level with the other inspired volumes). A noticeable peculiarity of this Dialogue is, that any alleged incident in Christ's life is taken as true, not because it is authenticated as historical, but simply because it was prophesied of; Justin's Christ is, in fact, an ideal, composed out of the prophecies of the Jews, and fitted on to a Jew named Jesus.

Christ was the offspring truly brought forth from the Father, before the creation of anything else, the Word begotten of God, before all his works, and he appeared before his birth, sometimes as a flame of fire, sometimes as an angel, as at Sodom, to Moses, to Joshua. He was called by Solomon,

Wisdom; and by the Prophets and by Christians, the King, the Eternal Priest, God, Lord, Angel, Man, the Flower, the Stone, the Cornerstone, the Rod, the Day, the East, the Glory, the Rock, the Sword, Jacob, Israel, the Captain, the Son, the Helper, the Redeemer. He was born into the World by the over-shadowing of God the Holy Ghost, who is none other than the Word himself, and produced without sexual union by a virgin of the seed of Jacob, Judah, Phares, Jesse, and David, his birth being announced by an angel, who told the Virgin to call his name Jesus, for he should save his people from their sins. Joseph, the spouse of Mary, desired to put her away, but was commanded in a vision not to put away his wife, the angel telling him that what was in her womb was of the Holy Ghost. At the first census taken in Judæa, under Cyrenius, the first Roman Procurator, he left Nazareth where he lived, and went to Bethlehem, to which he belonged, his family being of the tribe of Judah, and then was ordered to proceed to Egypt with Mary and the child, and remain there until another revelation warned them to return to Judæa. At Bethlehem Joseph could find no lodging in the village, so took up his quarters in a cave near, where Christ was born and placed in a manger. Here he was found by the Magi from Arabia, who had been to Jerusalem inquiring what king was born there, they having seen a star rise in heaven. They worshipped the child and gave him gold, frankincense, and myrrh, and warned by a revelation, went home without telling Herod where they had found the child. So Herod, when Joseph, Mary, and the child had gone into Egypt, as they were commanded, ordered the whole of the children then in Bethlehem to be massacred. Archelaus succeeded Herod, and was succeeded himself by another Herod. The child grew up like all other men, and was a man without comeliness, and inglorious, working as a carpenter, making ploughs and yokes, and when he was thirty years of age, more or less, he went to Jordan to be baptised by John, who was the herald of his approach. When he stepped into the water a fire was kindled in the Jordan, and when he came out of the water the Holy Ghost lighted on him like a dove, and at the same instant a voice came from the heavens: "Thou art my son; this day have I begotten thee." He was tempted by Satan, and of like passions with men; he was spotless and sinless, and the blameless and righteous man; he made whole the lame, the paralytic, and those born blind, and he raised the dead; he was called, because of his mighty works, a magician, and a deceiver of the people. He stood in the midst of his brethren the Apostles, and when living with them sang praises unto God. He changed the names of the sons of Zebedee to Boanerges, and of another of the Apostles to Peter. He ordered his acquaintance to bring him an ass, and the foal of an ass which stood bound to a vine, and he mounted and rode into Jerusalem. He overthrew the tables of the money-changers in the temple. He gave us bread and wine in remembrance of his taking our flesh and of shedding his blood. He took upon him the curses of all, and by his stripes the human race is healed. On the day in which he was to be crucified (elsewhere called the night before) he took three disciples to the hill called Olivet, and prayed; his sweat fell to the ground like drops, his heart and also his bones trembling; men went to the Mount of Olives to seize him; he was seized on the day of the Passover, and crucified during the Passover; Pilate sent Jesus bound to Herod; before Pilate he kept silence; they set Christ on the judgment seat, and said: "Judge us;" he was crucified under Pontius Pilate; his hands and feet were pierced; they cast lots for his vesture, and divided it; they that saw him crucified, shook their heads and mocked him, saying: "Let him who raised the dead save himself." "He said he was the Son of God; let him come down; let God save him." He gave up his spirit to the Father, and after he was crucified all his acquaintance forsook him, having denied him. He rose on the third day; he was crucified on Friday, and rose on "the day of the Sun," and appeared to the Apostles and taught them to read the prophecies, and they repented of their flight, after they were persuaded by himself that he had beforehand warned them of his sufferings, and that these sufferings were prophesied of. They saw him ascend. The rulers in heaven were commanded to admit the King of Glory, but seeing him uncomely and dishonoured they asked, "Who is this King of Glory?" God will keep Christ in heaven until he has subdued his enemies the devils. He will return in glory, raise the bodies of the dead, clothe the good with immortality, and send the bad, endued with eternal sensibility into everlasting fire. He has the everlasting kingdom.

These references to Jesus are scattered up and down through Justin's writings, without any chronological order, a phrase here, a phrase there; only in one or two instances are two or three things related even in the same chapter. They are arranged here connectedly, as nearly as possible in the usually accepted order, and the greatest care has been taken not to omit any. It will be worth while to note the differences between this and our Gospels, and also the allusions to other Gospels which it contains. Christ is clearly subsequent in time to the Father, being brought forth from him; he conceives himself, he being here identified with the Holy Ghost; it is the virgin who descends from David, a fact of which there is no hint given in our Gospels; the reason of the name Jesus is told to the Virgin instead of to Joseph; we hear nothing of the shepherds and the glory of the Lord round the chanting angels; Jesus is uncomely, and works making ploughs and yokes, of which, we hear nothing in the Gospels; the fire at the baptism is not mentioned in the Gospels, and the voice from heaven speaks in words not found in them; he is called a magician, of which accusation we know nothing from the four; the colt of the ass is tied to a vine, a circumstance omitted in the canonical writings; it is no where said in the New Testament that the bread at the Lord's supper is given in remembrance of the incarnation, but, on the contrary, it is in remembrance of the death of Christ; the crucifixion is not stated to have taken place during the Passover, but on the contrary the Fourth Gospel places it before, the others after, the Passover; we hear nothing of Christ set on the judgment seat in the Gospels: the vesture is not divided according to John, who draws a distinction between the vesture and the raiment which is not recognised by Justin; the taunts of the crowd are different; the denial of Christ by all the Apostles is uncanonical, as is also their forsaking him after the crucifixion; we do not hear of the "day of the Sun" in our Gospels, nor of the rulers of heaven and their reception of Christ. In fact, there are more points of divergence than of coincidence between the details of the story of Jesus given by Justin and that given in the Four Gospels, and yet Paley says that: "all the references in Justin are made without mentioning the author; which proves that these books were perfectly notorious, and that there were no other accounts of Christ then extant, or, at least, no others so received and credited, as to make it necessary to distinguish these from the rest" ("Evidences," p. 123). And Paley has actually the hardihood to state that what "seems extremely to be observed is, that in all Justin's works, from which might be extracted almost a complete life of Christ, there are but two instances in which he refers to anything as said or done by Christ, which is not related concerning him in our present Gospels; which shows that these Gospels, and these, we may say, alone, were the authorities from which the Christians of that day drew the information upon which they depended" (Ibid pp. 122, 123). Paley, probably, never intended that a life of Christ should "be extracted" from "all Justin's works." It is done above, and the reader may judge for himself of Paley's truthfulness. One of the "two instances" is given as follows: "The other, of a circumstance in Christ's baptism, namely, a fiery or luminous appearance upon the water, which, according to Epiphanius, is noticed in the Gospel of the Hebrews; and which might be true; but which, whether true or false, is mentioned by Justin with a plain mark of diminution when compared with what he quotes as resting upon Scripture authority. The reader will advert to this distinction. 'And then, when Jesus came to the river Jordan, where John was baptising, as Jesus descended into the water, a fire also was kindled in Jordan; and when he came up out of the water, the apostles of this our Christ have written, that the Holy Ghost lighted upon him as a dove'" (Ibid, p. 123). The italics here are Paley's own. Now let the reader turn to the passage itself, and he will find that Paley

94

has deliberately altered the construction of the phrases, in order to make a "distinction" that Justin does not make, inserting the reference to the apostles in a different place to that which it holds in Justin. Is it credible that such duplicity passes to-day for argument? one can only hope that the large majority of Christians who quote Paley are ignorant, and are, therefore, unconscious of the untruthfulness of the apologist; the passage quoted is taken from the "Dialogue with Trypho," chap. 88, and runs as follows: "Then, when Jesus had gone to the river Jordan, where John was baptising, and when he had stepped into the water, a fire was kindled in the Jordan; and when he came out of the water, the Holy Ghost lighted on him like a dove; the apostles of this very Christ of ours wrote" [thus]. The phrase italicised by Paley concludes the account, and if it refers to one part of the story, it refers to all; thus the reader can see for himself that Justin makes no "mark of diminution" of any kind, but gives the whole story, fire, Holy Ghost, and all, as from the "Memoirs." The mockery of Christ on the cross is worded differently in Justin and in the Gospels, and he distinctly says that he quotes from the "Memoirs." "They spoke in mockery the words which are recorded in the memoirs of his Apostles: 'He said he was the Son of God; let him come down: let God save him'" ("Dial." chap. ci.).

If we turn to the Clementines, we find, in the same way, passages not to be found in the Canonical Gospels. "And Peter said: We remember that our Lord and Teacher, as commanding us, said: Keep the mysteries for me, and the sons of my house" ("Hom." xix. chap. 20). "And Peter said: If, therefore, of the Scriptures some are true and some are false, our Teacher rightly said: 'Be ye good money-changers,' as in the Scriptures there are some true sayings and some spurious" ("Hom." ii. chap. 51; see also iii. chap. 50. and xviii. chap. 20). This saying of Christ is found in many of the Fathers. "To those who think that God tempts, as the Scriptures say he [Jesus] said: 'The tempter is the wicked one, who also tempted himself'" ("Hom." iii. chap. 55).

Of the Clementine "Homilies" Mr. Sanday remarks, "several apocryphal sayings, and some apocryphal details, are added. Thus the Clementine writer calls John a 'Hemerobaptist,' i.e., member of a sect which practised daily baptism. He talks about a rumour which became current in the reign of Tiberius, about the 'vernal equinox,' that at the same time a King should arise in Judæa who should work miracles, making the blind to see, the lame to walk, healing every disease, including leprosy, and raising the dead; in the incident of the Canaanite woman (whom, with Mark, he calls a Syrophoenician) he adds her name, 'Justa,' and that of her daughter 'Bernice.' He also limits the ministry of our Lord to one year" ("Gospels in the Second Century," pp. 167, 168). But it is needless to multiply such passages; three or four would be enough to prove our position: whence were they drawn, if not from records differing from the Gospels now received? We, therefore, conclude that in the numerous Evangelical passages quoted by the

Fathers, which are not in the Canonical Gospels, we find evidence that the earlier records were not the Gospels now esteemed Canonical.

I. That the books themselves show marks of their later origin. We should draw this conclusion from phrases scattered throughout the Gospels, which show that the writers were ignorant of local customs, habits, and laws, and therefore could not have been Jews contemporary with Jesus at the date when he is alleged to have lived. We find a clear instance of this ignorance in the mention made by Luke of the census which is supposed to have brought Joseph and Mary to Bethlehem immediately before the birth of Jesus. If Jesus was born at the time alleged "the Roman census in question must have been made either under Herod the Great, or at the commencement of the reign of Archelaus. This is in the highest degree improbable, for in those countries which were not reduced in formam provinciæ, but were governed by regibus sociis, the taxes were levied by these princes, who paid a tribute to the Romans; and this was the state of things in Judæa prior to the deposition of Archelaus.... The Evangelist relieves us from a further inquiry into this more or less historical or arbitrary combination by adding that this taxing was first made when Cyrenius (Quirinus) was Governor of Syria [Greek: haegemoneuontos taes Surias Kuraeniou] for it is an authenticated point that the assessment of Quirinus did not take place either under Herod or early in the reign of Archelaus, the period at which, according to Luke, Jesus was born. Quirinus was not at that time Governor of Syria, a situation held during the last years of Herod by Lentius Saturninus, and after him by Quintilius Varus; and it was not till long after the death of Herod that Quirinus was appointed Governor of Syria. That Quirinus undertook a census of Judæa we know certainly from Josephus, who, however, remarks that he was sent to execute this measure when Archelaus' country was laid to the province of Syria (compare "Ant.," bk. xvii. ch. 13, sec. 5; bk. xviii. ch. 1, sec. 1; "Wars of the Jews," bk. ii. ch. 8, sec. 1; and ch. 9, sec. 1) thus, about ten years after the time at which, according to Matthew and Luke, Jesus must have been born" (Strauss's "Life of Jesus," vol. i., pp. 202-204).

The confusion of dates, as given in Luke, proves that the writer was ignorant of the internal history of Judæa and the neighbouring provinces. The birth of Jesus, according to Luke, must have taken place six months after the birth of John Baptist, and as John was born during the reign of Herod, Jesus must also have been born under the same King, or else at the commencement of the reign of Archelaus. Yet Luke says that he was born during the census in Judæa, which, as we have seen just above, took place ten years later. "The Evangelist, therefore, in order to get a census, must have conceived the condition of things such as they were after the deposition of Archelaus; but in order to get a census extending to Galilee, he must have imagined the kingdom to have continued undivided, as in the time of Herod the Great. [Strauss had explained that the reduction of the kingdom of Archelaus into a Roman province did not affect Galilee, which was still ruled by Herod Antipas as an allied prince, and that a census taken by the Roman Governor would, therefore, not extend to Galilee, and could not affect Joseph, who, living at Nazareth, would be the subject of Herod. See, as illustrative of this, Luke xxiii. 6, 7.] Thus he deals in manifest contradictions; or, rather, he has an exceedingly sorry acquaintance with the political relations of that period; for he extends the census not only to the whole of Palestine, but also (which we must not forget) to the whole Roman world" (Strauss's "Life of Jesus," vol. i., p. 206).

After quoting one of the passages of Josephus referred to above, Dr. Giles says: "There can be little doubt that this is the mission of Cyrenius which the Evangelist supposed to be the occasion of the visit of Christ's parents to Bethlehem. But such an error betrays on the part of the writer a great ignorance of the Jewish history, and of Jewish politics; for, if Christ was born in the reign of Herod the Great, no Roman census or enrolment could have taken place in the dominions of an independent King. If, however, Christ was born in the year of the census, not only Herod the Great, but Archelaus, also, his son, was dead. Nay, by no possibility can the two events be brought together; for even after the death of Archelaus, Judæa alone became a Roman province; Galilee was still governed by Herod Antipas as an independent prince, and Christ's parents would not have been required to go out of their own country to Jerusalem, for the purpose of a census which did not comprise their own country, Galilee. Besides which, it is notorious that the Roman census was taken from house to house, at the residence of each, and not at the birth-place or family rendezvous of each tribe" ("Christian Records," pp. 120, 121). Another "striking witness to the late composition of the Gospels is furnished by expressions, denoting ideas that could not have had any being in the time of Christ and his disciples, but must have been developed afterwards, at a time when the Christian religion was established on a broader and still increasing basis" (Ibid, p. 169). Dr. Giles has collected many of these, and we take them from his pages. In John i. 15, 16, we read: "John bare witness of him, and cried, saying, This was he of whom I spake, He that cometh after me is preferred before me: for he was before me. And of his fulness have all we received, and grace for grace." At that time none had received of the "fulness of Christ," and the saying in the mouth of John Baptist is an anachronism. The word "cross" is several times used symbolically by Christ, as expressing patience and self-denial; but before his own crucifixion the expression would be incomprehensible, and he would surely not select a phraseology his disciples could not understand; "Bearing the cross" is a later phrase, common among Christians. Matthew xi. 12, Jesus, speaking while John the Baptist is still living, says: "From the days of John the Baptist until now"—an expression that implies a lapse of time.

The word "gospel" was not in use among Christians before the end of the second century; yet we find it in Matthew iv. 23, ix. 35, xxiv. 14, xxvi. 13; Mark i. 14, viii. 35, x. 29, xiii. 10, xiv. 9; Luke ix. 6. The unclean spirit, or rather spirits, who were sent into the swine (Mark v. 9, Luke viii. 30), answered to the question, "What is thy name?" that his name was Legion. "The Four Gospels are written in Greek, and the word 'legion' is Latin; but in Galilee and Peraea the people spoke neither Latin nor Greek, but Hebrew, or a dialect of it. The word 'legion' would be perfectly unintelligible to the disciples of Christ, and to almost everybody in the country" (Ibid, p. 197). The account of Matthew, that Jesus rode on the ass and the colt, to fulfil the prophecy, "Behold thy king cometh unto thee, meek, and sitting upon an ass, and a colt the foal of an ass" (xxi. 5. 7), shows that Matthew did not understand the Hebrew idiom, which should be rendered "sitting upon an ass, even upon a colt, the foal of an ass," and related an impossible riding feat to fulfil the misunderstood prophecy. The whole trial scene shows ignorance of Roman customs: the judge running in and out between accused and people, offering to scourge him and let him go—a course not consistent with Roman justice; then presenting him to the people with a crown of thorns and purple robe. The Roman administration would not condescend to a procedure so unjust and so undignified. The mass of contradictions in the Gospels, noticed under k, show that they could not have been written by disciples possessing personal knowledge of the events narrated; while the fact that they are written in Greek, as we shall see below, under j, proves that they were not written by "unlearned and ignorant" Jews, and were not contemporary records, penned by the immediate followers of Jesus. From these facts we draw the conclusion. that the books themselves show marks of their later origin.

J. That the language in which they are written is presumptive evidence against their authenticity. We are here dealing with the supposed history of a Jewish prophet written by Jews, and yet we find it written in Greek, a language not commonly known among the Jews, as we learn from the testimony of Josephus: "I have so completely perfected the work I proposed to myself to do, that no other person, whether he were a Jew or a foreigner, had he ever so great an inclination to it, could so accurately deliver these accounts to the Greeks as is done in these books. For those of my own nation freely acknowledge that I far exceed them in the learning belonging to the Jews. I have also taken a great deal of pains to obtain the learning of the Greeks, and understand the elements of the Greek language, although I have so long accustomed myself to speak our own tongue, that I cannot pronounce Greek with sufficient exactness; for our nation does not encourage those that learn the languages of many nations ... on which account, as there have been many who have done their endeavours with great patience to obtain this learning, there have yet hardly been so many as two or three that have succeeded therein, who were immediately well rewarded for their pains" ("Ant." bk. xx. ch. 11, sec 2). He further tells us that "I grew weary, and went on slowly, it being a large subject, and a difficult thing to translate our history into a foreign and, to us, unaccustomed language" (Ibid, Preface). The chief reason, perhaps, for this general ignorance of Greek was the barbarous aversion of the Rabbis to foreign literature. "No one will be partaker of eternal life who reads foreign literature. Execrable is he, as the swineherd, execrable alike, who teaches his son the wisdom of the Greeks" (translated from Latin translation of Rabbi Akiba, as given in note in Keim's "Jesus of Nazara," vol. i. p, 295). It is noteworthy, also, that the Evangelists quote generally from the Septuagint, and that loyal Jews would have avoided doing so, since "the translation of the Bible into Greek had already been the cause of grief, and even of hatred, in Jerusalem" (Ibid, p. 294). In the face of this we are asked to believe that a Galilean fisherman, by the testimony of Acts iv. 13, unlearned and ignorant, outstripped his whole nation, save the "two or three that have succeeded" in learning Greek, and wrote a philosophical and historical treatise in that language. Also that Matthew, a publican, a member of the most degraded class of the Jews, was equally learned, and published a history in the same tongue. Yet these two marvels of erudition were unknown to Josephus, who expressly states that the two or three who had learned Greek, were "immediately well rewarded for their pains." The argument does not tell against Mark and Luke, as no one knows anything about these two writers, and they may have been Greeks, for anything we know to the contrary. If Mark, however, is to be identified with John Mark, sister's son to Barnabas, then it will lie also against him. Leaving aside the main difficulty, pointed out above, it is grossly improbable, on the face of it, that these Jewish writers should employ Greek, even if they knew it, instead of their own tongue. They were writing the story of a Jew; why should they translate all his sayings instead of writing them down as they fell from his lips? Their work lay among the Jews. Eight years after the death of Jesus they rebuked one of their number, Peter, who eat with "men uncircumcised" (Acts xi. 3); nineteen years afterwards they still went only "unto the circumcision" (Gal. ii. 9); twenty-seven years afterwards they were still in Jerusalem, teaching Jews, and carefully fulfilling the law (Acts xxi. 18-24); after this, we hear no more of them, and they must all have been old men, not likely to then change the Jewish habits of their lives. Besides, why should they do so? their whole sphere of work was entirely Jewish, and, if they were educated enough to write at all, they would surely write for the benefit of those amongst whom they worked. The only parallel for so curious a phenomenon as these Greek Gospels, written by ignorant Jews, would be found if a Cornish fisherman and a low London attorney, both perfectly ignorant of German, wrote in German the sayings and doings of a Middlesex carpenter, and as their work was entirely confined to the lower classes of the people, who knew nothing of German, and they desired to place within their reach full knowledge of the carpenter's life, they circulated it among them in German only, and never wrote anything about him in English. The Greek text of the Gospels proves that they were written in later times, when Christianity found its adherents among the Gentile populations. It might, indeed, be fairly urged that the Greek text is a suggestion that the creed did not originate in Judæa at all, but was the offshoot of Gentile thought rather than of Jewish. However that may be, the Greek text forbids us to believe that these Gospels were written by the Jewish contemporaries of Jesus, and we conclude that the language in which they are written is presumptive evidence against their authenticity.

K. That they are in themselves utterly unworthy of credit from (1) the miracles with which they abound. (2) The numerous contradictions of each by the others. (3) The fact that the story of the hero, the doctrines, the miracles, were current long before the supposed dates of the Gospels, so that these Gospels are simply a patchwork composed of older materials.

(1) The miracles with which they abound. Paley asks: "Why should we question the genuineness of these books? Is it for that they contain accounts of supernatural events? I apprehend that this, at the bottom, is the real, though secret cause of our hesitation about them; for, had the writings, inscribed with the names of Matthew and John, related nothing but ordinary history, there would have been no more doubt whether these writings were theirs, than there is concerning the acknowledged works of Josephus or Philo; that is, there would have been no doubt at all" ("Evidences," pp. 105, 106). There is a certain amount of truth in this argument. We do—openly, however, and not secretly—doubt any and every book which is said to be a record of miracles, written by an eye-witness of them; the more important the contents of a book, the more keenly are its credentials scrutinised; the more extraordinary the story it contains, the more carefully are its evidences sifted. In dealing with Josephus, we examine his authenticity before relying at all on his history; finding there is little doubt that the book was written by him, we value it as the account of an apparently careful writer. When we come to passages like one in "Wars of the Jews," bk. vi. ch. 5, sec. 3—which tells us among the portents which forewarned the Jews of the fall of the temple: "A heifer, as she was led by the high priest to be sacrificed, brought forth a lamb in the midst of the temple"—we do not believe it, any more than we believe that the devils went into the swine. If such fables, instead of forming excrescences here and there on the history of Josephus, which may be cut off without injury to the main record, were so interwoven with the history as to be part and parcel of it, so that no history would remain if they were all taken away, then we should reject Josephus as a teller of fables, and not a writer of history. If it were urged that Josephus was an

eye-witness, and recorded what he saw, then we should answer: Either your history is not written by Josephus at all, but is falsely assigned to him in order to give it the credit of being written by a contemporary and an eye-witness; or else your Josephus is a charlatan, who pretended to have seen miracles in order to increase his prestige. If this supposed history of Josephus were widely spread and exercised much influence over mankind, then its authenticity would be very carefully examined and every weak point in the evidences for it tested, just as the Gospels are to-day. We may add, that it is absurd to parallel the Evangelists and Josephus, as though we knew of the one no more than we do of the others. Josephus relates his own life, giving us an account of his family, his childhood, and his education; he then tells us of his travels, of all he did, and of the books he wrote, and the books themselves bear his own announcement of his authorship; for instance, we read: "I, Joseph, the son of Matthias, by birth an Hebrew, a priest also, and one who at first fought against the Romans myself, and was forced to be present at what was done afterwards, am the author of this work" ("Wars of the Jews," Preface, sec. I). To which of the Gospels is such an announcement prefixed? even in Luke, where the historian writes a preface, it is not said: "I, Luke," and anonymous writings must be of doubtful authenticity. Which of the Evangelists has related for us his own life, so that we may judge of his opportunities of knowing what he tells? To which of their histories is such external testimony given as that of Tacitus to Josephus, in spite of the contempt felt by the polished Roman towards the whole Jewish race? Nothing can be more misleading than to speak of Josephus and of the Evangelists as though their writings stood on the same level; every mark of authenticity is present in the one; every mark of authenticity is absent in the other.

We shall argue as against the miraculous accounts of the Gospels—first, that the evidence is insufficient and far below the amount of evidence brought in support of more modern miracles; secondly, that the power to work miracles has been claimed by the Church all through her history, and is still so claimed, and it is, therefore, impossible to mark any period wherein miracles ceased; and, thirdly, that not only are Christian miracles unproven, but that all miracles are impossible, as well as useless if possible.

Paley, arguing for the truth of Christian miracles, and of these only, endeavours to lay down canons which shall exclude all others. Thus, he excludes: "I. Such accounts of supernatural events as are found only in histories by some ages posterior to the transaction.... II. Accounts published in one country of what passed in a distant country, without any proof that such accounts were known or received at home.... III. Transient rumours.... IV. Naked history (fragments, unconnected with subsequent events dependent on the miracles).... V. In a certain way, and to a certain degree, particularity, in names, dates, places, circumstances, and in the order of events preceding or

101

following.... VI. Stories on which nothing depends, in which no interest is involved, nothing is to be done or changed in consequence of believing them.... VII. Accounts which come merely in affirmation of opinions already formed.... It is not necessary to admit as a miracle, what can be resolved into a false perception (such miracles as healing the blind, lame, etc., cannot be reduced under this head), ... or imposture ... or tentative miracles (where, out of many attempts, one succeeds) ... or doubtful (possibly explainable as coincidence, or effect of imagination) ... or exaggeration" ("Evidences," pp. 199-218). Paley then criticises some miracles alleged by Hume, and argues against them. He very fairly criticises and disposes of them, but fails to see that the same style of argument would dispose of his Gospel ones. The Cardinal de Retz sees, at a church in Saragossa, a man who lighted the lamps, and the canons told him "that he had been several years at the gate with one leg only. I saw him with two." Paley urges that "it nowhere appears that he (the Cardinal) either examined the limb, or asked the patient, or indeed any one, a single question about the matter" ("Evidences," page 224). Well argued, Dr. Paley; and in the man who sat outside the beautiful gate of the Temple, who examined the limb, or questioned the patient? Canons I. and II. exclude the Gospel miracles, unless the Gospels are proved to be written by those whose names they bear, and even then there is no proof that either Matthew, Mark, Luke, or John, published their Gospels in Judæa, or that their accounts were "received at home." The doubt and obscurity hanging over the origin of the Gospels themselves, throws the like doubt and obscurity on all that they relate. "Transient rumours," "false perception," "imposture," "doubtful," and "exaggeration"—there is a door open to all these things in the slow and gradual putting together of the collection of legends now known as "the Gospels." We argue that the witness of the Gospels to the miracles cannot be accepted until the Gospels themselves are authenticated, and that the evidence in support of the miracles is, therefore, insufficient. Strauss shows us very clearly how the miracles recorded in the Gospels became ascribed to Jesus. "That the Jewish people in the time of Jesus expected miracles from the Messiah is in itself natural, since the Messiah was a second Moses, and the greatest of the prophets, and to Moses and the prophets the national legend attributed miracles of all kinds.... But not only was it pre-determined in the popular expectation that the Messiah should work miracles in general—the particular kinds of miracles which he was to perform were fixed, also in accordance with Old Testament types and declarations. Moses dispensed meat and drink to the people in a supernatural manner (Ex. xvi. xvii.): the same was expected, as the rabbis explicitly say, from the Messiah. At the prayer of Elisha, eyes were in one case closed, in another, opened supernaturally (2 Kings vi.): the Messiah also was to open the eyes of the blind. By this prophet and his master, even the dead had been raised (1 Kings xvii; 2 Kings iv.); hence to the Messiah also power over death could not be wanting. Among the prophecies, Is. xxxv, 5, 6 (comp. xlii. 7), was especially influential in forming this part of the Messianic idea. It is here said of the Messianic times: Then shall the eyes of the blind be opened and the ears of the deaf unstopped; then shall the lame man leap as a hart, and the tongue of the dumb shall sing" ("Life of Jesus," vol. ii., pp. 235, 236.) In dealing with the alleged healing of the blind, Strauss remarks: "How should we represent to ourselves the sudden restoration of vision to a blind eye by a word or a touch? as purely miraculous and magical? That would be to give up thinking on the subject. As magnetic? There is no precedent of magnetism having influence over a disease of this nature. Or, lastly, as psychical? But blindness is something so independent of the mental life, so entirely corporeal, that the idea of its removal at all, still less of its sudden removal by means of a mental operation, is not to be entertained. We must, therefore, acknowledge that an historical conception of these narratives is more than merely difficult to us; and we proceed to inquire whether we cannot show it to be probable that legends of this kind should arise unhistorically.... That these deeds of Elisha were conceived, doubtless with reference to the passage of Isaiah, as a real opening of the eyes of the blind, is proved by the above rabbinical passage [stating that the Messiah would do all that in ancient times had been done by the hands of the righteous, vol. i., p. 81, note], and hence cures of the blind were expected from the Messiah. Now, if the Christian community, proceeding as it did from the bosom of Judaism, held Jesus to be the Messianic personage, it must manifest the tendency to ascribe to him every Messianic predicate, and, therefore, the one in question" (Ibid, 292, 293).

Not only, then, are the miracles rendered doubtful by the dubious character of the records in which they are found, but there is a clear and reasonable explanation why we should expect to find them in any history of a supposed Messiah. Christian apologists appear to have overlooked the statement in the Gospels that Jesus objected to publicity being given to his supposed miracles; the natural conclusion that sceptics draw from this assertion, is that the miracles never took place at all, and that the supposed modesty of Jesus is invented in order to account for the ignorance of the people concerning the alleged marvels. Judge Strange fairly remarks: "The appeal to miracles is a very questionable resort. Now, as Jesus is repeatedly represented to have exhorted those on whose behalf they were wrought to keep the matter secret to themselves, and as when such signs, upon being asked for, were refused to be accorded by him, and the desire to have them was repressed as sinful, it is to be gathered, in spite of the sayings to the contrary, that the writers were aware that there was no such public sense of the occurrence of these marvels as must have attached to them had they really been enacted, and we are left to the conclusion that there were in fact no such demonstrations" ("The Portraiture and

Mission of Jesus," p. 23). Clearly, miracles are useless, as evidence, unless they are publicly performed, and the secresy used by Jesus suggests fraud rather than miraculous power, and savours of the conjuror rather than of the "God." But, further, there is far stronger evidence for later Church miracles than for those of Christ, or of the apostles, and if evidence in support of miracles is good for anything, these more modern miracles must command our belief. Eusebius relates the following miracle of Narcissus, the thirtieth Bishop of Jerusalem, A.D. 180, as one among many: "Whilst the deacons were keeping the vigils the oil failed them; upon which all the people being very much dejected, Narcissus commanded the men that managed the lights to draw water from a neighbouring well, and to bring it to him. They having done it as soon as said, Narcissus prayed over the water, and then commanded them, in a firm faith in Christ, to pour it into the lamps. When they had also done this, contrary to all natural expectation, by an extraordinary and divine influence, the nature of the water was changed into the quality of oil, and by most of the brethren a small quantity was preserved from that time until our own, as a specimen of the wonder then performed" ("Eccles. Hist," bk. vi., chap. 9). St. Augustine bears personal witness to more than one miracle which happened in his own presence, and gives a long list of cures performed in his time. "One thing may be affirmed, that nothing of importance is omitted, and in regard to essential details they are as explicit as the mass of other cases reported. In every instance names and addresses are stated, and it will have been observed that all these miracles occurred in, or near to, Hippo, and in his own diocese. It is very certain that in every case the fact of the miracle is asserted in the most direct and positive terms" ("Sup. Rel.," vol. i., pp. 167, 168).

None can deny that miraculous powers have been claimed by Christian Churches from the time of Christ down to the present day, and that there is no break which can be pointed to as the date at which these powers ceased. "From the first of the Fathers to the last of the Popes a succession of bishops, of saints, and of martyrs, and of miracles, is continued without interruption; and the progress of superstition was so gradual, and almost imperceptible, that we know not in what particular link we should break the chain of tradition. Every age bears testimony to the wonderful events by which it was distinguished; and its testimony appears no less weighty and respectable than that of the preceding generation, till we are insensibly led on to accuse our own inconsistency, if in the eighth or in the twelfth century we deny to the venerable Bede, or to the holy Bernard, the same degree of confidence which, in the second century, we had so liberally granted to Justin or to Irenæus. If the truth of any of those miracles is appreciated by their apparent use and propriety, every age had unbelievers to convince, heretics to confute, and idolatrous nations to convert; and sufficient motives might always be produced to justify the interposition of heaven. And yet, since every friend to revelation is persuaded of the reality, and every reasonable man is convinced of the cessation, of miraculous powers, it is evident that there must have been some period in which they were either suddenly or gradually withdrawn from the Christian Church. Whatever era is chosen for that purpose, the death of the Apostles, the conversion of the Roman empire, or the extinction of the Arian heresy, the insensibility of the Christians who lived at that time will equally afford a just matter of surprise. They still supported their pretensions after they had lost their power. Credulity performed the office of faith; fanaticism was permitted to assume the language of inspiration; and the effects of accident or contrivance were ascribed to supernatural causes. The recent experience of genuine miracles should have instructed the Christian world in the ways of Providence, and habituated their eye (if we may use a very inadequate expression) to the style of the Divine Artist" (Gibbon's "Decline and Fall," vol. ii., chap. xv., p. 145). The miraculous powers were said to have been given by Christ himself to his disciples. "These signs shall follow them that believe; in my name shall they cast out devils; they shall speak with mew tongues; they shall take up serpents; and, if they drink any deadly thing, it shall not hurt them; they shall lay hands on the sick, and they shall recover" (Mark xvi. 17, 18). This power is exercised by the Apostles (see Acts throughout), by believers in the Churches (1 Cor. xii. 9, 10; Gal. iii. 5; James v. 14, 15); at any rate, it was in force in the time with which these books treat, according to the Christians. Justus, surnamed Barsabas, drinks poison, and is unhurt (Eusebius, bk. iii., chap. xxxix.). Polycarp's martyrdom, supposed to be in the next generation, is accompanied by miracle (Epistle of Church of Smyrna; Apostolical Fathers, p. 92; see ante, pp. 220, 221). At Hierapolis the daughters of Philip the Apostle tell Papias how one was there raised from the dead (Eusebius, bk. iii., ch. xxxix.). Justin Martyr pleads the miracles worked in his own time in Rome itself (second "Apol.," ch. vi.). Irenæus urges that the heretics cannot work miracles as can the Catholics: "they can neither confer sight on the blind, nor hearing on the deaf, nor chase away all sorts of demons ... nor can they cure the weak, or the lame, or the paralytic" ("Against Heretics," bk. ii., ch. xxxi., sec. 2). Tertullian encourages Christians to give up worldly pleasures by reminding them of their grander powers: "what nobler than to tread under foot the gods of the nations, to exorcise evil spirits, to perform cures?" ("De Spectaculis," sec. 29). "Origen claims for Christians the power still to expel demons, and to heal diseases, in the name of Jesus; and he states that he had seen many persons so cured of madness, and countless other evils" (quoted from "Origen against Celsus" in "Sup. Rel.," vol. i., p. 154. A mass of evidence on this subject will be found in chap. v. of this work, on "The Permanent Stream of Miraculous Pretension"). St. Augustine's testimony has been already referred to. St. Ambrose discovered the bones of SS. Gervasius and Protasius; and "these relics were laid in the Faustinian Basilic, and the next morning were translated into the Ambrosian Basilic; during which translation a blind man, named Severus, a butcher by trade, was cured by touching the bier on which the relics lay with a handkerchief, and then applying it to his eyes. He had been blind several years, was known to the whole city, and the miracle was performed before a prodigious number of people; and is testified also by St. Austin [Augustine], who was then at Milan, in three several parts of his works, and by Paulinus in the Life of St. Ambrose" ("Lives of the Fathers, Martyrs, etc.," by Rev. Alban Butler, vol. xii., pp. 1001, 1002; ed. 1838; published in two vols., each containing six vols.). The sacred stigmata of St. Francis d'Assisi (died 1226) were seen and touched by St. Bonaventure, Pope Alexander IV., Pope-Gregory IX., fifty friars, many nuns, and innumerable crowds (Ibid, vol. x., pp. 582, 583). This same saint underwent the operation of searing, and, "when the surgeon was about to apply the searing-iron, the saint spoke to the fire, saying: 'Brother fire, I beseech thee to burn me gently, that I may be able to endure thee.' He was seared very deep, from the ear to the eyebrow, but seemed to feel no pain at all" (Ibid, p. 575). The miracles of St. Francis Xavier (died 1552) are borne witness to on all sides, and resulted in the conversion of crowds of Indians; even so late as 1744, when the Archbishop of Goa, by order of John V. of Portugal, attended by the Viceroy, the Marquis of Castel Nuovo, visited the saint's relics, "the body was found without the least bad smell," and had "not suffered the least alteration, or symptom of corruption" (Ibid, vol. xii., p. 974). The chain of miracles extends right down to the present day. At Lourdes, in this year (1876), the Virgin was crowned by the Cardinal Archbishop of Paris in the presence of thirty-five prelates and one hundred thousand people. During the mass performed at the Grotto by the Nuncio, Madeleine Lancereau, of Poictiers, aged 61, known by a large number of the pilgrims as having been unable to walk without crutches for nineteen years, was radically cured. Here is a better authenticated miracle than anyone in the Gospel story; yet no Protestant even cares to investigate the matter, or believes its truth to be within the limits of possibility. Thus we see that not a century has, passed since A.D. 30 which has not been thickly sown with miracles, and there is no reason why we should believe in the miracles of the first century, and reject those of the following eighteen; nor is the first century even "the beginning of miracles," for before that date Jewish and Pagan miracles are to be found in abundance. Why should Bible miracles be severed from their relations all over the world, so that belief in them is commendable faith, while belief in the rest is reprehensible credulity? "The fact is, however, that the Gospel miracles were preceded and accompanied by others of the same type; and we may here merely mention exorcism of demons, and the miraculous cure of disease, as popular instances; they were also followed by a long succession of others, quite as well authenticated, whose occurrence only became less frequent in proportion as the diffusion of knowledge dispelled popular credulity. Even at the present day a stray miracle is from time to time reported in outlying districts, where the ignorance and superstition which formerly produced so abundant a growth of them are not yet entirely dispelled" ("Sup. Rel.," vol. i., p. 148). "Ignorance, and its invariable attendant, superstition, have done more than mere love of the marvellous to produce and perpetuate belief in miracles, and there cannot be any doubt that the removal of ignorance always leads to the cessation of miracles" (Ibid, p. 144).

Special objection has often been raised against one class of miracles—common to the Gospels and to all miraculous narratives—which has severely taxed the faith even of the Christians themselves—that class, namely, which consists of the healing of those "possessed with devils." Exorcism has always been a favourite kind of miracle, but, in these days, very few believe in the possibility of possession, and the language of the Evangelists on the subject has consequently given rise to much trouble of mind. Prebendary Row, in a work on "The Supernatural in the New Testament Possible, Credible, and Historical"—one of the volumes issued by the Christian Evidence Society in answer to "Supernatural Religion"—deals fully with this difficulty; it has been urged that possession was simply a form of mania, and on this Mr. Row say: "Now, on the assumption that possession was simple mania, and nothing more, the following suppositions are the only possible ones. First, that our Lord really distinguished between mania and possession; but that the Evangelists have inaccurately reported his words and actions, through the media of their own subjective impressions, or, in short, have attributed to him language that he did not really utter. Second, that our Lord knew that possession was a form of mania, and adopted the current notions of the time in speaking of it, and that the words were really uttered by him. Third, that with similar knowledge, he adopted the language as part of the curative process. Fourth, that he accepted the validity of the distinction, and that it was a real one during those times" ("Supernatural in the New Testament," pp. 251, 252). Mr. Row argues that: "If possession be mania, there is nothing in the language which the Evangelists have attributed to our Lord which compromises the truthfulness of his character. If, on the other hand, we assume that possession was an objective fact, there is nothing in our existing scientific knowledge of the human mind which proves that the possessions of the New Testament were impossible" (Ibid). Mr. Row rejects the first alternative, and accepts the accuracy of the Evangelic records. But he considers that if possession were simply mania, Jesus, knowing the nature of the disease, might reasonably use language suited to the delusion, as most likely to effect a cure; he could not argue with a maniac that he was under a delusion, but would rightly use whatever method was best fitted to ensure recovery. If this idea be rejected, and the reality of demoniacal possession maintained as most consonant with the behaviour of Jesus, then Mr. Row argues that there is no reason to consider it impossible that either good or evil spirits should be able to influence man, and that psychological science does not warrant us in a denial of the possibility of such influence.

The utter uselessness of miracles—supposing them to be possible—is worthy of remembrance. They must not be accepted as proofs of a divine mission, for false prophets can work them as well as true (Deut. xiii., 1-5; Matt. xxiv., 24; 2 Thess. ii., 9; Rev. xiii., 13-15, etc.) and it may be that God himself works them to deceive (Deut. xiii., 3). Satan can work miracles to authenticate the false doctrines of his emissaries, and there is no test whereby to distinguish the miracle worked by God from the miracle worked by Satan. Hence a miracle is utterly useless, for the credibility of a teacher rests on the morality that he teaches, and if this is good, it is accepted without a miracle to attest its goodness, so that the attesting miracle is superfluous. If it is bad, it is rejected in spite of a miracle to attest its authority, so that the attesting miracle is deceptive. The only use of a miracle might be to attest a revelation of otherwise unknowable facts, which had nothing to do with any moral teaching; and seeing that such revelation could not be investigated, as it dealt with the unknowable, it would be highly dangerous—and, perhaps, blasphemous—to accept it on the faith of the miracle, for it might quite as likely be a revelation made by Satan to injure, as by God to benefit, mankind. Allowing that God and Satan exist, it would seem likely—judging Christianity by its fruits—that the Christian religion is such a malevolent revelation of the evil one.

The objection we raise is, however, of far wider scope than the assertion of the lack of evidence for the New Testament miracles; it is against all, and not only against Christian, miracles. "As far as the impossibility of supernatural occurrences is concerned, Pantheism and Atheism occupy precisely the same grounds. If either of them propounds a true theory of the universe, any supernatural occurrence, which necessarily implies a supernatural agent to bring it about, is impossible, and the entire controversy as to whether miracles have ever been actually performed is a foregone conclusion. Modern Atheism, while it does not venture in categorical terms to affirm that no God exists, definitely asserts that there is no evidence that there is one. It follows that, if there is no evidence that there is a God, there can be no evidence that a miracle ever has been performed, for the very idea of a miracle implies the idea of a God to work one. If, therefore, Atheism is true, all controversy about miracles is useless. They are simply impossible, and to inquire whether an impossible event has happened is absurd. To such a person the historical inquiry, as far as a miracle is concerned, must be a foregone conclusion. It might have a little interest as a matter of curiosity; but even if the most unequivocal evidence could be adduced that an occurrence such as we call supernatural had taken place, the utmost that it could prove would be that some most extraordinary and abnormal fact had taken place in nature of which we did not know the cause. But to prove a miracle to any person who consistently denies that he has any evidence that any being exists which is not a portion of and included in the material universe, or developed out of it, is impossible" ("The Supernatural in the New Testament," by Prebendary Row, pp. 14, 15). We maintain that Nature includes everything, and that, therefore, the supernatural is an impossibility. Every new fact, however marvellous, must, therefore, be within Nature; and while our ignorance may for awhile prevent us from knowing in what category the newly-observed phenomenon should be classed, it is none the less certain that wider knowledge will allot to it its own place, and that more careful observation will reduce it under law, i.e., within the observed sequence or concurrence of phenomena. The natural, to the unthinking, coincides with their own knowledge, and supernatural, to them, simply means super-known; therefore, in ignorant ages, miracles are every-day occurrences, and as knowledge widens the miraculous diminishes. The books of unscientific ages—that is, all early literature—are full of miraculous events, and it may be taken as an axiom of criticism that the miraculous is unhistorical.

(2). The numerous contradictions of each by the others.—We shall here only present a few of the most glaring contradictions in the Gospels, leaving untouched a mass of minor discrepancies. We find the principal of these when we compare the three synoptics with the Fourth Gospel, but there are some irreconcilable differences even between the three. The contradictory genealogies of Christ given in Matthew and Luke—farther complicated, in part, by a third discordant genealogy in Chronicles—have long been the despair of Christian harmonists. "On comparing these lists, we find that between David and Christ there are only two names which occur in both Matthew and Luke—those of Zorobabel and of Joseph, the reputed father of Jesus. In tracing the list downwards from David there would be less difficulty in explaining this, at least, to a certain point, for Matthew follows the line of Solomon, and Luke that of Nathan—both of whom were sons of David. But even in the downward line, on reaching Salathiel, where the two genealogies again come into contact, we find, to our astonishment, that in Luke he is the son of Neri, whilst in Matthew his father's name is Jechonias. From Zorobabel downwards, the lists are again divergent, until we reach Joseph, who in St. Luke is placed as the son of Heli, whilst in St. Matthew his father's name is Jacob" ("Christian Records," Dr. Giles, p. 101). According to Chronicles, Jotham is the great-great-grandson of Ahaziah; according to Matthew, he is his son (admitting that the Ahaziah of Chronicles is the Ozias of Matthew); according to Chronicles, Jechonias is the grandson of Josiah, according to Matthew, he is his son; according to Chronicles, Zorababel is the son of Pedaiah,

109

according to Matthew, he is the son of Salathiel, according to Luke, he is the son of Neri; according to Chronicles, Zorobabel left eight children, but neither Matthew's Abiud, nor Luke's Rhesa, are among them. The same discordance is found when Matthew and Luke again touch each other in Joseph, the husband of Mary; according to the one, Jacob begat Joseph, according to the other, Joseph was the son of Heli. To crown the absurdity of the whole, we are given two genealogies of Joseph, who is no relation to Jesus at all, if the story of the virgin-birth be true, while none is given of Mary, through whom alone Jesus is said to have derived his humanity. We have, therefore, no genealogy at all of Jesus in the Gospels. Various theories have been put forward to reconcile the irreconcilable; some say that the genealogy in Luke is that of Mary, of which supposition it is enough to remark that "Mary, the daughter of," can scarcely be indicated by "Joseph, the son of." It is also said that Joseph was legally the son of Jacob, although naturally the son of Heli, it being supposed that Jacob died childless, and that his brother Heli according to the Levitical law, married the widow of Jacob; but here Joseph's grand-fathers and great-grand-fathers should be the same, Heli and Jacob being supposed to be brothers. Besides, if Joseph were legally the son of Jacob, only the genealogy of Jacob should be given, since that only would be Joseph's genealogy. No man can reckon his paternal ancestry through two differing lines. To make matters in yet more hopeless confusion, we find Chronicles giving twenty-two generations where Matthew gives seventeen, and Luke twenty-three; while, from David to Christ, Matthew reckons twenty-eight and Luke forty-three, a most marvellous discrepancy.

"If we compare the genealogies of Matthew and Luke together, we become aware of still more striking discrepancies. Some of these differences indeed are unimportant, as the opposite direction of the two tables.... More important is the considerable difference in the number of generations for equal periods, Luke having forty-one between David and Jesus, whilst Matthew has only twenty-six. The main difficulty, however, lies in this: that in some parts of the genealogy in Luke totally different persons are made the ancestors of Jesus from those in Matthew. It is true, both writers agree in deriving the lineage of Jesus through Joseph from David and Abraham, and that the names of the individual members of the series correspond from Abraham to David, as well as two of the names in the subsequent portion: those of Salathiel and Zorobabel. But the difficulty becomes desperate when we find that, with these two exceptions about midway, the whole of the names from David to the foster father of Jesus are totally different in Matthew and in Luke. In Matthew the father of Joseph is called Jacob; in Luke, Heli. In Matthew the son of David through whom Joseph descended from that King is Solomon; in Luke, Nathan; and so on, the line descends, in Matthew, through the race of known Kings; in Luke, through an unknown collateral branch, coinciding only with respect to Salathiel and Zorobabel, whilst they still differ in the names of the father of Salathiel and the son of Zorobabel.... A consideration of the insurmountable difficulties, which unavoidably embarrass every attempt to bring these two genealogies into harmony with one another, will lead us to despair of reconciling them, and will incline us to acknowledge, with the more free-thinking class of critics, that they are mutually contradictory. Consequently, they cannot both be true.... In fact, then, neither table has any advantage over the other. If the one is unhistorical, so also is the other, since it is very improbable that the genealogy of an obscure family like that of Joseph, extending through so long a series of generations, should have been preserved during all the confusion of the exile, and the disturbed period that followed.... According to the prophecies, the Messiah could only spring from David. When, therefore, a Galilean, whose lineage was utterly unknown, and of whom consequently no one could prove that he was not descended from David, had acquired the reputation of being the Messiah; what more natural than that tradition should, under different forms, have early ascribed to him a Davidical descent, and that genealogical tables, corresponding with this tradition, should have been formed? which, however, as they were constructed upon no certain data, would necessarily exhibit such differences and contradictions as we find actually existing between the genealogies in Matthew and in Luke" ("Life of Jesus," by Strauss, vol. i., pp. 130, 131, and 137-139).

The accounts of the several angelic warnings to Mary and to Joseph appear to be mutually exclusive. Most theologians, says Strauss, "maintaining, and justly, that the silence of one Evangelist concerning an event which is narrated by the other, is not a negation of the event, they blend the two accounts together in the following manner: , the angel makes known to Mary her approaching pregnancy (Luke); 2, she then journeys to Elizabeth (the same Gospel); 3, after her return, her situation being discovered, Joseph takes offence (Matthew); whereupon, 4, he likewise is visited by an angelic apparition (the same Gospel). But this arrangement of the incidents is, as Schliermacher has already remarked, full of difficulty; and it seems that what is related by one Evangelist is not only pre-supposed, but excluded, by the other. For, in the first place, the conduct of the angel who appears to Joseph is not easily explained, if the same, or another, angel had previously appeared to Mary. The angel (in Matthew) speaks altogether as if his communication were the first in this affair. He neither refers to the message previously received by Mary, nor reproaches Joseph because he had not believed it; but, more than all, the informing Joseph of the name of the expected child, and the giving him a full detail of the reasons why he should be so called (Mat. i. 21), would have been wholly superfluous had the angel (according to Luke i. 31) already indicated this name to Mary. Still more incomprehensible is the conduct of the betrothed parties, according to this arrangement of events. Had Mary been visited by an angel, who had made known to her an approaching supernatural pregnancy, would not the first impulse of a delicate woman have been to hasten to impart to her betrothed the import of the divine message, and by this means to anticipate the humiliating discovery of her situation, and an injurious suspicion on the part of her affianced husband? But exactly this discovery Mary allows Joseph to make from others, and thus excites suspicion; for it is evident that the expression [Greek: heurethae en gastri echousa] (Mat. i. 18) signifies a discovery made independent of any communication on Mary's part, and it is equally clear that in this manner only does Joseph obtain the knowledge of her situation, since his conduct is represented as the result of that discovery [Greek: (euriskesthai)]" ("Life of Jesus," v. i., pp. 146, 147).

Strauss gives a curious list, showing the gradual growth of the myth relating to the birth of Jesus (we may remark No. 3 is distinctly out of place when referred to Olshausen: it should be referred to the early Fathers, from whom Olshausen derived it):—

"**1.** Contemporaries of Jesus and composers of the genealogies: Joseph and Mary man and wife—Jesus the offspring of their marriage.

"**2.** The age and authors of our histories of the birth of Jesus: Mary and Joseph betrothed only; Joseph having no participation in the conception of the child, and, previous to his birth, no conjugal connection with Mary.

"**3.** Olshausen and others: subsequent to the birth of Jesus, Joseph, though then the husband of Mary, relinquishes his matrimonial rights.

"**4.** Epiphanius, Protevangelium, Jacobi, and others: Joseph a decrepit old man, no longer to be thought of as a husband; the children attributed to him are of a former marriage. More especially it is not as a bride and wife that he receives Mary; he takes her merely under his guardianship.

"**5.** Protevang., Chrysostom, and others: Mary's virginity was not only not destroyed by any subsequent births of children by Joseph, it was not in the slightest degree impaired by the birth of Jesus.

"**6.** Jerome: Not Mary only, but Joseph also, observed an absolute virginity, and the pretended brothers of Jesus were not his sons, hut merely cousins to Jesus" ("Life of Jesus," vol. i., p. 188).

Thus we see how a myth gradually forms itself, bit after bit being added to it, until the story is complete.

The account given by Luke of the meeting of Elizabeth and Mary is clearly mythical, and not historical: "Apart from the intention of the narrator, can it be thought natural that two friends visiting one another should, even in the midst of the most extraordinary occurrences, break forth into long hymns, and that their conversation should entirely lose the character of dialogue, the natural form on such occasions? By a supernatural influence alone could the minds of the two friends be attuned to a state of elevation, so foreign to their every-day life. But if indeed Mary's hymn is to be understood as the work of the Holy Spirit, it is surprising that a speech emanating immediately from the divine source of inspiration should not be more striking for its originality, but should be so interlarded with reminiscences from the Old Testament, borrowed from the song of praise spoken by the mother of Samuel (1 Sam. ii) under analogous circumstances. Accordingly, we must admit that the compilation of this hymn, consisting of recollections from the Old Testament, was put together in a natural way; but allowing its composition to have been perfectly natural, it cannot be ascribed to the artless Mary, but to him who poetically wrought out the tradition in circulation respecting the scene in question" ("Life of Jesus," by Strauss, vol. i., pp. 196, 197).

The notes of time given for the birth of Christ are irreconcilable. According to Matthew he is born in the reign of Herod the King: according to Luke, he is born six months after John Baptist, whose birth is referred to the reign of the same monarch; yet in Luke, he is also born at the time of the census, which must have taken place at least ten years later; thus Luke contradicts Matthew, and also contradicts himself. The discrepancies surrounding the birth are not yet complete; passing the curious differences between Matthew and Luke, Matthew knowing nothing about the visit of the shepherds, and Luke nothing of the visit of the Magi, and the consequent slaughter of the babes, we come to a direct conflict between the Evangelists; Matthew informs us that Joseph, Mary, and the child, fled into Egypt from Bethlehem to avoid the wrath of King Herod, and that they were returning to Judæa, when Joseph, hearing that Archelaus was ruling there, turned aside to Galilee, and came and dwelt "in a city called Nazareth." Luke, on the contrary, says that when the days of Mary's purification were accomplished they took the child up to Jerusalem, and presented him in the Temple, and then, after this, returned to Galilee, to "their own city, Nazareth." Moreover, had Herod wanted to find him, he could have taken him at the Temple, where his presentation caused much commotion. In Matthew, the turning into Galilee is clearly a new thing; in Luke, it is returning home; and in Luke there is no space of time wherein the flight into Egypt can by any possibility be inserted. We may add a wonder why Galilee was a safer residence than Judæa, since Antipas, its ruler, was a son of Herod, and would, primâ facie, be as dangerous as his brother Archelaus.

The conduct of Herod is incredible if we accept Matthew's account: "Herod's first anxious question to the magi is to ascertain the time of the appearance of the star. He 'inquires diligently' (ii. 7); and he must have had a motive for so doing. What was this motive? Could he have any other purpose than that of determining the age under which no infants in the neighbourhood of Bethlehem should be allowed to

113

live? But, according to the narrative, Herod never conceived the idea of slaughtering the children till he found that he had been 'mocked of the wise men;' and the mythical nature of the story is betrayed by this anticipation of motives which, at the time spoken of could have no existence. Yet, further, Herod, who, though in a high degree cruel, unjust, and unscrupulous, is represented as a man of no slight sagacity, clearness of purpose, and strength of will, and who feels a deadly jealousy of an infant whom he knows to have been recently born in Bethlehem, a place only a few miles distant from Jerusalem, is here described not as sending his own emissaries privately to put him to death, or despatching them with the Magi, or detaining the Magi at Jerusalem, until he had ascertained the truth of their tale, and the correctness of the answer of the priests and scribes, but as simply suffering the Magi to go by themselves, at the same time charging them to return with the information for which he had shown himself so feverishly anxious. This strange conduct can be accounted for only on the ground of a judicial blindness; but they who resort to such an explanation must suppose that it was inflicted in order to save the new-born Christ from the death thus threatened; and if they adopt this hypothesis, they must further believe that this arrangement likewise ensured the death of a large number of infants instead of one. A natural reluctance to take up such a notion might prompt the question, Why were the Magi brought to Jerusalem at all? If they knew that the star was the star of Christ (ii. 2), and were by this knowledge conducted to Jerusalem, why did it not suffice to guide them straight to Bethlehem, and thus prevent the slaughter of the innocents? Why did the star desert them after its first appearance, not to be seen again till they issued from Jerusalem? or, if it did not desert them, why did they ask of Herod and the priests the road which they should take, when, by the hypothesis, the star was ready to guide?" ("The English Life of Jesus," by Thomas Scott, pp. 34, 35; ed. 1872). To these improbabilities must be added the remarkable fact that Josephus, who gives a very detailed history of Herod, entirely omits any hint of this stupendous crime.

The story of the temptation of Jesus is full of contradictions. Matthew iv. 2, 3, implies that the first visit of the tempter was made after the forty days' fast, while Mark and Luke speak of his being tempted for forty days. According to Matthew, the angels came to him when the Devil left him; but, according to Mark, they ministered to him throughout. According to Matthew, the temptation to cast himself down is the second trial, and the offer of the kingdoms of the world the third: in Luke the order is reversed. In additions to these contradictions, we must note the absurdity of the story. The Devil "set him on a pinnacle of the temple." Did Jesus and the Devil go flying through the air together, till the Devil put Jesus down? What did the people in the courts below think of the Devil and a man standing on a point of the temple in the full sight of Jerusalem? Did so unusual an

114

occurrence cause no astonishment in the city? Where is the high mountain from which Jesus and the Devil saw all round the globe? Is it true that the Devil gives power to whom he will? If so, why is it said that the powers are "ordained of God"?

Another "discrepancy, concerning the denial of Christ by Peter, furnishes a still stronger proof that these records have not come down to us with the exactness of a contemporary character, much less with the authority of inspiration. The four accounts of Peter's denial vary considerably. The variations will be more intelligible, exhibited in a tabular form" (Giles' "Christian Records," p. 228). We present the table, slightly altered in arrangement, and corrected in some details :—

	MATTHEW	MARK	LUKE	JOHN
1st.	Seated without in the palace, to a damsel.	Beneath in the palace, by the fire, to a maid.	In the midst of the hall where Jesus was being tried, seated by the fire, to a maid.	On entering to the damsel that kept the door.
2nd.	Out in the porch, having left the room, in answer to a second maid.	Out in the porch, having left the room, in answer to a second maid.	Still in the hall, in answer to a man.	In the hall, standing by the fire, in answer to the bystanders.
3rd.	Out in the porch, to the bystanders.	Out in the porch, to the bystanders.	Still in the hall, to a man.	Still in the hall, to a man.

In addition to these discrepancies, we find that Jesus prophesies that Peter shall deny him thrice "before the cock crow," while in Mark the cock crows immediately after the first denial: in Luke, Jesus and Peter remain throughout the scene of the denial in the same hall, so that the Lord may turn and look upon Peter; while Matthew and Mark place him "beneath" or "without," and make the third denial take place in the porch outside—a place where Jesus, by the context, certainly could not see him.

How long did the ministry of Jesus last? Luke places his baptism in the fifteenth year of Tiberius (iii. 1), and he might have been crucified under Pontius Pilate at any time within the seven years following. The Synoptics mention but one Passover, and at that Jesus was crucified, thus limiting his ministry to one year, unless he broke the Mosaic law, and disregarded the feast; clearly his triumphal entry into Jerusalem is his first visit there in his manhood, since we find all

115

the city moved and the people asking: "Who is this? And the multitude said, This is Jesus the Prophet of Nazareth of Galilee" (Matt. xxi. 10, 11). His person would have been well known, had he visited Jerusalem before and worked miracles there. If, however, we turn to the Fourth Gospel, his ministry must extend over at least two years. According to Irenæus, he "did not want much of being fifty years old" when the Jews disputed with him ("Against Heresies," bk. ii., ch. 22, sec. 6), and he taught for nearly twenty years. Dr. Giles remarks that "the first three Gospels plainly exhibit the events of only one year; to prove them erroneous or defective in so important a feature as this, would be to detract greatly from their value" ("Christian Records," p. 112). "According to the first three Gospels, Christ's public life lasted only one year, at the end of which he went up to Jerusalem and was crucified" (Ibid, p. 11). "Would this questioning [on the triumphal entry] have taken place if Jesus had often made visits to Jerusalem, and been well known there? The multitude who answered the question, and who knew Jesus, consisted of those 'who had come to the feast,'—St. John indicates this [xii. 12]—but the people of Jerusalem knew him not, and, therefore, asked 'Who is this?'" (Ibid, p. 113). The fact is, that we know nothing certainly as to the birth, life, death, of this supposed Christ. His story is one tissue of contradictions. It is impossible to believe that the Synoptics and the fourth Gospel are even telling the history of the same person. The discourses of Jesus in the Synoptics are simple, although parabolical; in the Fourth they are mystical, and are being continually misunderstood by the people. The historical divergences are marked. The fourth Gospel "tells us (ch. 1) that at the beginning of his ministry Jesus was at Bethabara, a town near the junction of the Jordan with the Dead Sea; here he gains three disciples, Andrew and another, and then Simon Peter: the next day he goes into Galilee and finds Philip and Nathanael, and on the following day—somewhat rapid travelling—he is present, with these disciples, at Cana, where he performs his first miracle, going afterwards with them to Capernaum and Jerusalem. At Jerusalem, whither he goes for 'the Jews' passover,' he drives out the traders from the temple and remarks, 'Destroy this temple, and in three days I will raise it up:' which remark causes the first of the strange misunderstandings between Jesus and the Jews peculiar to this Gospel, simple misconceptions which Jesus never troubles himself to set right. Jesus and his disciples then go to the Jordan, baptising, whence Jesus departs into Galilee with them, because he hears that the Pharisees know he is becoming more popular than the Baptist (ch. iv., 1, 3). All this happens before John is cast into prison, an occurrence which is a convenient note of time. We turn to the beginning of the ministry of Jesus as related by the three. Jesus is in the south of Palestine, but, hearing that John is cast into prison, he departs into Galilee, and resides at Capernaum. There is no mention of any ministry in Galilee and Judæa before this; on the contrary, it is only 'from that time' that

116

'Jesus began to preach.' He is alone, without disciples, but, walking by the sea, he comes upon Peter, Andrew, James, and John, and calls them. Now if the fourth Gospel is true, these men had joined him in Judæa, followed him to Galilee, south again to Jerusalem, and back to Galilee, had seen his miracles and acknowledged him as Christ, so it seems strange that they had deserted him and needed a second call, and yet more strange is it that Peter (Luke v. 1-11) was so astonished and amazed at the miracle of the fishes. The driving out of the traders from the temple is placed by the Synoptics at the very end of his ministry, and the remark following it is used against him at his trial: so was probably made just before it. The next point of contact is the history of the 5,000 fed by five loaves (ch. vi.); the preceding chapter relates to a visit to Jerusalem unnoticed by the three: indeed, the histories seem written of two men, one the 'prophet of Galilee' teaching in its cities, the other concentrating his energies on Jerusalem. The account of the miraculous feeding is alike in all: not so the succeeding account of the multitude. In the fourth Gospel, Jesus and the crowd fall to disputing, as usual, and he loses many disciples: among the three, Luke says nothing of the immediately following events, while Matthew and Mark tell us that the multitudes—as would be natural—crowded round him to touch even the hem of his garment. This is the same as always: in the three the crowd loves him; in the fourth it carps at and argues with him. We must again miss the sojourn of Jesus in Galilee according to the three, and his visit to Jerusalem according to the one, and pass to his entry into Jerusalem in triumph. Here we notice a most remarkable divergence: the Synoptics tell us that he was going up to Jerusalem from Galilee, and, arriving on his way at Bethphage, he sent for an ass and rode thereon into Jerusalem: the fourth Gospel relates that he was dwelling at Jerusalem, and leaving it, for fear of the Jews, he retired, not into Galilee, but 'beyond Jordan, into a place where John at first baptised,' i.e., Bethabara, 'and there he abode.' From thence he went to Bethany and raised to life a putrefying corpse: this stupendous miracle is never appealed to by the earlier historians in proof of their master's greatness, though 'much people of the Jews' are said to have seen Lazarus after his resurrection; this miracle is also given as the reason for the active hostility of the priests, 'from that day forward.' Jesus then retires to Ephraim near the wilderness, from which town he goes to Bethany, and thence in triumph to Jerusalem, being met by the people 'for that they heard that he had done this miracle.' The two accounts have absolutely nothing in common except the entry into Jerusalem, and the preceding events of the Synoptics exclude those of the fourth Gospel, as does the latter theirs. If Jesus abode in Bethabara and Ephraim, he could not have come from Galilee; if he started from Galilee, he was not abiding in the south. John xiii.-xvii. stand alone, with the exception of the mention of the traitor. On the arrest of Jesus, he is led (ch. xviii. 13) to Annas, who sends him to

Caiaphas, while the others send him direct to Caiaphas, but this is immaterial. He is then taken to Pilate: the Jews do not enter the judgment-hall, lest, being defiled, they could not eat the passover, a feast which, according to the Synoptics, was over, Jesus and his disciples having eaten it the night before. Jesus is exposed to the people at the sixth hour (ch. xix. 14), while Mark tells us he was crucified three hours before—at the third hour—a note of time which agrees with the others, since they all relate that there was darkness from the sixth to the ninth hour, i.e., there was thick darkness at the time when, 'according to St. John,' Jesus was exposed. Here our evangelist is in hopeless conflict with the three. The accounts about the resurrection are irreconcilable in all the Gospels, and mutually destructive. It remains to notice, among these discrepancies, one or two points which did not come in conveniently in the course of the narrative. During the whole of the fourth Gospel, we find Jesus constantly arguing for his right to the title of Messiah. Andrew speaks of him as such (i. 41); the Samaritans acknowledge him (iv. 42); Peter owns him (vi. 69); the people call him so (vii. 26, 31, 41); Jesus claims it (viii. 24); it is the subject of a law (ix. 22); Jesus speaks of it as already claimed by him (x. 24, 25); Martha recognises it (xi. 27). We thus find that, from the very first, this title is openly claimed by Jesus, and his right to it openly canvassed by the Jews. But—in the three—the disciples acknowledge him as Christ, and he charges them to 'tell no man that he was Jesus the Christ" (Matt. xvi. 20; Mark viii. 29, 30; Luke ix. 20, 21); and this in the same year that he blames the Jews for not owning this Messiahship, since he had told them who he was 'from the beginning' (ch. viii. 24, 25): so that, if 'John' was right, we fail to see the object of all the mystery about it, related by the Synoptics. We mark, too, how Peter is, in their account, praised for confessing him, for flesh and blood had not revealed it to him, while in the fourth Gospel, 'flesh and blood,' in the person of Andrew, reveal to Peter that the Christ is found; and there seems little praise due to Peter for a confession which had been made two or three years earlier by Andrew, Nathanael, John Baptist, and the Samaritans. Contradiction can scarcely be more direct. In John vii. Jesus owns that the Jews know his birthplace (28), and they state (41, 42) that he comes from Galilee, while Christ should be born at Bethlehem. Matthew and Luke distinctly say Jesus was born at Bethlehem; but here Jesus confesses the right knowledge of those who attribute his birthplace to Galilee, instead of setting their difficulty at rest by explaining that though brought up at Nazareth he was born in Bethlehem. But our writer was apparently ignorant of their accounts ("According to St John," by Annie Besant. Scott Series, pp. 11-14, ed. 1873). These are but a few of the contradictions in the Gospels, which compel us to reject them as historical narratives.

(3) The fact that the story of the hero, the doctrines, the miracles, were current long before the supposed dates of the Gospels, etc. There

are two mythical theories as to the growth of the story of Jesus, which demand our attention; the first, that of which Strauss is the best known exponent, which acknowledges the historical existence of Jesus, but regards him as the figure round which has grown a mythus, moulded by the Messianic expectations of the Jews: the second, which is indifferent to his historical existence, and regards him as a new hero of the ancient sun-worship, the successor of Mithra, Krishna, Osiris, Bacchus, etc. To this school, it matters not whether there was a Jesus of Nazareth or not, just as it matters not whether a Krishna or an Osiris had an historical existence or not; it is Christ, the Sun-god, not Jesus, the Jewish peasant, whom they find worshipped in Christendom, and who is, therefore, the object of their interest.

According to the first theory, whatever was expected of the Messiah has been attributed to Jesus. "When not merely the particular nature and manner of an occurrence is critically suspicious, its external circumstances represented as miraculous and the like; but where likewise the essential substance and groundwork is either inconceivable in itself, or is in striking harmony with some Messianic idea of the Jews of that age, then not the particular alleged course and mode of the transaction only, but the entire occurrence must be regarded as unhistorical" (Strauss' "Life of Jesus," vol. i., p. 94). The mythic theory accepts an historical groundwork for many of the stories about Jesus, but it does not seek to explain the miraculous by attenuating it into the natural—as by explaining the story of the transfiguration to have been developed from the fact of Jesus meeting secretly two men, and from the brilliancy of the sunlight dazzling the eyes of the disciples—but it attributes the incredible portions of the history to the Messianic theories current among the Jews. The Messiah would do this and that; Jesus was the Messiah; therefore, Jesus did this and that—such, argue the supporters of the mythical theory, was the method in which the mythus was developed. The theory finds some support in the peculiar attitude of Justin Martyr, for instance, who believes a number of things about Jesus, not because the things are thus recorded of him in history, but because the prophets stated that such things should happen to the Messiah. Thus, Jesus is descended from David, because the Messiah was to come of David's lineage. His birth is announced by an angelic visitant, because the birth of the Messiah must not be less honoured than that of Isaac or of Samson; he is born of a virgin, because God says of the Messiah, "this day have I begotten thee," implying the direct paternity of God, and because the prophecy in Is. vii. 14 was applied to the Messiah by the later Jews (see Septuagint translation, [Greek: parthenos], a pure virgin, while the Hebrew word [Hebrew: almah] signifies a young woman; the Hebrew word for virgin [Hebrew: betulah] not being used in the text of Isaiah), the ideas of "son of God" and "son of a virgin" completing each other; born at Bethlehem, because there the Messiah was to be born (Micah v.

1); announced to shepherds, because Moses was visited among the flocks, and David taken from the sheepfolds at Bethlehem; heralded by a star, because a star should arise out of Jacob (Num. xxiv. 17), and "the Gentiles shall come to thy light" (Is. lx. 3); worshipped by magi, because the star was seen by Balaam, the magus, and astrologers would be those who would most notice a star; presented with gifts by these Eastern sages, because kings of Arabia and Saba shall offer gifts (Ps. lxxii. 10); saved from the destruction of the infants by a jealous king, because Moses, one of the great types of the Messiah, was so saved; flying into Egypt and thence returning, because Israel, again a type of the Messiah, so fled and returned, and "out of Egypt have I called my son" (Hos. xi. 1); at twelve years of age found in the temple, because the duties of the law devolved on the Jewish boy at that age, and where should the Messiah then be found save in his Father's temple? recognised at his baptism by a divine voice, to fulfil Is. xlii. 1; hovered over by a dove, because the brooding Spirit (Gen. i. 2) was regarded as dove-like, and the Spirit was to be especially poured on the Messiah (Is. xlii. 1); tempted by the devil to test him, because God tested his greatest servants, and would surely test the Messiah; fasting forty days in the wilderness, because the types of the Messiah—Moses and Elijah—thus fasted in the desert; healing all manner of disease, because Messiah was to heal (Is. xxxv. 5, 6); preaching, because Messiah was to preach (Is. lxi. 1, 2); crucified, because the hands and feet of Messiah were to be pierced (Ps. xxii. 16); mocked, because Messiah was to be mocked (Ibid 6-8); his garments divided, because thus it was spoken of Messiah (Ibid, 18); silent before his judges, because Messiah was not to open his mouth (Is. liii. 7); buried by the rich, because Messiah was thus to find his grave (Ib. 9); rising again, because Messiah's could not be left in hell (Ps. xvi. 10); sitting at God's right hand, because there Messiah was to sit as king (Ps. cx. 1). Thus the form of the Messiah was cast, and all that had to be done was to pour in the human metal; those who alleged that the Messiah had come in the person of Jesus of Nazareth, adapted his story to the story of the Messiah, pouring the history of Jesus into the mould already made for the Messiah, and thus the mythus was transformed into a history.

This theory is much strengthened by a study of the prophecies quoted in the New Testament, since we find that they are very badly "set;" take as a specimen those referred to in Matthew i. and ii. "Now all this was done, that it might be fulfilled which was spoken of the Lord by the prophet, saying, Behold a virgin shall be with child," etc (i. 22, 23). If we refer to Is. vii., from whence the prophecy is taken, we shall see the wresting of the passage which is necessary to make it into a "Messianic prophecy." Ahaz, king of Judah, is hard pressed by the kings of Samaria and Syria, and he is promised deliverance by the Lord, before the virgin's son, Immanuel, should be of an age to discern between good and evil. How Ahaz could be given as a sign of a birth which was not to take place until more than 700 years afterwards, it is hard to say, nor can we believe that Ahaz was not delivered from his enemies until Jesus was old enough to know right from wrong. According to the Gospels, the name "Immanuel" was never given to Jesus, and in the prophecy is bestowed on the child simply as a promise that, "God" being "with us," Judah should be delivered from its foes. The same child is clearly spoken of as the child of Isaiah and his wife in Is. viii. 3, 4; and in verses 6-8 we find that the two kings of Samaria and Syria are to be conquered by the king of Assyria, who shall fill "thy land, O Immanuel!" thus referring distinctly to the promised child as living in that time. The Hebrew word translated "virgin" does not, as we have already shown, mean "a pure virgin," as translated in the Septuagint. It is used for a young woman, a marriageable woman, or even to describe a woman who is being embraced by a man. Micah's supposed prophecy in Matt. ii. 5, 6, is as inapplicable to Christ as that of Isaiah. Turning back to Micah, we find that he "that is to be ruler in Israel" shall be born in Bethlehem, but Jesus was never ruler in Israel, and the description cannot therefore be applied to him; besides, finishing the passage in Micah (v. 5) we read that this same ruler "shall be the peace when the Assyrian shall come into our land," so that the prophecy has a local and immediate fulfilment in the circumstances of the time. Matthew ii. 15 is only made into a prophecy by taking the second half of a historical reference in Hosea to the Exodus of Israel from Egypt; it would be as reasonable to prove in this fashion that the Bible teaches a denial of God, "as is spoken by David the prophet, There is no God." The fulfilment of the saying of Jeremy the prophet is as true as all the preceding (verses 17, 18); Jeremy bids Rahel not to weep for the children who are carried into bondage, "for they shall come again from the land of the enemy ... thy children shall come again to their own border" (Jer. xxxi. 16, 17). Very applicable to the slaughtered babes, and so honest of "Matthew" to quote just so much of the "prophecy" as served his purpose, leaving out that which altered its whole meaning. After these specimens, we are not surprised to find that—unable to find a prophecy fit to twist to suit his object—our evangelist quietly invents one, and (verse 23) uses a prophecy which has no existence in what was "spoken by the prophets." It is needless to go through all the other passages known as Messianic prophecies, for they may all be dealt with as above; the guiding rule is to refer to the Old Testament in each case, and not to trust to the quotation as given in the New, and then to read the whole context of the "prophecy," instead of resting content with the few words which, violently wrested from their natural meaning, are forced into a superficial resemblance with the story recorded in the Gospels.

The second theory, which regards Jesus as a new hero of the ancient sun-worship, is full of intensest interest. Dupuis, in his great work on sun-worship ("Origines de Tous les Cultes") has drawn out in detail the various sun-myths, and has pointed to their common features. Briefly stated, these points are as follows: the hero is born about Dec. 25th, without sexual intercourse, for the sun, entering the winter solstice, emerges in the sign of Virgo, the heavenly virgin. His mother remains ever-virgin, since the rays of the sun, passing through the zodiacal sign, leave it intact. His infancy is begirt with dangers, because the new-born sun is feeble in the midst of the winter's fogs and mists, which threaten to devour him; his life is one of toil and peril, culminating at the spring equinox in a final struggle with the powers of darkness. At that period the day and the night are equal, and both fight for the mastery; though the night veil the sun, and he seems dead; though he has descended out of sight, below the earth, yet he rises again triumphant, and he rises in the sign of the Lamb, and is thus the Lamb of God, carrying away the darkness and death of the winter months. Henceforth, he triumphs, growing ever stronger and more brilliant. He ascends into the zenith, and there he glows, "on the right hand of God," himself God, the very substance of the Father, the brightness of his glory, and the "express image of his person," "upholding all things" by his heat and his life-giving power; thence he pours down life and warmth on his worshippers, giving them his very self to be their life; his substance passes into the grape and the corn, the sustainers of health; around him are his twelve followers, the twelve signs of the zodiac, the twelve months of the year; his day, the Lord's Day, is Sunday, the day of the Sun, and his yearly course, ever renewed, is marked each year, by the renewed memorials of his career. The signs appear in the long array of sun-heroes, making the succession of deities, old in reality, although new-named.

It may be worth noting that Jesus is said to be born at Bethlehem, a word that Dr. Inman translates as the house "of the hot one" ("Ancient Faiths," vol. i., p. 358; ed. 1868); Bethlehem is generally translated "house of bread," and the doubt arises from the Hebrew letters being originally unpointed, and the points—equivalent to vowel sounds—being inserted in later times; this naturally gives rise to great latitude of interpretation, the vowels being inserted whenever the writer or translator thinks they ought to come in, or where the traditionary reading requires them (see Part 1., pp. 13, and 31, 32).

Each point in the story of Jesus may be paralleled in earlier tales; the birth of Krishna was prophesied of; he was born of Devaki, although she was shut up in a tower, and no man was permitted to approach her. His birth was hymned by the Devas—the Hindoo equivalent for angels—and a bright light shone round where he was. He was pursued by the wrath of the tyrant king, Kansa, who feared that Krishna would supplant him in the kingdom. The infants of the district were massacred, but Krishna miraculously escaped. He was brought up among the poor until he reached maturity. He preached a pure morality, and went about doing good. He healed the leper, the sick, the injured, and he raised the dead. His head was anointed by a woman; he washed the feet of the Brahmins; he was persecuted, and finally slain, being crucified. He went down into hell, rose again from the dead, and ascended into heaven (see "Asiatic Researches," vol. i.; on "The Gods of Greece, Italy, and India," by Sir William Jones, an essay which, though very imperfect, has much in it that is highly instructive). He is pictorially represented as standing on the serpent, the type of evil; his foot crushes its head, while the fang of the serpent pierces his heel; also, with a halo round his head, this halo being always the symbol of the Sun-god; also, with his hands and feet pierced—the sacred stigmata—and with a hole in his side. In fact, some of the representations of him could not be distinguished from the representations of the crucified Jesus.

The name of "Krishna" is by Sir William Jones, and by many others written "Crishna," and I have seen it spelt "Cristna." The resemblance it bears, when thus written, to "Christ" is apparent only, there is no etymological similarity. Krishna is derived from the Sanscrit "Krish," to scrape, to draw, to colour. Krishna means black, or violet-coloured; Christ comes from the Greek [Greek: christos] the anointed. Colonel Vallancy, Sir W. Jones tells us, informed him that "Crishna" in Irish means the Sun ("As. Res.," p. 262; ed. 1801); and there is no doubt that the Hindu Krishna is a Sun-god; the "violet-coloured" might well be a reference to the deep blue of the summer sky.

If Moses be a type of Christ, must not Bacchus be admitted to the same honour? In the ancient Orphic verses it was said that he was born in Arabia; picked up in a box that floated on the water; was known by the name of Mises, as "drawn from the water;" had a rod which he could change into a serpent, and by means of which he performed miracles; leading his army, he passed the Red Sea dryshod; he divided the rivers Orontes and Hydaspes with his rod; he drew water from a rock; where he passed the land flowed with wine, milk, and honey (see "Diegesis," pp. 178, 179).

The name Christ Jesus is simply the anointed Saviour, or else Chrestos Jesus, the good Saviour; a title not peculiar to Jesus of Nazareth. We find Hesus, Jesous, Yes or Ies. This last name, [Greek: Iaes], was one of the titles of Bacchus, and the simple termination "us" makes it "Jesus;" from this comes the sacred monogram I.H.S., really the Greek [Greek: UAeS]—IES; the Greek letter [Greek: Ae], which is the capital E, has by ignorance been mistaken for the Latin H, and the ancient name of Bacchus has been thus transformed into the Latin monogram of Jesus. In both cases the letters are surrounded with a halo, the sun-rays, symbolical of the sun-deity to whom they refer. This halo surrounds the heads of gods who typify the sun, and is continually met with in Indian sculptures and paintings.

Hercules, with his twelve labours, is another source of Christian fable. "It is well known that by Hercules, in the physical mythology of the heathens, was meant the Sun, or solar light, and his twelve famous labours have been referred to the sun's passing through the twelve zodiacal signs; and this, perhaps, not without some foundation. But the labours of Hercules seem to have had a still higher view, and to have been originally designed as emblematic memorials of what the real Son of God and Saviour of the world was to do and suffer for our sakes— [Greek: Noson Theletaeria panta komixon]—'Bringing a cure for all our ills,' as the Orphic hymn speaks of Hercules" (Parkhurst's "Hebrew Lexicon," page 520; ed. 1813). As the story of Hercules came first in time, it must be either a prophecy of Christ, an inadmissible supposition, or else of the sources whence the story of Christ has been drawn.

Aesculapius, the heathen "Good Physician," and "the good Saviour," healed the sick and raised the dead. He was the son of God and of Coronis, and was guarded by a goatherd.

Prometheus is another forerunner of Christ, stretched in cruciform position on the rocks, tormented by Jove, the Father, because he brought help to man, and winning for man, by his agony, light and knowledge.

Osiris, the great Egyptian God, has much in common with the Christian Jesus. He was both god and man, and once lived on earth. He was slain by the evil Typhon, but rose again from the dead. After his resurrection he became the Judge of all men. Once a year the Egyptians used to celebrate his death, mourning his slaying by the evil one: "this grief for the death of Osiris did not escape some ridicule; for Xenophanes, the Ionian, wittily remarked to the priests of Memphis, that if they thought Osiris a man they should not worship him, and if they thought him a God they need not talk of his death and suffering.... Of all the gods Osiris alone had a place of birth and a place of burial. His birthplace was Mount Sinai, called by the Egyptians Mount Nyssa. Hence was derived the god's Greek name Dionysus, which is the same as the Hebrew Jehovah-Nissi" ("Egyptian Mythology and Egyptian Christianity," by Samuel Sharpe, pp. 10, 11; ed. 1863). Various places claimed the honour of his burial. "Serapis" was a god's name, formed out of "Osiris" and "Apis," the sacred bull, and we find (see ante, p. 206) that the Emperor Adrian wrote that the "worshippers of Serapis are Christians," and that bishops of Serapis were bishops of Christ; although the stories differ in detail, as is natural, since the Christian tale is modified by other myths—Osiris, for instance, is married—the general outline is the same. We shall see, in Section II., how thoroughly Pagan is the origin of Christianity.

We find the Early Fathers ready enough to claim these analogies, in order to recommend their religion. Justin Martyr argues: "When we say that the word, who is the first birth of God, was produced without sexual union, and that he, Jesus Christ, our teacher, was crucified and died, and rose again, and ascended into heaven, we propound nothing different from what you believe regarding those whom you esteem sons of Jupiter. For you know how many sons your esteemed writers ascribe to Jupiter; Mercury, the interpreting word and teacher of all; Aesculapius, who, though he was a great physician, was struck by a thunderbolt, and so ascended to heaven; and Bacchus too, after he had been torn limb from limb; and Hercules, when he had committed himself to the flames to escape his toils; and the sons of Leda, the Dioscuri; and Perseus, son of Danae; and Bellerophon, who, though sprung from mortals, rose to heaven on the horse Pegasus" ("First Apology," ch. xxi.). "If we assert that the Word of God was born of God in a peculiar manner, different from ordinary generation, let this, as said above, be no extraordinary thing to you, who say that Mercury is the angelic word of God. But if anyone objects that he was crucified, in this also he is on a par with those reputed sons of Jupiter of yours, who suffered as we have now enumerated.... And if we even affirm that he was born of a virgin, accept this in common with what you accept of Perseus. And in that we say that he made whole the lame, the paralytic, and those born blind, we seem to say what is very similar to the deeds said to have been done by AEsculapius" (Ibid, ch. xxi.). "Plato, in like manner, used to say that Rhadamanthus and Minos would punish the wicked who came before them; and we say that the same thing will be done, but at the hand of Christ" (Ibid, ch. viii.) In ch. liv. Justin argues that the devils invented all these gods in order that when Christ came his story should be thought to be another marvellous tale like its predecessors! On the whole, we can scarcely wonder that Caecilius (about A.D. 211) taunted the early Christians with those facts: "All these figments of cracked-brained opiniatry and silly solaces played off in the sweetness of song by deceitful poets, by you, too credulous creatures, have been shamefully reformed, and made over to your own God" (as quoted in R. Taylor's "Diegesis," p. 241). That the doctrines of Christianity had the same origin as the story of Christ, and the miracles ascribed to him, we shall prove under section ii., while section iii. will prove the same as to his morality. Judge Strange fairly says: "The Jewish Scriptures and the traditionary teaching of their doctors, the Essenes and Therapeuts, the Greek philosophers, the neo-platonism of Alexandria, and the Buddhism of the East, gave ample supplies for the composition of the doctrinal portion of the new faith; the divinely procreated personages of the Grecian and Roman pantheons, the tales of the Egyptian Osiris, and of the Indian Rama, Krishna, and Buddha, furnished the materials for the image of the new saviour of mankind; and every surrounding mythology poured forth samples of the 'mighty works' that were to be attributed to him to attract and enslave his followers: and thus, first from Judaism, and finally from the bosom of heathendom, we have our matured expression of Christianity" ("The Portraiture and Mission of Jesus," p. 27). From the mass of facts brought together above, we contend that the Gospels are in themselves

125

utterly unworthy of credit, from (1) the miracles with which they abound, (2) the numerous contradictions of each by the others, (3) the fact that the story of the hero, the doctrines, the miracles, were current long before the supposed dates of the Gospels; so that these Gospels are simply a patchwork composed of older materials.

We have thus examined, step by step, the alleged evidences of Christianity, both external and internal; we have found it impossible to rely on its external witnesses, while the internal testimony is fatal to its claims; it is, at once, unauthenticated without, and incredible within. After earnest study, and a careful balancing of proofs, we find ourselves forced to assert that THE EVIDENCES OF CHRISTIANITY ARE UNRELIABLE.

APPROXIMATE DATES CLAIMED FOR THE CHIEF CHRISTIAN AND HERETICAL AUTHORITIES

A.D.

Between 92 and 125	Clement of Rome	Very doubtful
Between 90 and 138	Barnabas	" "
Said to be martyred 107	Ignatius	" "
Between 117 and 138	Quadratus	" "
Possibly 138	Hermas	" "
About 150-170	Papias	" "
About 135-145	Basilides and Valentinus	" "
About 140-160	Marcion	
Said to be martyred 166	Polycarp	Very doubtful
Said to be martyred 166	Justin Martyr	
After 166	Hegesippus	
About 177	Epistle of Lyons and Vienne	
Between 150 and 290	Clementines	Real date quite unknown
Between 166 and 176	Dionysius of Corinth	
About 176	Athenagoras	
Between 170 and 175	Tatian	
177 to about 200	Irenæus	
About 193	Tertullian	
About 200	Celsus	Very doubtful
205	Clement of Alexandria succeeded as head of School	
About 205	Porphyry	
205-249	Origen	

THE SO-CALLED TEN PERSECUTIONS

A.D.

61 under Nero
81" Domitian
107" Trajan
166" Marcus Aurelius
193" Severus

A.D.

235 under Maximin
249" Decius
254" Valerian
272 " Aurelian
303" Diocletian

DATES OF ROMAN EMPERORS AT ALLEGED BIRTH OF CHRIST

Augustus Cæsar
A.D.
14 Tiberius
33 Caligula
41 Claudius
54 Nero
68 Galba
  Otho
69 Vitellius
69 Vespasian
79 Titus
81 Domitian
96 Nerva
98 Trajan associated
117 Hadrian
138 Antoninus Pius
161 Marcus Aurelius
180 Commodus
192 Pertinax
193 Julian
   Severus
211 Caracalla and Geta
217 Macrinus
218 Heliogabalus
222 Alexander Severus
235 Maximin

237 The Gordians
   Maximus and Galbinus
238 Maximus, Galbinus, and Gordian
238 Gordian alone
244 Philip
249 Decius
251 Gallus
253 Valerian
260 Gallienus
268 Claudius
270 Aurelian
275 Tacitus
276 Florianus
276 Probus
282 Carus
283 Carinus and Numerian
285 Diocletian
286 Maximian associated
305 Galerius and Constantius
305 Severus and Maximin
306 Constantine
   Licinius
   Maxentius
324 Constantine alone

SECTION II

ITS ORIGIN PAGAN

There are two ancient and widely-spread creeds to which we must chiefly look for the origin of Christianity, namely, Sun-worship and Nature-worship. It is doubtful which of the twain is the elder, and they are closely intertwined, the central idea of each being the same; personally, I am inclined to think that Nature-worship is the older of the two, because it is the simpler and the nearer; the barbarian, slowly emerging into humanity, would be more likely to worship the force which was the most immediately wonderful to him, the power of generation of new life; to recognise the sun as the great life producer seems to imply some little growth of reason and of imagination; sun-worship seems the idealisation of nature-worship, for the same generative force is adored in both, and round the idea of this production of new life all creeds revolve. Christian symbols and Christian ceremonies speak as plainly to the student of ancient religions as the stars speak to the astronomer, and the rocks to the geologian; Christian Churches are as full of the fossil relics of the old creeds as are the earth's strata of the bones of extinct animals. We shall expect to find, then, a family resemblance running through all Eastern creeds—of which Christianity is one—and we shall not be surprised to find similar symbols expressing similar ideas; there are, in fact, cardinal symbols re-appearing in all these allied religions; the virgin and child; the trinity in unity; the cross; these have their roots struck deep in human nature, and are found in every Eastern creed. So also can we trace sacraments and ceremonies, and many minor dogmas. In looking back into those ancient creeds it is necessary to get rid of the modern fashion of regarding any natural object as immodest. Sir William Jones justly remarks that in Hindustan "it never seems to have entered the heads of the legislators, or people, that anything natural could be offensively obscene; a singularity which pervades all their writings and conversation, but is no proof of depravity in their morals" ("Asiatic Researches," vol. i., p. 255). Gross injustice is sometimes done to ancient creeds by contemplating them from a modern point of view; in those days every power of Nature was thought divine, and most divine of all was deemed the power of creation, whether worshipped in the sun, whose beams impregnated the earth, or in the male and female organs of generation, the universal creators of life in the animal world; thus we find in all ancient sculptures carvings of the phallus and the yoni, expressed both naturally and symbolically, the representations becoming more and more conventional and refined as civilisation

128

advanced; of the infant world it may be said that it was "naked, and was not ashamed;" as it grew older, and clothed the human form, it also draped its religious symbols, but as the body remains unaltered under its garments, so the idea concealed beneath the emblems remains the same.

The union of male and female is, then, the foundation of all religions; the heaven marries the earth, as man marries woman, and that union is the first marriage. Saturn is the sky, the male, or active energy; Rhea is the earth, the female, or receptive; and these are the father and the mother of all. The Persians of old called the sky Jupiter, or Jupater, "Ju the Father." The sun is the agent of the generative power of the sky, and his beams fecundate the earth, so that from her all life is produced. Thus the sun becomes worshipped as the Father of all, and the sun is the emblem which crowns the images of the Supreme God; the vernal equinox is the resurrection of the sun, and the sign of the zodiac in which he then is becomes the symbol of his life-producing power; thus the bull, and afterwards the ram, became his sign as Life-Giver, and the Sun-god was pictured as bull, or as ram (or lamb), or else with the horns of his, emblem, and the earthly animals became sacred for his sake. Mithra, the Sun-god of Persia, is sculptured as riding on a bull; Osiris, the Sun-god of Egypt, wears the horns of the bull, and is worshipped as Osiris-Apis, or Serapis, the Sun-god in the sign of Apis, the bull. Later, by the precession of the equinoxes, the sun at the vernal equinox has passed into the sign of the ram (called in Persia, the lamb), and we find Jupiter Ammon, Jupiter with ram's horns, and Jesus the Lamb of God. These symbols all denote the sun victorious over darkness and death, giving life to the world. The phallus is the other great symbol of the Life-Giver, generating life in woman, as the sun in the earth. Bacchus, Adonis, Dionysius, Apollo, Hercules, Hermes, Thammuz, Jupiter, Jehovah, Jao, or Jah, Moloch, Baal, Asher, Mahadeva, Brahma, Vishnu, Mithra, Atys, Ammon, Belus, with many another, these are all the Life-Giver under different names; they are the Sun, the Creator, the Phallus. Red is their appropriate colour. When the sun or the Phallus is not drawn in its natural form, it is indicated by a symbol: the symbol must be upright, hard, or else burning, either conical, or clubbed at one end. Thus—the torch, flame of fire, cone, serpent, thyrsus, triangle, letter T, cross, crosier, sceptre, caduceus, knobbed stick, tall tree, upright stone, spire, tower, minaret, upright pole, arrow, spear, sword, club, upright stump, etc., are all symbols of the generative force of the male energy in Nature of the Supreme God.

One of the most common, and the most universally used, is THE CROSS. Carved at first simply as phallus, it was gradually refined; we meet it as three balls, one above the two; the letter T indicated it, which, by the slightest alteration, became the cross now known as the Latin: thus "Barnabas" says that "the cross was to express the grace by the letter T" (ante, p. 233). We find the cross in India, Egypt, Thibet,

Japan, always as the sign of life-giving power; it was worn as an amulet by girls and women, and seems to have been specially worn by the women attached to the temples, as a symbol of what was, to them, a religious calling. The cross is, in fact, nothing but the refined phallus, and in the Christian religion is a significant emblem of its Pagan origin; it was adored, carved in temples, and worn as a sacred emblem by sun and nature worshippers, long before there were any Christians to adore, carve, and wear it. The crowd kneeling before the cross in Roman Catholic and in High Anglican Churches, is a simple reproduction of the crowd who knelt before it in the temples of ancient days, and the girls who wear it amongst ourselves, are—in the most innocent unconsciousness of its real signification—exactly copying the Indian and Egyptian women of an elder time. Saturn's symbol was a cross and a ram's horn. Jupiter bore a cross with a horn. Venus a circle with a cross. The Egyptian deities a cross and oval. (The signification of these will be dealt with below.) The Druids sought oak trees with two main arms growing in shape of a cross, and, if they failed to find such, nailed a beam cross-wise. The chief pagodas in India are built, like many Christian churches, in the form of a cross. I have read in a book on church architecture that churches should be built either in the form of a cross, or else in that of a ship, typifying the ark; i.e., they should either be built in the form of the phallus or the yoni, the ship or ark being one of the symbols of the female energy (see below, p. 361).

The CRUCIFIX, or cross with human figure stretched upon it, is also found in ancient times, although not so frequently as the simple cross. The crucifix appears to have arisen from the circle of the horizon being divided into four parts, North, South, East, and West, and the Sun-god, drawn within, or on, the circle, came into contact with each cardinal point, his feet and head touching, or intersecting, two, while his outstretched arms point to the other quarters. Plato says that the "next power to the Supreme God was decussated, or figured in the shape of a cross, on the universe." Krishna is painted and sculptured on a cross. The Egyptians thus drew Osiris, and sometimes we find a circle drawn with the dividing lines, and in the midst is stretched the dead body of Osiris. Robert Taylor gives another origin for the crucifix: "The ignorant gratitude of a superstitious people, while they adored the river [Nile] on whose inundations the fertility of their provinces depended, could not fail of attaching notions of sanctity and holiness to the posts that were erected along its course, and which, by a transverse beam, indicated the height to which, at the spot where the beam was fixed, the waters might be expected to rise. This cross at once warned the traveller to secure his safety, and formed a standard of the value of land. Other rivers may add to the fertility of the country through which they pass, but the Nile is the absolute cause of that great fertility of the Lower Egypt, which would be all a desert, as bad as the most sandy parts of Africa without this river. It supplies it both with soil and moisture, and was therefore gratefully addressed, not merely as an ordinary river-god, but by its express title of the Egyptian Jupiter. The crosses, therefore, along the banks of the river would naturally share in the honour of the stream, and be the most expressive emblem of good fortune, peace, and plenty. The two ideas could never be separated: the fertilising flood was the waters of life, that conveyed every blessing, and even existence itself, to the provinces through which they flowed. One other and most obvious hieroglyph completed the expressive allegory. The Demon of Famine, who, should the waters fail of their inundation, or not reach the elevation indicated by the position of the transverse beam upon the upright, would reign in all his horrors over their desolated lands. This symbolical personification was, therefore, represented as a miserable emaciated wretch, who had grown up 'as a tender plant, and as a root out of a dry ground, who had no form nor comeliness; and when they should see him, there was no beauty that they should desire him.' Meagre were his looks; sharp misery had worn him to the bone. His crown of thorns indicated the sterility of the territories over which he reigned. The reed in his hand, gathered from the banks of the Nile, indicated that it was only the mighty river, by keeping within its banks, and thus withholding its wonted munificence, that placed an unreal sceptre in his gripe. He was nailed to the cross, in indication of his entire defeat. And the superscription of his infamous title, 'THIS IS THE KING OF THE JEWS,' expressively indicated that Famine, Want, or Poverty, ruled the destinies of the most slavish, beggarly, and mean race of men with whom they had the honour of being acquainted" ("Diegesis," p. 187). While it may very likely be true that the miserable aspect given to Jesus crucified is copied from some such original as Mr. Taylor here sketches, we are tolerably certain that the general idea of the crucifix had the solar origin described above.

Very closely joined to the notion of the cross is the idea of the TRINITY IN UNITY, and we need not delay upon it long. It is as universal in Eastern religions as the cross, and comes from the same idea; all life springs from a trinity in unity in man, and, therefore, God is three in one. This trinity is, of course, symbolised by the cross, and especially by the lotus, and any "three in one" leaf; from this has come to Christianity the conventional triple foliage so constantly seen in Church carvings, the fleur-de-lis, the triangle, etc., which are now—as of old—accepted as the emblems of the trinity. The persons of the trinity are found each with his own name; in India, Brahma, Vishnu, Siva, and it is Vishnu who becomes incarnate; in Egypt different cities had different trinities, and "we have a hieroglyphical inscription in the British Museum as early as the reign of Sevechus of the eighth century before the Christian era, showing that the doctrine of Trinity in Unity already formed part of their religion, and that in each of the two groups last mentioned the three gods only made one person" ("Egyptian Mythology and Egyptian Christology," by S. Sharpe, p. 14). Mr. Sharpe

131

might have gone to much earlier times and "already" have found the adoration of the trinity in unity; as far back as the first who bowed in worship before the generative force of the male three in one. Osiris, Horus, and Ra form one of the Egyptian trinities; Horus the Son, is also one of a trinity in unity made into an amulet, and called the Great God, the Son God, and the Spirit God. Horus is the slayer of Typhon, the evil one, and is sometimes represented as standing on its head, and as piercing its head with a spear, reminding us of Krishna, the incarnation of Vishnu, the second person of the Indian Trinity.

These trinities, however, were not complete in themselves, for the female element is needed for the production of life; hence, we find that in most nations a fourth person is joined to the trinity, as Isis, the mother of Horus, in Egypt, and Mary, the mother of Jesus, in Christendom; the Egyptian trinity is often represented as Osiris, Horus, and Isis, but we more generally find the female constituting the fourth element, in addition to the triune, and symbolised by an oval, or circle, typical of the female organ of reproduction; thus the crux ansata of the Egyptians, the "symbol of life" held in the hand by the Egyptian deities, is a cross or oval, i.e., the T with an oval at the top; the circle with the cross inside, symbolises, again, the male and female union; also the six-rayed star, the pentacle, the double triangle, the triangle and circle, the pit with a post in it, the key, the staff with a half-moon, the complicated cross. The same union is imaged out in all androgynous deities, in Elohim, Baalim, Baalath, Arba-il, the bearded Venus, the feminine Jove, the virgin and child. In countries where the Yoni worship was more popular than that of the Phallus, the VIRGIN and CHILD was a favourite deity, and to this we now turn.

Here, as in the history of the cross, we find sun and nature worship intertwined. The female element is sometimes the Earth, and sometimes the individual. The goddesses are as various in names as the gods. Is, Isis, Ishtar, Astarte, Mylitta, Sara, Mrira, Maia, Parvati, Mary, Miriam, Eve, Juno, Venus, Diana, Artemis, Aphrodite, Hera, Rhea, Cybele, Ceres, and others, are the earth under many names; the receptive female, the producer of life, the Yoni. Black is the special colour of female deities, and the black Isis and Horus, the black Mary and Jesus are of peculiar sanctity. Their emblems are: the earth, moon, star of the sea, circle, oval, triangle, pomegranate, door, ark, fish, ship, horseshoe, chasm, cave, hole, celestial virgin, etc. They bore first the titles now worn by Mary, the virgin mother of Jesus, and were reverenced as the "queen of heaven." Ishtar, of Babylonia, was the "Mother of the Gods," and the "Queen of the Stars." Isis, of Egypt, was "our Immaculate Lady." She was figured with a crown of stars, and with the crescent moon. Venus was an ark brooded over by a dove, or the moon floating on the water. They are "the mother," "mamma," "emma," "ummah," or "the woman." The symbols are everywhere the same, though given with different names. Everywhere it is Mary, the

132

mother; the female principle in nature, adored side by side with the male. She shares in the work of creation and salvation, and has a kind of equality with the Father of all; hence we hear of the immaculate conception. She produces a child alone in some stories, without even divine co-operation. The Virgo of the Zodiac is represented in ancient sculptures and drawings as a woman suckling a child, and the Paamylian feasts were celebrated at the spring equinox, and were the equivalent of the Christian feast of the Annunciation, when the power of the highest overshadowed Mary of Nazareth. Thus in India, we have Devaki and Krishna; in Egypt, Osiris and Horus—the "Saviour of the World;" in Christendom, Mary and Christ; the pictures and carvings of India and Egypt would be indistinguishable from those of Europe, were it not for the differences of dress. Apis, the sacred Egyptian bull, was always born without an earthly father, and his mother never had a second calf. So the later Sun-god, Jesus, is born without sexual intercourse, and Mary never bears another child. Jupiter visits Leda as a swan; God visits Mary as an overshadowing dove. The salutation of Gabriel to Mary is curiously like that of Mercury to Electra: "Hail, most happy of all women, you whom Jupiter has honoured with his couch; your blood will give laws to the world, I am the messenger of the gods." The mother of Fohi, the great Chinese God, became enceinte by walking in the footsteps of a giant. The mother of Hercules did not lose her virginity. The savages of St. Domingo represented the chief divinity by a female figure called the "mother of God." On Friday, the day of Freya, or Venus, many Christians still eat only fish, fish being sacred to the female deity.

In Comtism we find the latest development of woman-worship, wherein the "emotional sex" becomes the sacred sex, to be guarded, cherished, sustained, adored; and thus in the youngest religion the stamp of the eldest is found.

Thus womanhood has been worshipped in all ages of the world, and maternity has been deified by all creeds: from the savage who bowed before the female symbol of motherhood, to the philosophic Comtist who adores woman "in the past, the present, and the future," as mother, wife, and daughter, the worship of the female element in nature has run side by side with that of the male; the worship is one and the same in all religions, and runs in an unbroken thread from the barbarous ages to the present time.

The doctrines of the mediation, and the divinity of Christ, and of the immortality of the soul, are as pre-Christian as the symbols which we have examined.

The idea of the Mediator comes to us from Persia, and the title was borne by Mithra before it was ascribed to Christ. Zoroaster taught that there was existence itself, the unknown, the eternal, "Zeruane Akerne," "time without bounds." From this issued Ormuzd, the good, the light, the creator of all. Opposite to Ormuzd is Ahriman, the bad,

133

the dark, the deformer of all. Between these two great deities comes Mithra, the Mediator, who is the Reconciler of all things to God, who is one with Ormuzd, although distinct from him. Mithra, as we have seen, is the Sun in the sign of the Bull, exactly parallel to Jesus, the Sun in the sign of the Lamb, both the one and the other being symbolised by that sign of the zodiac in which the sun was at the spring equinox of his supposed date. "Mithras is spiritual light contending with spiritual darkness, and through his labours the kingdom of darkness shall be lit with heaven's own light; the Eternal will receive all things back into his favour, the world will be redeemed to God. The impure are to be purified, and the evil made good, through the mediation of Mithras, the reconciler of Ormuzd and Ahriman. Mithras is the Good, his name is Love. In relation to the Eternal he is the source of grace, in relation to man he is the life-giver and mediator. He brings the 'Word,' as Brahma brings the Vedas, from the mouth of the Eternal. (See Plutarch 'De Isid. et Osirid.;' also Dr. Hyde's 'De Religione Vet. Pers.,' ch. 22; see also 'Essay on Pantheism,' by Rev. J. Hunt.) It was just prior to the return of the Jews from living among the people who were dominated by these ideas, that the splendid chapter of Isaiah (xl.), or indeed the series of chapters which form the closing portion of the book, were written: 'Comfort ye, comfort ye my people, saith your God. Prepare ye the way of the Lord, make straight in the desert a highway for our God. Every valley shall be exalted, and every mountain and hill shall be made low, and the crooked shall be made straight, and the rough places plain.' And then follows a magnificent description of the greatness and supremacy of God, and this is followed by chapters which tell of a Messiah, or conquering prince, who will redeem the nation from its enemies, and restore them to the light of the divine favour, and which predict a millennium, a golden age of purified and glorified humanity. It is thus manifest that the inspiration of these writings came to the Jewish people from their contact with the religious thought of the Persians, and not from any supernatural source. From this time the Jews began to hold worthier ideas concerning God, and to cherish expectations of a golden age, a kingdom of heaven, which the Messiah, who was to be the sent messenger of God, should inaugurate. And this kingdom was to be a kingdom of righteousness, a day of marvellous light, a rule under which all evil and darkness were to perish" ("Plato, Philo, and Paul," Rev. J.W. Lake, pp. 15, l6.)

The growth of the philosophical side of the dogma of the Divinity of Christ is as clearly traceable in Pagan and Jewish thought as is the dogma of the incarnation of the Saviour-God in the myths of Krishna, Osiris, etc. Two great teachers of the doctrine of the "Logos," the "Word," of God, stand out in pre-Christian times—the Greek Plato and the Jewish Philo. We borrow the following extract from pp. 19, 20, of the pamphlet by Mr. Lake above referred to, as showing the general theological position of Plato; its resemblance to Christian teaching will be at once apparent (it must not be forgotten that Plato lived B.C. 400):—

"The speculative thought and the religious teaching of Plato are diffused throughout his voluminous writings; but the following is a popular summary of them, by Madame Dacier, contained in her introduction to what have been classed as the 'Divine Dialogues:'—

"'That there is but one God, and that we ought to love and serve him, and to endeavour to resemble him in holiness and righteousness; that this God rewards humility and punishes pride.

"'That the true happiness of man consists in being united to God, and his only misery in being separated from him.

"'That the soul is mere darkness, unless it be illuminated by God; that men are incapable even of praying well, unless God teaches them that prayer which alone can be useful to them.

"'That there is nothing solid and substantial but piety; that this is the source of all virtues, and that it is the gift of God.

"'That it is better to die than to sin.

"'That it is better to suffer wrong than to do it.

"'That the "Word" ([Greek: Logos]) formed the world, and rendered it visible; that the knowledge of the Word makes us live very happily here below, and that thereby we obtain felicity after death.

"'That the soul is immortal, that the dead shall rise again, that there shall be a final judgment—both of the righteous and of the wicked, when men shall appear only with their virtues or vices, which shall be the occasion of their eternal happiness or misery.'"

It is this Logos who was "figured in the shape of a cross on the universe" (ante, p. 358). The universe, which is but the materialised thought of God, is made by his Logos, his Word, which is the expression of his thought. In the Christian creed it is the Logos, the Word of God, by whom all things are made (John i. 1-3). The very name, as well as the thought, is the same, whether we turn over the pages of Plato or those of John. Philo, the great Jewish Platonist, living in Alexandria at the close of the last century B.C. and in the first half of the first century after Christ, speaks of the Logos in terms that, to our ears, seem purely Christian. Philo was a man of high position among the Jews in Alexandria, being "a man eminent on all accounts, brother to Alexander the alabarch [governor of the Jews], and one not unskilful in philosophy" (Josephus' "Antiquities of the Jews," bk. xviii., ch. 8, sec. 1). This "Alexander was a principal person among all his contemporaries both for his family and wealth" (Ibid, bk. xx, ch. 5, sec. 2). He was the principal man in the Jewish embassage to Caius (Caligula) A.D. 39-40, and was then a grey-headed old man. Keim speaks of him as about sixty or seventy years old at that time, and puts his birth at about B.C. 20. He writes: "The Theology of Philo is in great measure founded on his peculiar combination of the Jewish, the Platonic, and the Neo-Platonic conception of God. The God of the Old

Testament, the exalted God, as he is called by the modern Hegelian philosophy, stood in close relations to the Greek Philosophers' conception of God, which believed that the Supreme Being could be accurately defined by the negative of all that was finite. In accordance with this, Philo also described God as the simple Entity; he disclaimed for him every name, every quality, even that of the Good, the Beautiful, the Blessed, the One. Since he is still better than the good, higher than the Unity, he can never be known as, but only that, he is: his perfect name is only the four mysterious letters (Jhvh)—that is, pure Being. By such means, indeed, neither a fuller theology nor God's influence on the world was to be obtained. And yet it was the problem of philosophy, as well as of religion, to shed the light of God upon the world, and to lead it again to God. But how could this Being which was veiled from the world be brought to bear upon it? By Philo, as well as by all the philosophy of the time, the problem could only be solved illogically. Yet, by modifying his exalted nature, it might be done. If not by his being, yet by his work he influences the world; his powers, his angels, all in it that is best and mightiest, the instrument, the interpreter, the mediator and messenger of God; his pattern and his first-born, the Son of God, the Second God, even himself God, the divine Word or Logos communicate with the world; he is the ideal and actual type of the world and of humanity, the architect and upholder of the world, the manna and the rock in the wilderness" ("Jesus of Nazara," vol. i., pp. 281, 282).

"Man is fallen.... There is no man who is without sin, and even the perfect man, if he should be born, does not escape from it.... Yet there is a redemption, willed by God himself, and brought to pass by the act of a wise man. Adam's successors still preserve the types of their relationship to the Father, although in an obscure form, each man possesses the knowledge of good and evil and an incorruptible judgment, subject to reason; his spiritual strength is even now aided by the Divine Logos, the image, copy, and reflection of the blessed nature. Hence it follows that man can discern and see all the stains with which he has wilfully or involuntarily defiled his life, that man by means of his self-knowledge can decide to subdue his passions, to despise his pleasures and desires, to wage the battle of repentance, and to be just at any cost, and by the fundamental virtues of humanity, piety, and justice, to imitate the virtues of the Father.... In such perfection as is possible to all, even to women and to slaves, since no one is a slave by nature, the wise man is truly rich. He is noble and free who can proudly utter the saying of Sophocles, God is my ruler, not one among men! Such a one is priest, king, and prophet, he is no longer merely a son and scholar of the Logos, he is the companion and son of God.... God is the eternal guide and director of the world, himself requiring nothing, and giving all to his children. It is of his goodness that he does not punish as a judge, but that, as the giver of grace, he bears with all. With him all things are possible; he deals with all, even with that which is almost beyond redemption. From him all the world hopes for forgiveness of sins, the Logos, the high priest, and intercessor, and the patriarchs pray for it; he grants it, not for the world's sake, but of his own gracious nature, to those who can truly believe. He loves the humble, and saves those whom he knows to be worthy of healing. His grace elects the pious before they are born, giving them victory over sensuality, and steadfastness in virtue. He reveals himself to holy souls by his Spirit, and by his divine light leads those who are too weak by nature even to understand the external world, beyond the limits of human nature to that which is divine" ("Jesus of Nazara," pp. 283-287). Such are the most important passages of Keim's résumé of Philo's philosophy, and its resemblance to Christian doctrine is unmistakeable, and adds one more proof to the fact that Christianity is Alexandrian rather than Judæan. It will be well to add to this sketch the passages carefully gathered out of Philo's works by Jacob Bryant, who endeavoured to prove, from their resemblance to passages in the New Testament, that Philo was a Christian, forgetting that Philo's works were mostly written when Jesus was a child and a youth, and that he never once mentions Jesus or Christianity. It must not be forgotten that Philo lived in Alexandria, not in Judæa, and that between the Canaanitish and the Hellenic Jews there existed the most bitter hostility, so that—even were the story of Jesus true—it could not have reached Philo before A.D. 40, at which time he was old and gray-headed. We again quote from Mr. Lake's treatise, who prints the parallel passages, and we would draw special attention to the similarity of phraseology as well as of idea:

"Identity of the Christ of the New Testament with the Logos of Philo.

Philo, describing the Logos, says:—

The New Testament, speaking of Jesus says:—

'The Logos is the Son of God the Father.'—De Profugis.

'This is the Son of God.' John i. 34.

'The first begotten of God.'—De Somniis.

'And when he again bringeth his first-born into the world.'—Heb. i. 6.

'And the most ancient of all beings.'—De Conf. Ling

'That he is the first-born of every creature.'—Col. i. 15.

'The Logos is the image and likeness of God.'—De Monarch.

'Christ, the image of the invisible God.'—Col. i. 15. 'The brightness of his (God's) glory, and the express image of his person.'—Heb. i. 3.

'The Logos is superior to the angels.'—De Profugis.

'The Logos is superior to all beings

'Being made so much better that

137

in the world.'—De Leg. Allegor.

'The Logos is the instrument by whom the world was made.'—De Leg. Allegor.
'The divine word by whom all things were ordered and disposed.'—De Mundi Opificio.

'the Logos is the light of the world, and the intellectual sun.'—De Somniis.

'The Logos only can see God.'—De Confus. Ling.
'He is the most ancient of God's works.'—De Confus Ling.
'And was before all things.'—De Leg. Allegor.
'The Logos is esteemed the same as God.'—De Somniis.

'The Logos was eternal.'—De Plant. Noë.

'The Logos supports the world, is the connecting power by which all things are united.'—De Profugis.
'The Logos is nearest to God, without any separation; being, as it were, fixed upon the only true existing Deity, nothing coming between to disturb that unity.'—De Profugis.

'The Logos is free from all taint of sin, either voluntary or involuntary.'—De Profugis.

'The Logos the fountain of life.
'It is of the greatest consequence to every person to strive without remission to approach to the divine Logos, the Word of God above, who is the fountain of all wisdom; that

the angels. Let all the angels of God worship him.'—Heb. i. 4, 6.
'Thou hast put all things in subjection under his feet.'—Heb. ii. 8.
'All things were made by him (the Word or Logos), and without him was not anything made that was made.'—John i. 3
'Jesus Christ, by whom are all things.'—1 Cor. viii. 6.

'By whom also he made the worlds.'—Heb. i. 2.
'The Word (Logos) was the true light.'—John i. 9.
'The life and the light of men.'—John i. 4.
'I am the light of the world.'—John viii. 12.
'He that is of God, he hath seen the Father.'—John vi. 46.

'No man hath seen God at any time. The only begotten Son which is in the bosom of the Father, he hath declared him."—John i. 18.

'Now, O Father, glorify thou me with thine own self with the glory which I had with thee before the world was.'—John xvii. 5.

'He was in the beginning with God.'—John i. 2.
'Before all worlds.'—2 Tim. i. 9.

'Christ, who is over all, God blessed for evermore.'—Rom. ix. 5.
'Who, being in the form of God. thought it no robbery to be equal with God.'—Phil. ii. 6.
'Christ abideth for ever.—John xii. 34.

by drinking largely of that sacred spring, instead of death, he may be rewarded with everlasting life.'—De Profugis.

'The Logos is the shepherd of God's flock.

'The deity, like a shepherd, and at the same time like a monarch, acts with the most consummate order and rectitude, and has appointed his First-born, the upright Logos, like the substitute of a mighty prince, to take care of his sacred flock.'—De Agricult.

The Logos, Philo says, is 'The great governor of the world; he is the creative and princely power, and through these the heavens and the whole world were produced.' —De Profugis.

'The Logos is the physician that heals all evil.'—De Leg. Allegor.

The Logos the Seal of God.
'The Logos, by whom the world was framed, is the seal, after the impression of which everything is made, and is rendered the similitude and image of the perfect Word of God.'—De Profugis.

'The soul of man is an impression of a seal, of which the prototype and original characteristic is the everlasting Logos.'—De Plantatione Noë.

The Logos the source of immortal life.
Philo says 'that when the soul strives after its best and noblest life, then the Logos frees it from all corruption, and confers upon it the gift of immortality.'—De C.Q. Erud. Gratiâ.'

'But to the Son he saith, Thy throne, O God, is for ever and ever.'—Heb. i. 8.

'Upholding all things by the word of his power.'—Heb. i. 3.
'By him all things consist.'—Col. i. 17.

'I and my Father are one.'—John x. 30.

'That they may be one as we are.'—John xvii. 11.
'The only begotten Son, who is in the bosom of the Father.'—John i. 18.

'The blood of Christ, who offered himself without spot to God.'—Heb. ix. 14.

'Who did no sin, neither was guile found in his mouth.' —1 Pet. ii. 22.
'Whosoever shall drink of the water that I shall give him, shall never thirst, but the water that I shall give him shall be in him a well of water, springing up into everlasting life.'—John iv. 14.

'The great shepherd of the flock... our Lord Jesus.'— Heb. xiii. 20.

'I am the good shepherd, and know my sheep, and am known of mine.—John x. 14.
'Christ ... the shepherd and guardian of your souls.' 1 Pet. ii. 25.

'For Christ must reign till he hath put all his enemies under his feet.'—1 Cor. xv. 25
'Christ, above all principality,

Philo speaks of the Logos not only as the Son of God and his first begotten, but also styles him 'his beloved Son.'—De Leg. Allegor

Philo says 'that good men are admitted to the assembly of the saints above.

'Those who relinquish human doctrines, and become the well-disposed disciples of God, will be one day translated to an incorruptible and perfect order of beings."—De Sacrifices.

Philo says 'that the just man, when he dies is translated to another state by the Logos, by whom the world was created. For God by his said Word (Logos), by which he made all things, will raise the perfect man from the dregs of this world, and exalt him near himself. He will place him near his own person.'—De Sacrificiis.

Philo says that the Logos is the true High Priest, who is without sin and anointed by God:—

'It is the world, in which the Logos, God's First-born, that great High Priest, resides. And I assert that this High Priest is no man, but the Holy Word of God; who is not capable of either voluntary or involuntary sin, and hence his head is anointed with oil.'—De Profugis.

Philo mentions the Logos as the great High Priest and Mediator for the sins of the world. Speaking of the rebellion of Korah, he

and might, and dominion, and every name that is named, not only in this world, but in the world to come ... and God hath put all things under his feet.'—Eph. i. 21, 22

'The spirit of the Lord is upon me, because he hath anointed me to heal the broken-hearted.'—Luke iv. 18.

Christ the Seal of God.

'In whom also, after that ye believed, ye were sealed with the holy seal of promise.'—Eph. i. 13
'In whom also, after that ye believed, ye were sealed with the holy seal of promise.'—Eph. i. 13

'Jesus, the son of man ... him hath God the Father sealed.'—John vi. 27.

'Christ, the brightness of his (God's) glory, and the express image of his person.—Heb. i. 3.

Christ the source of eternal life.
'The dead (in Christ) shall be raised incorruptible.'—1 Cor. xv. 52
'Because the creature itself also shall be delivered from the bondage of corruption into the glorious liberty of the children of God.'—Rom. vii. 21.

The New Testament callsChrist the Beloved Son:—'This is my beloved Son in whom I am well pleased.'—Matt. iii. 17; Luke ix. 35; 2 Pet. i. 17
'The Son of his love.'—Col. i. 13.
'But ye are come unto mount

introduces the Logos as saying:—

'It was I who stood in the middle between the Lord and you.

'The sacred Logos pressed with zeal and without remission that he might stand between the dead and the living.—Quis Rerum Div. Haeres.

The Logos, the Saviour God, who brings salvation as the reward of repentance and righteousness.

'If then men have from their very souls a just contrition, and are changed, and have humbled themselves for their past errors, acknowledging and confessing their sins, such persons shall find pardon from the Saviour and merciful God, and receive a most choice and great advantage of being like the Logos of God, who was originally the great archetype after which the soul of man was formed.'—De Execrationibus.

Zion, and to the city of the living God, and to an innumerable company of angels, and to the spirits of just men made perfect.'—Heb. xii. 22, 23.

'Giving thanks unto the Father which hath made us meet to be the partakers of the inheritance of the saints in light.'—Col. i. 12.

'No man can come to me, except the Father which hath sent me draw him; and I will raise him up at the last day.'—John vi. 44.

'No man cometh to the Father but by me.'—John xvi. 6.

'Where I am, there also shall my servant be ... him will my father honour.'—

The New Testament speaks of Jesus as the High Priest:

'Seeing then that we have a great High Priest that is passed into the heavens, Jesus, the Son of God, let us hold fast our profession.'—Heb. iv. 14.

'For such an High Priest became us, who is holy, harmless, undefiled, separate from sinners.'—Heb. vii. 26.

The New Testament says of Christ:—

'We have such an High Priest, who is set on the right hand of the throne of the majesty in the heavens, a mediator of a better covenant.'—Heb. viii. 1-6.

'But Christ being come an High Priest ... entered at once into the holy place, having obtained eternal redemption for us,—Heb. ix. 11, 12.

The New Testament says of

John, the forerunner of Jesus, that he preached 'the baptism of repentance for the remission of sins.'—Mark i. 4.

Jesus says :—

'Ye will not come to me, that ye might have life.'—John v. 40.

'Beloved, we be now the sons of God; and it doth not yet appear what we shall be; but we know that when he doth appear we shall be like him.'—1 John iii. 2.

'As we have born the image of the earthy, we shall also bear the image of the heavenly.'—1 Cor. xv. 49.

'For if we have been planted together in the likeness of his death, we shall be also in the likeness of his resurrection.'—Rom. vi. 5."

Here, then, we get, complete, the idea of Christ as the Word of God, and we see that Christianity is as lacking in originality on these points as in everything else. We may note, also, that this Platonic idea was current among the Jews before Philo, although he gives it to us more thoroughly and fully worked out: in the apocryphal books of the Jews we find the idea of the Logos in many passages in Wisdom, to take but a single case.

The widely-spread existence of this notion is acknowledged by Dean Milman in his "History of Christianity." He says: "This Being was more or less distinctly impersonated, according to the more popular or more philosophic, the more material or the more abstract, notions of the age or people. This was the doctrine from the Ganges, or even the shores of the Yellow Sea to the Ilissus; it was the fundamental principle of the Indian religion and the Indian philosophy; it was the basis of Zoroastrianism; it was pure Platonism; it was the Platonic Judaism of the Alexandrian school. Many fine passages might be quoted from Philo, on the impossibility that the first self-existing Being should become cognisable to the sense of man; and even in Palestine, no doubt, John the Baptist and our Lord himself spoke no new doctrine, but rather the common sentiment of the more enlightened, when they declared that 'no man had seen God at any time.' In conformity with this principle, the Jews, in the interpretation of the older Scriptures, instead of direct and sensible communication from the one great Deity, had interposed either one or more intermediate beings as the channels

142

of communication. According to one accredited tradition alluded to by St. Stephen, the law was delivered by the 'disposition of angels;' according to another, this office was delegated to a single angel, sometimes called the angel of the Law (see Gal. iii. 19); at others, the Metatron. But the more ordinary representative, as it were, of God, to the sense and mind of man, was the Memra, or the Divine Word; and it is remarkable that the same appellation is found in the Indian, the Persian, the Platonic, and the Alexandrian systems. By the Targumists, the earliest Jewish commentators on the Scriptures, this term had been already applied to the Messiah; nor is it necessary to observe the manner in which it has been sanctified by its introduction into the Christian scheme. This uniformity of conception and coincidence of language indicates the general acquiescence of the human mind in the necessity of some mediation between the pure spiritual nature of the Deity and the moral and intellectual nature of man" (as quoted by Lake). And "this uniformity of conception and coincidence of language indicates," also, that Christianity has only received and repeated the religious ideas which existed in earlier times. How can that be a revelation from God which was well known in the world long before God revealed it? The acknowledgment of the priority of Pagan thought is the destruction of the supernatural claims of Christianity based on the same thought; that cannot be supernatural after Christ which was natural before him, nor that sent down from heaven which was already on earth as the product of human reason. The Rev. Mr. Lake fairly says: "We have evidence—clear, conclusive, irrefutable evidence—as to what this doctrine really is. We can trace its birth-place in the philosophic speculations of the ancient world, we can note its gradual development and growth, we can see it in its early youth passing (through Philo and others) from Grecian philosophy into the current of Jewish thought; then, after resting awhile in the Judaism of the period of the Christian era, we see it slightly changing its character, as it passes through Gamaliel, Paul—the writers of the Fourth Gospel and of the Epistle to the Hebrews—through Justin Martyr and Tertullian, into the stream of early Christian thought, and now from a sublime philosophical speculation it becomes dwarfed and corrupted into a church dogma, and finally gets hardened as a frozen mass of absurdity, stupidity, and blasphemy, in the Nicene and Athanasian creeds" ("Philo, Plato, and Paul," pp. 71, 72).

The idea of IMMORTALITY was by no means "brought to light" by Christ, as is pretended. The early Jews had clearly no idea of life after death; "for in death there is no remembrance of thee; in the grave who shall give thee thanks?" (Ps. vi. 5). "Like the slain that lie in the grave, whom thou rememberest no more.... Wilt thou shew wonders to the dead? Shall the dead arise and praise thee? Shall thy lovingkindness be declared in the grave? or thy faithfulness in destruction? Shall thy wonders be known in the dark? and thy righteousness in the land of forgetfulness?" (Ps. lxxxviii. 5, 10-12). "The dead praise not the Lord" (Ps. cxv. 17). "I said in mine heart concerning the estate of the sons of men, that God might manifest them, and that they might see that they themselves are beasts. For that which befalleth the sons of men befalleth beasts; even one thing befalleth them: as the one dieth, so dieth the other; yea, they have all one breath; so that man hath no pre-eminence above a beast" (Eccles. iii. 18, 19). "There is no work, nor device, nor knowledge, nor wisdom, in the grave" (Ibid, ix. 10). "The grave cannot praise thee, death cannot celebrate thee: they that go down into the pit cannot hope for thy truth. The living, the living, he shall praise thee" (Is. xxxviii. 18, 19). In strict accordance with this belief, that death was the end of man, the pre-captivity Jews regarded wealth, strength, prosperity, and all earthly blessings, as the reward of virtue. After the captivity they change their tone; in the post-Babylonian Psalms life after death is distinctly spoken of: "My flesh also shall rest in hope. For thou wilt not leave my soul in hell" (Ps. xvi. 9, 10); together with other passages. In the apocryphal Jewish Scriptures the belief in immortality appears over and over again.

To say that Jesus "brought life and immortality to light through the Gospel," even to the Jews, is to contend for a position against all evidence. If from the Jews we turn to the Pagan thinkers, immortality is proclaimed by them long before the Jews have dreamed about it. The Egyptians, in their funeral ritual, went through the judgment of the soul before Osiris: "The resurrection of the dead to a second life had been a deep-rooted religious opinion among the Egyptians from the earliest times ("Egyptian Mythology," Sharpe, p. 52), and they appear to have believed in a transmigration of souls through the lower animals, and an ultimate return to the original body; to this end they preserved the body as a mummy, so that the soul, on its return, might find its original habitation still in existence: any who believe in the resurrection of the body should clearly follow the example of the ancient Egyptians. In later times, the more instructed Egyptians believed in a spiritual resurrection only, but the mass of the people clung to the idea of a bodily resurrection (Ibid, p. 54). "It is to the later times of Egyptian history, perhaps to the five centuries immediately before the Christian era, that the religious opinions contained in the funeral papyri chiefly belong. The roll of papyrus buried with the mummy often describes the funeral, and then goes on to the return of the soul to the body, the resurrection, the various trials and difficulties which the deceased will meet and overcome in the next world, and the garden of paradise in which he awaits the day of judgment, the trial on that day, and it then shows the punishment which would have awaited him if he had been found guilty" (Ibid, p. 64). We have already seen that the immortality of the soul was taught by Plato (ante, p. 364). The Hindus taught that happiness or misery hereafter depended upon the life here. "If duty is performed, a good name will be obtained, as well as happiness, here and after death" ("Mahabharata," xii., 6,538, in "Religious and Moral Sentiments from Indian Writers," by J. Muir, p. 22). The "Mahabharata" was written, or rather collected, in the second century before Christ. "Poor King Rantideva bestowed water with a pure mind, and thence ascended to heaven.... King Nriga gave thousands of largesses of cows to Brahmans; but because he gave away one belonging to another person, he went to hell" (Ibid, xiv. 2,787 and 2,789. Muir, pp, 31, 32). "Let us now examine into the theology of India, as reported by Megasthenes, about B.C. 300 (Cory's 'Ancient Fragments,' p. 226, et seq.). 'They, the Brahmins, regard the present life merely as the conception of persons presently to be born, and death as the birth into a life of reality and happiness, to those who rightly philosophise: upon this account they are studiously careful in preparing for death'" (Inman's "Ancient Faiths," vol. ii., p. 820). Zoroaster (B.C. 1,200, or possibly 2,000) taught: "The soul, being a bright fire, by the power of the Father remains immortal, and is the mistress of life" (Ibid, p. 821). "The Indians were believers in the immortality of the soul, and conscious future existence. They taught that immediately after death the souls of men, both good and bad, proceed together along an appointed path to the bridge of the gatherer, a narrow path to heaven, over which the souls of the pious alone could pass, whilst the wicked fall from it into the gulf below; that the prayers of his living friends are of much value to the dead, and greatly help him on his journey. As his soul enters the abode of bliss, it is greeted with the word, 'How happy art thou, who hast come here to us, mortality to immortality!' Then the pious soul goes joyfully onward to Ahura-Mazdao, to the immortal saints, the golden throne, and Paradise" (Ibid, p. 834). From these notions the writer of the story of Jesus drew his idea of the "narrow way" that led to heaven, and of the "strait gate" through which many would be unable to pass. Cicero (bk. vi. "Commonwealth," quoted by Inman) says: "Be assured that, for all those who have in any way conducted to the preservation, defence, and enlargement of their native country, there is a certain place in heaven, where they shall enjoy an eternity and happiness." It is needless to further multiply quotations in order to show that our latest development of these Eastern creeds only reiterated the teaching of the earlier phases of religious thought.

"But, at least," urge the Christians, "we owe the sublime idea of the UNITY OF GOD to revelation, and this is grander than the Polytheism of the Pagan world." Is it not, however, true, that just as Christians urge that the Father, Son, and Holy Ghost, are but one God, so the thinkers of old believed in one Supreme Being, while the multitudinous gods were but as the angels and saints of Christianity, his messengers, his subordinates, not his rivals? All savages are Polytheists, just as were the Hebrews, whose god "Jehovah" was but their special god, stronger than the gods of the nations around them,

145

gods whose existence they never denied; but as thought grew, the superior minds in each nation rose over the multitude of deities to the idea of one Supreme Being working in many ways, and the loftiest flights of the "prophets" of the Jewish Scriptures may be paralleled by those of the sages of other creeds. Zoroaster taught that "God is the first, indestructible, eternal, unbegotten, indivisible, dissimilar" ("Ancient Fragments," Cory, p. 239, quoted by Inman). In the Sabaean Litany (two extracts only of this ancient work are preserved by El Wardi, the great Arabic historian) we read: "Thou art the Eternal One, in whom all order is centred.... Thou dost embrace all things. Thou art the Infinite and Incomprehensible, who standest alone" ("Sacred Anthology," by M.D. Conway, pp. 74, 75). "There is only one Deity, the great soul. He is called the Sun, for he is the soul of all beings. That which is One, the wise call it in divers manners. Wise poets, by words, make the beautiful-winged manifold, though he is One" ("Rig-Veda," B.C. 1500, from "Anthology," p.76). "The Divine Mind alone is the whole assemblage of the gods.... He (the Brahmin) may contemplate castle, air, fire, water, the subtile ether, in his own body and organs; in his heart, the Star; in his motion, Vishnu; in his vigour, Hara; in his speech, Agni; in digestion, Mitra; in production, Brahma; but he must consider the supreme Omnipresent Reason as sovereign of them all" ("Manu," about B.C. 1200; his code collected about B.C. 300; from "Anthology," p. 81). On an ancient stone at Bonddha Gaya is a Sanscrit inscription to Buddha, in which we find: "Reverence be unto thee, an incarnation of the Deity and the Eternal One. OM! [the mysterious name of God, equivalent to pure existence, or the Jewish Jhvh] the possessor of all things in vital form! Thou art Brahma, Veeshnoo, and Mahesa!... I adore thee, who art celebrated by a thousand names, and under various forms" ("Asiatic Researches," Essay xi., by Mr. Wilmot; vol. i., p. 285). Plato's teaching is, "that there is but one God" (ante, p. 364), and wherever we search, we find that the more thoughtful proclaimed the unity of the Deity. This doctrine must, then, go the way of the rest, and it must be acknowledged that the boasted revelation is, once more, but the speculation of man's unassisted reason.

Turning from these cardinal doctrines to the minor dogmas and ceremonies of Christianity, we shall still discover it to be nothing but a survival of Paganism.

BAPTISM seems to have been practised as a religious rite in all solar creeds, and has naturally, therefore, found its due place in the latest solar faith. "The idea of using water as emblematic of spiritual washing, is too obvious to allow surprise at the antiquity of this rite. Dr. Hyde, in his treatise on the 'Religion of the Ancient Persians,' xxxiv. 406, tells us that it prevailed among that people. 'They do not use circumcision for their children, but only baptism or washing for the inward purification of the soul. They bring the child to the priest into the church, and place him in front of the sun and fire, which ceremony

146

being completed, they look upon him as more sacred than before. Lord says that they bring the water for this purpose in bark of the Holm-tree; that tree is in truth the Haum of the Magi, of which we spoke before on another occasion. Sometimes also it is otherwise done by immersing him in a large vessel of water, as Tavernier tells us. After such washing, or baptism, the priest imposes on the child the name given by his parents'" ("Christian Records," Rev. Dr. Giles, p. 129).

"The Baptismal fonts in our Protestant churches, and we can hardly say more especially the little cisterns at the entrance of our Catholic chapels, are not imitations, but an unbroken and never interrupted continuation of the same aquaminaria, or amula, which the learned Montfaucon, in his 'Antiquities,' shows to have been vases of holy water, which were placed by the heathens at the entrance of their temples, to sprinkle themselves with upon entering those sacred edifices" ("Diegesis," R. Taylor, p. 219). Among the Hindus, to bathe in the Ganges is to be regenerated, and the water is holy because it flows from Brahma's feet. Tertullian, arguing that water, as being God's earliest and most favoured creation, and brooded over by the spirit— Vishnu also is called Narayan, "moving on the waters"—was sanctifying in its nature, says: "'Well, but the nations, who are strangers to all understanding of spiritual powers, ascribe to their idols the imbuing of waters with the self-same efficacy.' So they do, but these cheat themselves with waters which are widowed. For washing is the channel through which they are initiated into some sacred rites of some notorious Isis or Mithra; and the gods themselves likewise they honour by washings.... At the Appollinarian and Eleusinian games they are baptised; and they presume that the effect of their doing that is the regeneration, and the remission of the penalties due to their perjuries.... Which fact, being acknowledged, we recognise here also the zeal of the devil rivalling the things of God, while we find him, too, practising baptism in his subjects" ("On Baptism," chap. v.). As "the devil" did it first, it seems scarcely fair to accuse him of copying.

Closely allied to baptism is the idea of regeneration, being born again. In baptism the purification is wrought by the male deity, typified in the water flowing from the throne or the feet of the god. In regeneration without water the purification is wrought by the female deity. The earth is the mother of all, and "as at birth the new being emerges from the mother, so it was supposed that emergence from a terrestrial cleft was equivalent to a new birth" (Inman's "Ancient Faiths," vol. i., p. 415; ed. 1868). Hence the custom of squeezing through a hole in a rock, or passing through a perforated stone, or between and under stones set up for the purpose; a natural cleft in a rock or in the earth was considered as specially holy, and to some of these long pilgrimages are still made in Eastern lands. On emerging from the hole, the devotee is re-born, and the sins of the past are no longer counted against him.

CONFIRMATION was also a rite employed by the ancient Persians. "Afterwards, in the fifteenth year of his age, when he begins to put on the tunic, the sudra and the girdle, that he may enter upon religion, and is engaged upon the articles of belief, the priest bestows upon him confirmation, that he may from that time be admitted into the number of the faithful, and may be looked upon as a believer himself" (Dr. Hyde on "Religion of the Ancient Persians," tr. by Dr. Giles in "Christian Records," pp. 129, 130).

LORD'S SUPPER.—Bread and wine appear to have been a regular offering to the Sun-god, whose beams ripen the corn and the grape, and who may indeed, by a figure, be said to be transubstantiated thus for the food of man. The Persians offered bread and wine to Mithra; the people of Thibet and Tartary did the same. Cakes were made for the Queen of heaven, kneaded of dough, and were offered up to her with incense and drink-libations (Jer. vii. 18, and xliv. 19). Ishtar was worshipped with cakes, or buns, made out of the finest flour, mingled with honey, and the ancient Greeks offered the same: this bread seems to have been sometimes only offered to the deity, sometimes also eaten by the worshippers; in the same way the bread and the wine are offered to God in the Eucharist, and he is prayed to accept "our alms and oblations." The Easter Cakes presented by the clergyman to his parishioners—an old English custom, now rarely met with—are the cakes of Ishtar, oval in form, symbolising the yoni. We have already dealt fully with the apparent similarity between the Christian Agapae, and the Bacchanalian mysteries (ante, pp. 222-227). The supper of Adoneus, Adonai, literally, the "supper of the Lord," formed part of these feasts, identical in name with the supper of the Christian mysteries. The Eleusinian mysteries, celebrated at Eleusis, in honour of Ceres, goddess of corn, and Bacchus, god of wine, compel us to think of bread and wine, the very substance of the gods, as it were, there adored. And Mosheim gives us the origin of many of the Christian eucharistic ceremonies. He writes: "The profound respect that was paid to the Greek and Roman mysteries, and the extraordinary sanctity that was attributed to them, was a further circumstance that induced the Christians to give their religion a mystic air, in order to put it upon an equal foot, in point of dignity, with that of the Pagans. For this purpose they gave the name of mysteries to the institutions of the gospel, and decorated particularly the holy Sacrament with that solemn title. They used in that sacred institution, as also in that of baptism, several of the terms employed in the heathen mysteries; and proceeded so far, at length, as even to adopt some of the rites and ceremonies of which these renowned mysteries consisted. This imitation began in the Eastern provinces; but after the time of Adrian, who first introduced the mysteries among the Latins, it was followed by the Christians, who dwelt in the Western parts of the Empire. A great part, therefore, of the service of the church, in this century [A.D. 100-200], had a certain air of the heathen mysteries, and resembled them considerably in many particulars" ("Eccles. Hist.," 2nd century, p. 56).

The whole system of THE PRIESTHOOD was transplanted into Christianity from Paganism; the Egyptian priesthood, however, was in great part hereditary, and in this differs from the Christian, while resembling the Jewish. The priests of the temple of Dea (Syria) were, on the other hand, celibate, and so were some orders of the Egyptian priests. Some classes of priests closely resembled Christian monks, living in monasteries, and undergoing many austerities; they prayed twice a day, fasted often, spoke little, and lived much apart in their cells in solitary meditation; in the most insignificant matters the same similarity may be traced. "When the Roman Catholic priest shaves the top of his head, it is because the Egyptian priest had done the same before. When the English clergyman—though he preaches his sermon in a silk or woollen robe—may read the Liturgy in no dress but linen, it is because linen was the clothing of the Egyptians. Two thousand years before the Bishop of Rome pretended to hold the keys of heaven and earth, there was an Egyptian priest with the high-sounding title of Appointed keeper of the two doors of heaven, in the city of Thebes" ("Egyptian Mythology," S. Sharpe, preface, p. xi.). The white robes of modern priests are remnants of the same old faith; the more gorgeous vestments are the ancient garb of the priests officiating in the temple of female deities; the stole is the characteristic of woman's dress; the pallium is the emblem of the yoni; the alb is the chemise; the oval or circular chasuble is again the yoni; the Christian mitre is the high cap of the Egyptian priests, and its peculiar shape is simply the open mouth of the fish, the female emblem. In old sculptures a fish's head, with open mouth pointing upwards, is often worn by the priests, and is scarcely distinguishable from the present mitre. The modern crozier is the hooked staff, emblem of the phallus; the oval frame for divine things is the female symbol once more. Thus holy medals are generally oval, and the Virgin is constantly represented in an oval frame, with the child in her arms. In some old missals, in representations of the Annunciation, we see the Virgin standing, with the dove hovering in front above her, and from the dove issues a beam of light, from the end of which, as it touches her stomach, depends an oval containing the infant Jesus.

The tinkling bell—used at the Mass at the moment of consecration—is the symbol of male and female together—the clapper, the male, within the hollow shell, the female—and was used in solar services at the moment of sacrifice. The position of the fingers of the priest in blessing the congregation is the old symbolical position of the fingers of the solar priest. The Latin form, with the two fingers and thumb upraised—copied in Anglican churches—is said rightly by ecclesiastical writers to represent the trinity; but the trinity it represents is the real human trinity: the more elaborate Greek form is intended to represent the cross as well. The decoration of the cross with flowers, specially at Easter-tide, was practised in the solar temples, and there the phallus, upright on the altar, was garlanded with spring blossoms, and was adored as the "Lord and Giver of Life, proceeding from the Father," and indeed one with him, his very self. The sacred books of the Egyptians were written by the god Thoth, just as the sacred books of the Christians were written by the god the Holy Ghost. The rosary and cross were used by Buddhists in Thibet and Tartary. The head of the religion in those countries, the Grand Llama, is elected by the priests of a certain rank, as the Pope by his Cardinals. The faithful observe fasts, offer sacrifice for the dead, practise confession, use holy water, honour relics, make processions; they have monasteries and convents, whose inmates take vows of poverty and chastity; they flagellate themselves, have priests and bishops—in fact, they carry out the whole system of Catholicism, and have done so, since centuries before Christ, so that a Roman Catholic priest, on his first mission among them, exclaimed that the Devil had invented an imitation of Christianity in order to deceive and ruin men. As with baptism, the imitation is older than the original!

"The rites and institutions, by which the Greeks, Romans, and other nations, had formerly testified their religious veneration for fictitious deities, were now adopted, with some slight alterations, by Christian bishops, and employed in the service of the true God. [This is the way a Christian writer accounts for the resemblance his candour forces him to confess; we should put it, that Christianity, growing out of Paganism, naturally preserved many of its customs.].... Hence it happened that in these times the religion of the Greeks and Romans differed very little in its external appearance from that of the Christians. They had both a most pompous and splendid ritual. Gorgeous robes, mitres, tiaras, wax-tapers, crosiers, processions, lustrations, images, gold and silver vases, and many such circumstances of pageantry, were equally to be seen in the heathen temples and the Christian churches" (Mosheim's "Eccles. Hist.," fourth century, p. 105). Says Dulaure: "These two Fathers [Justin and Tertullian] are in no fashion embarrassed by this astonishing resemblance; they both say that the devil, knowing beforehand of the establishment of Christianity, and of the ceremonies of this religion, inspired the Pagans to do the same, so as to rival God and injure Christian worship" ("Histoire Abrégée de Differens Cultes," t. i., p. 522; ed. 1825).

The idea of angels and devils has also spread from the far East; the Jews learned it from the Babylonians, and from the Jews and the Egyptians it passed into Christianity. The Persian theology had seven angels of the highest order, who ever surrounded Ormuzd, the good creator; and from this the Jews derived the seven archangels always before the Lord, and the Christians the "seven spirits of God" (Rev. iii.

1), and the "seven angels which stood before God" (Ibid, viii. 2). The Persians had four angels—one at each corner of the world; Revelation has "four angels standing on the four corners of the earth" (vii. 1). The Persians employed them as Mediators with the Supreme; the majority of Christians now do the same, and all Christians did so in earlier times. Origen, Tertullian, Chrysostom, and other Fathers, speak of angels as ruling the earth, the planets, etc. Michael is the angel of the Sun, as was Hercules, and he fights with and conquers the dragon, as Hercules the Python, Horus the monster Typhon, Krishna the serpent. The Persians believed in devils as well as in angels, and they also had their chief, Ahriman, the pattern of Satan. These devils—or dews, or devs—struggled against the good, and in the end would be destroyed, and Ahriman would be chained down in the abyss, as Satan in Rev. xx. Ahriman flew down to earth from heaven as a great dragon (Rev. xii. 3 and 9), the angels arming themselves against him (Ibid, verse 7). Strauss remarks: "Had the belief in celestial beings, occupying a particular station in the court of heaven, and distinguished by particular names, originated from the revealed religion of the Hebrews—had such a belief been established by Moses, or some later prophet—then, according to the views of the supranaturalist, they might—nay, they must—be admitted to be correct. But it is in the Maccabaean Daniel and in the apocryphal Tobit that this doctrine of angels, in its more precise form, first appears; and it is evidently a product of the influence of the Zend religion of the Persians on the Jewish mind. We have the testimony of the Jews themselves that they brought the names of the angels with them from Babylon" ("Life of Jesus," vol. i., p. 101).

Dr. Kalisch, after having remarked that "the notions [of the Jews] concerning angels fluctuated and changed," says that "at an early period, the belief in spirits was introduced into Palestine from eastern Asia through the ordinary channels of political and commercial interchange," and that to the Hebrew "notions heathen mythology offers striking analogies;" "it would be unwarranted," the learned doctor goes on, "to distinguish between the 'established belief of the Hebrews' and 'popular superstition;' we have no means of fixing the boundary line between both; we must consider the one to coincide with the other, or we should be obliged to renounce all historical inquiry. The belief in spirits and demons was not a concession made by educated men to the prejudices of the masses, but a concession which all—the educated as well as the uneducated—made to Pagan Polytheism" ("Historical and Critical Commentary on the Old Testament." Leviticus, part ii., pp. 284-287. Ed. 1872). "When the Jews, ever open to foreign influence in matters of faith, lived under Persian rule, they imbibed, among many other religious views of their masters, especially their doctrines of angels and spirits, which, in the region of the Euphrates and Tigris, were most luxuriantly developed." Some of the angels are now "distinguished by names, which the Jews themselves admit to have borrowed from their heathen rulers;" "their chief is Mithron, or Metatron, corresponding to the Persian Mithra, the mediator between eternal light and eternal darkness; he is the embodiment of divine omnipotence and omnipresence, the guardian of the world, the instructor of Moses, and the preserver of the law, but also a terrible avenger of disobedience and wickedness, especially in his capacity of Supreme Judge of the dead" (Ibid, pp. 287, 288). This is "the angel of the Lord" who went before the children of Israel, of whom God said "my name is in him" (see Ex. xxiii. 20-23), and who is identified by many Christian commentators as the second person in the Trinity. The belief in devils is the other side of the belief in angels, and "we see, above all, Satan rise to greater and more perilous eminence both with regard to his power and the diversity of his functions." "This remarkable advance in demonology cannot be surprising, if we consider that the Persian system known as that of Zoroaster, and centering in the dualism of a good and evil principle, flourished most and attained its fullest development, just about the time of the Babylonian exile" (Ibid, pp. 292, 293). The Persian creed supplies us, as Dr. Kalisch has well said, with "the sources from which the demonology of the Talmud, the Fathers and the Catholic Church has been derived" (Ibid, p. 318).

The whole ideas of the judgment of the dead, the destruction of the world by fire, and the punishment of the wicked, are also purely Pagan. Justin Martyr says truly that as Minos and Rhadamanthus would punish the wicked, "we say that the same thing will be done, but by the hand of Christ" ("Apology" 1, chap. viii). "While we say that there will be a burning up of all, we shall seem to utter the doctrine of the Stoics; and while we affirm that the souls of the wicked, being endowed with sensation even after death, are punished, and that those of the good being delivered from punishment spend a blessed existence, we shall seem to say the same things as the poets and philosophers" (Ibid, chap. xx). In the Egyptian creed Osiris is generally the Judge of the dead, though sometimes Horus is represented in that character; the dead man is accused before the Judge by Typhon, the evil one, as Satan is the "accuser of the brethren;" forty-two assessors declare the innocence of the accused of the crimes they severally note; the recording angel writes down the judgment; the soul is interceded for by the lesser gods, who offer themselves as an atoning sacrifice (see Sharpe's "Egyptian Mythology," pp. 49-52). A pit, or lake of fire, is the doom of the condemned. The good pass to Paradise, where is the tree of life: the fruit of this tree confers health and immortality. In the Persian mythology the tree of life is planted by the stream that flows from the throne of Ormuzd (Rev. xxii. i and 2). The Hindu creed has the same story, and it is also found among the Chinese.

The monastic life comes to us from India and from Egypt; in

both countries solitaries and communities are found. Bartholémy St. Hilaire, in his book on Buddha, gives an account of the Buddhist monasteries which is worthy perusal. From Egypt the contagion of asceticism spread over Christendom. "From Philo also we learn that a large body of Egyptian Jews had embraced the monastic rules and the life of self-denial, which we have already noted among the Egyptian priests. They bore the name of Therapeuts. They spent their time in solitary meditation and prayer, and only saw one another on the seventh day. They did not marry; the women lived the same solitary and religious life as the men. Fasting and mortification of the flesh were the foundation of their virtues" ("Egyptian Mythology," S. Sharpe, p. 79). In these Egyptian deserts grew up those wild and bigoted fanatics—some Jews, some Pagans, and apparently no difference between them—who, appearing later under the name of Christians, formed the original of the Western monasticism. It was these monks who tore Hypatia to pieces in the great church of Alexandria, and who formed the strength of "that savage and illiterate party, who looked upon all sorts of erudition, particularly that of a philosophical kind, as pernicious, and even destructive to true piety and religion" (Mosheim's "Eccles. Hist," p. 93). There can be no doubt of the identity of the Christians and the Therapeuts, and this identity is the real key to the spread of "Christianity" in Egypt and the surrounding countries. Eusebius tells us that Mark was said to be the first who preached the Gospel in Egypt, and "so great a multitude of believers, both of men and women, were collected there at the very outset, that in consequence of their extreme philosophical discipline and austerity, Philo has considered their pursuits, their assemblies, and entertainments, as deserving a place in his descriptions" ("Eccles. Hist," bk. ii., chap. xvi). We will see what Philo found in Egypt, before remarking on the date at which he lived. Eusebius states (we condense bk. ii., chap. xvii) that Philo "comprehends the regulations that are still observed in our churches even to the present time;" that he "describes, with the greatest accuracy, the lives of our ascetics;" these Therapeuts, stated by Eusebius to be Christians, were "everywhere scattered over the world," but they abound "in Egypt, in each of its districts, and particularly about Alexandria." In every house one room was set aside for worship, reading, and meditation, and here they kept the "inspired declarations of the prophets, and hymns," they had also "commentaries of ancient men," who were "the founders of the sect;" "it is highly probable that the ancient commentaries which he says they have, are the very Gospels and writings of the apostles;" Eusebius thinks that none can "be so hardy as to contradict his statement that these Therapeuts were Christians, when their practices are to be found among none but in the religion of Christians;" and "why should we add to these their meetings, and the separate abodes of the men and the women in these meetings, and the exercises performed by them, which are still in vogue among us at the present day, and which, especially at the festival of our Saviour's passion, we are accustomed to pass in fasting and watching, and in the study of the divine word? All these the above-mentioned author has accurately described and stated in his writings, and are the same customs that are observed by us alone, at the present day, particularly the vigils of the great festival, and the exercises in them, and the hymns that are commonly recited among us.... Besides this, he describes the grades of dignity among those who administer the ecclesiastical services committed to them, those of the deacons, and the presidencies of the episcopate as the highest." Thus Philo wrote of "the original practices handed down from the apostles." The important points to notice here are: that in the time of Philo, these Christians were scattered all over the world; that the commentaries they had, which Eusebius says were the Christian's gospels, were the works of ancient men, who founded the sect, so that the founders were men who lived long before Philo's time; that they were thoroughly organised, proving thereby that their sect was not a new one in his day; that the "discipline," organised association, ranks of priests, etc., implied a long existence of the sect before Philo studied it, and that such existence was clearly not consistent with any persecution being then directed against it. Philo writes of flourishing and orderly communities, founded by men who had long since passed away, and had bequeathed their writings to their followers for their instruction and guidance. And what was the date of Philo? He himself gives us a clear note of time; in A.D. 40 he was sent on an embassy to the Emperor Caligula at Rome, to complain of a persecution to which the Jews were being subjected by Flaccus; he describes himself as being, in A.D. 40, "a grey-headed old man." The Rev. J.W. Lake puts him at sixty-five or seventy years of age at that period, and consequently would place his birth twenty-five or thirty years before the birth of Jesus ("Plato, Philo, and Paul," by Rev. J.W. Lake, pp. 33, 34). Gibbon, in a note to chap. 15, vol. ii. (p. 180), says that "by proving it (the treatise on the Therapeuts) was composed as early as the time of Augustus, Basnage has demonstrated, in spite of Eusebius, and a crowd of modern Catholics, that the Therapeuts were neither Christians nor monks." Or rather, he has proved that Christians existed before the time of Christ, since Augustus died A.D. 14, and before that date Philo found a long-established sect holding Christian doctrines and practising "apostolic" customs. A man, who in A.D. 40 was grey-headed, spoke of the Christian Gospels as writings of ancient men, founders of a well-organised sect. Now we see why Christianity has so much in common with the Egyptian mythology. Because it grew out of Egypt; its Gospels came from thence; its ceremonies were learned there; its virgin is Isis; its Christ Osiris and Horus; the mask of the revelation of God drops from off it, and we see the true face, the ancient Egyptian religion, with a feature here and there moulded by the

154

cognate ideas of other Eastern creeds, all of which flowed into Alexandria, and mingled in its seething cauldron of thought.

There is also a Jewish sect which we must not overlook, in dealing with the sources of Christianity, that, namely, known as the Essenes. Gibbon regards the Therapeuts and the Essenes as interchangeable terms, but more careful investigation does not bear out this conclusion, although the two sects strongly resemble each other, and have many doctrines in common; he says, however, truly: "The austere life of the Essenians, their fasts and excommunications, the community of goods, the love of celibacy, their zeal for martyrdom, and the warmth, though not the purity of their faith, already offered a lively image of the primitive discipline" ("Decline and Fall," vol. ii., ch. xv., p. 180). It is to Josephus that we must turn for an account of the Essenes; a brief sketch of them is given in Antiquities of the Jews, bk. xviii., chap. i. He says: "The doctrine of the Essenes is this: That all things are best ascribed to God. They teach the immortality of souls, and esteem that the rewards of righteousness are to be earnestly striven for; and when they send what they have dedicated to God into the temple, they do not offer sacrifices, because they have more pure lustrations of their own; on which account they are excluded from the common court of the temple, but offer their sacrifices themselves; yet is their course of life better than that of other men; and they entirely addict themselves to husbandry." They had all things in common, did not marry and kept no servants, thus none called any master (Matt. xxiii. 8, 10). In the "Wars of the Jews," bk. ii., chap, viii., Josephus gives us a fuller account. "There are three philosophical sects among the Jews. The followers of the first of whom are the Pharisees; of the second the Sadducees; and the third sect who pretends to a severer discipline are called Essenes. These last are Jews by birth, and seem to have a greater affection for one another than the other sects [John xiii. 35]. These Essenes reject pleasures as an evil [Matt. xvi. 24], but esteem continence and the conquest over our passions to be virtue. They neglect wedlock.... They do not absolutely deny the fitness of marriage [Matt. xix. 12, last clause of verse, 1 Cor. vii. 27, 28, 32-35, 37, 38, 40].... These men are despisers of riches [Matt. xix. 21, 23, ... it is a law among them, that those who come to them must let what they have be common to the whole order [Acts iv. 32-37, v. 1-11].... They also have stewards appointed to take care of their common affairs [Acts vi. 1-6].... If any of their sect come from other places, what they have lies open for them, just as if it were their own [Matt. x. 11].... For which reason they carry nothing with them when they travel into remote parts [Matt. x. 9, 10].... As for their piety towards God, it is very extraordinary; for before sunrising they speak not a word about profane matters, but put up certain prayers which they have received from their forefathers, as if they made a supplication for its rising [the Essenes were then sun-worshippers].... A priest says grace before meat; and it is unlawful for

155

anyone to taste of the food before grace be said. The same priest, when he hath dined, says grace again after meat; and when they begin, and when they end, they praise God, as he that bestows their food upon them [Eph. v. 18-20. 1 Cor. x. 30, 31. 1 Tim. iv. 4, 5].... They dispense their anger after a just manner, and restrain their passion [Eph. iv. 26].... Whatsoever they say also is firmer than an oath; but swearing is avoided by them, and they esteem it worse than perjury; for they say, that he who cannot be believed without swearing by God, is already condemned [Matt. v. 34-37]." We insert these references into the account given by Josephus of the Essenes, in order to show the identity of teaching of the Gospels and the Essenes. The Essenes excommunicated those who sinned grievously; each promised, on entrance to the society, to exercise piety, observe justice, do no harm to any, show fidelity to all, and especially to those in authority, love truth, reprove lying, keep his hands clear from theft, and his soul from unlawful gains. The resemblance between the Essenes and the early Christians is on many points so strong that it is impossible to deny that the two are connected; if Jesus of Nazareth had any historical existence, he must have been one of the sect of the Essenes, who publicly preached many of their doctrines, and endeavoured to popularise them. We are thus led to conclude that the Jewish side of Christianity is simply Essenian, but that the major part of the religion is purely Pagan, and that its rise under the name of Christianity must be sought for in Alexandria rather than in Judæa.

The saints who play so great a part in the history of Christianity are, solely and simply, the old Pagan deities under new names. The ancient creeds were intertwined with the daily life of the people, and passed on, practically unchanged, although altered in name. "Ancient errors, in spite of the progress of knowledge, were respected. Civilisation, as it grew, only refined them, embellished them, or hid them under an allegorical veil" ("Histoire Abrégée de Differens Cultes," Dulauré, t. i., p. 20). "A remarkable passage in the life of Gregory, surnamed Thaumaturgus, i.e., the wonder-worker, will illustrate this point in the clearest manner. This passage is as follows [here it is given in Latin]: 'When Gregory perceived that the ignorant multitude persisted in their idolatry, on account of the pleasures and sensual gratifications which they enjoyed at the Pagan festivals, he granted them a permission to indulge themselves in the like pleasures, in celebrating the memory of the holy martyrs, hoping that, in process of time they would return, of their own accord, to a more virtuous and regular course of life.' There is no sort of doubt that, by this permission, Gregory allowed the Christians to dance, sport, and feast at the tombs of the martyrs upon their respective festivals, and to do everything which the Pagans were accustomed to do in their temples, during the feasts celebrated in honour of their gods" (Mosheim's "Eccles. Hist.," 2nd century; note, p. 56). "The virtues that had formerly been ascribed to the heathen temples, to their lustrations, to the statues of their gods and heroes, were now attributed to Christian churches, to water consecrated by certain forms of prayer, and to the images of holy men. And the same privileges that the former enjoyed under the darkness of Paganism, were conferred upon the latter under the light of the Gospel, or, rather, under that cloud of superstition that was obscuring its glory. It is true that, as yet, images were not very common [of this there is no proof]; nor were there any statues at all [equally unproven]. But it is, at the same time, as undoubtedly certain, as it is extravagant and monstrous, that the worship of the martyrs was modelled, by degrees, according to the religious services that were paid to the gods before the coming of Christ" (Ibid, 4th century; p. 98). The fact is, that wherever there was a popular god, he passed into the pantheon of Christendom under a new name, as "Christianity" spread. Dulaure, in his work above-quoted, gives a mass of details—mostly very unsavoury—which leave no doubt upon this point. The essence of the old worship was the worship of Nature, as we have seen, and a favourite deity was Priapus; this god was worshipped under the names of St. Fontin, St. Guerlichon, or Greluchon, St. Remi, St. Gilles, St. Arnaud, SS. Cosmo and Damian, etc., in the various provinces of France, Italy, and other Roman Catholic lands; and his worship, with its distinctive rites of the most indecent character, remained in practice up to, at least, 1740 in France, and 1780 in Italy. (See throughout the above work.) If Christians knew a little more about their creed they would be far less proud of it, and far less devout, than they are at present.

Mr. Glennie, in a pamphlet reprinted from "In the Morning Land," points out the resemblance between Christianity and "Osirianism," as he names the religion of Osiris: "'The peculiar character of Osiris,' says Sir Gardner Wilkinson, 'his coming upon earth for the benefit of mankind, with the titles of "Manifester of Good" and "Revealer of Truth;" his being put to death by the malice of the Evil One; his burial and resurrection, and his becoming the judge of the dead, are the most interesting features of the Egyptian religion. This was the great mystery; and this myth and his worship were of the earliest times, and universal in Egypt.' And, with this central doctrine of Osirianism, so perfectly similar to that of Christianism, doctrines are associated precisely analogous to those associated in Christianism with its central doctrine. In ancient Osirianism, as in modern Christianism, the Godhead is conceived as a Trinity, yet are the three Gods declared to be only one God. In ancient Osirianism, as in modern Christianism, we find the worship of a divine mother and child. In ancient Osirianism, as in modern Christianism, there is a doctrine of atonement. In ancient Osirianism, as in modern Christianism, we find the vision of a last judgment, and resurrection of the body. And finally, in ancient Osirianism, as in modern Christianism, the sanctions of morality are a lake of fire and tormenting demons on the one hand, and on the other, eternal life in the presence of God. Is it possible, then, that such similarities of doctrines should not raise the most serious questions as to the relation of the beliefs about Christ to those about Osiris; as to the cause of this wonderful similarity of the doctrines of Christianism to those of Osirianism; nay, as to the possibility of the whole doctrinal system of modern orthodoxy being but a transformation of the Osiris-myth?" ("Christ and Osiris," pp. 13, 14).

Thus we find that the cardinal doctrines and the ceremonies of Christianity are of purely Pagan origin, and that "Christianity" was in existence long ages before Christ. Christianity is only, as we have said, a patchwork composed of old materials; from the later Jews comes the Unity of God; from India and Egypt the Trinity in Unity; from India and Egypt the crucified Redeemer; from India, Egypt, Greece, and Rome, the virgin mother and the divine son; from Egypt its priests and its ritual; from the Essenes and the Therapeuts its ascetism; from Persia, India, and Egypt, its Sacraments; from Persia and Babylonia its angels and its devils; from Alexandria the blending into one of many lines of thought. There is nothing original in this creed, save its special appeal to the ignorant and to babes; "not many wise men after the flesh" are found among its adherents; it is an appeal to the darkness of the world, not to its light: to superstition, not to knowledge; to faith, not to reason. As its root is, so also are its fruits, and when—after glancing at its morality—we turn to its history, we shall see that the corrupt tree bears corrupt fruit, and that from the evil stem of a thinly disguised Paganism spring forth the death-bringing branches of the Upas-tree Christianity, stunting the growth of the young civilisation of the West, and drugging, with its poisonous dew-droppings, the Europe which lay beneath its shade, swoon-slumbering in the death stupor of the Ages of Darkness and of Faith.

SECTION III

ITS MORALITY FALLIBLE

How much may fairly be included under the title "Christian Morality"? Some of the more enlightened Christians would confine the term to the morality of the New Testament, and would exclude the Hebrew code as being the outcome of a barbarous age. But the Freethinker may fairly contend that any moral rules taught by the Bible are part of Christian morality. By the statute 9 and 10 William III, cap. 32, the "Holy Scriptures of the Old and New Testament" are declared to be "of divine authority," and there is no exclusion indicated of the Mosaic code; this statute is binding on all British subjects educated as Christians, and enacts penalties against those who infringe it. By Article VI. of the Church of England, Holy Scripture is defined as "those canonical books of the Old and New Testament, of whose authority was never any doubt in the Church," and a list is subjoined. In Article VII. we are instructed that the "Commandments which are called moral" are to be obeyed, but that the "civil precepts" of the Mosaic code ought not "of necessity to be received in any commonwealth;" from which we may conclude that the Church does not feel bound to enforce, as "of necessity," polygamy, prostitution, murder of heretics, and slavery. She does not venture to designate such precepts as immoral, but she does not feel bound in conscience to enforce them, for which small concession we must feel grateful. Passing from the law of the land to the Bible itself, we find that the Mosaic code must certainly be recognised as divine. Jesus himself proclaims: "Think not that I am come to destroy the law and the prophets, I am not come to destroy but to fulfil," and this is emphasised by the declaration: "Whosoever, therefore, shall break one of these least commandments, and shall teach men so, he shall be called least in the kingdom of heaven." The Broad Church party will be very little, if this be true. Turning to the Old Testament, we find that some of the most immoral precepts are spoken by God himself, immediately after the "Ten Commandments;" surely that which "The Lord said" out of "the thick darkness where God was," from the top of Sinai "on a smoke, with the thunderings and lightnings, and the noise of the trumpet," can scarcely be reverently designated as "the outcome of a barbarous age"? Yet it is under these circumstances that God taught that a Hebrew servant might be bought for seven years; that a wife might be given him by his master, and that the wife and the children proceeding from the union belonged to the master; that the servant could only go free by deserting his wife and his own children and leaving them in slavery (Ex. xxi. 1-6). It was under these circumstances that God taught that a man might sell his daughter to be

159

a "maid servant" (the translator's euphemism for concubine), and that, "if she please not her master" she may be bought back again, or if he "take him another" (translator supplying "wife" as throwing an air of respectability over the transaction) she may go free (Ibid. 7-11). It was under these circumstances that God taught that if a man should beat a male or female slave to death, he should not be punished, providing the slave did not die till "a day or two" after, because the slave was only "his money" (Ibid. 20, 21). Why blame a Legree, when he only acts on the permission given by God from Mount Sinai? Dr. Colenso writes: "I shall never forget the revulsion of feeling with which a very intelligent Christian native, with whose help I was translating these words into the Zulu tongue, first heard them as words said to be uttered by the same great and gracious Being whom I was teaching him to trust in and adore. His whole soul revolted against the notion, that the great and blessed God, the merciful Father of all mankind, would speak of a servant, or maid, as mere 'money,' and allow a horrible crime to go unpunished, because the victim of the brutal usage had survived a few hours. My own heart and conscience at the time fully sympathised with his" ("The Pentateuch and Book of Joshua," p. 9, ed. 1862). It was under these circumstances that God taught that a thief, who possessed nothing of his own, should "be sold for his theft" (Ex. xxii. 3). It was under these circumstances that God taught: "Thou shalt not suffer a witch to live" (Ibid 18). To this cruel and wicked command myriads of unfortunate human beings have been sacrificed; in the course of the Middle Ages hundreds of thousands perished; in France and Germany "many districts and large towns burned two, three, and four hundred witches every year, in some the annual executions destroyed nearly one per cent. of the whole population.... The Reformation, which swept away so many superstitions, left this, the most odious of all, in full activity. The Churchmen of England, the Lutherans of Germany, the Calvinists of Geneva, Scotland, and New England rivalled the most bigoted Roman Catholics in their severities. Indeed, the Calvinists, though the most opposite of all to the Church of Rome, were in this respect perhaps the most implicit imitators of her delusions" ("The Bible; What it is," by C. Bradlaugh, p. 262). "During the seventeenth century, 40,000 persons are said to have been put to death for witchcraft in England alone. In Scotland the number was probably, in proportion to the population, much greater; for it is certain that even in the last forty years of the sixteenth century the executions were not fewer than 17,000" (Ibid, p. 263). The Puritans in New England signalised themselves by their merciless severity towards wizards and witches. France was the first country to stem the tide of cruelty. In 1680 Louis XIV. "issued a proclamation prohibiting all future prosecutions for witchcraft; and directing that even those who might profess the art should only be punished as impostors." In England "the last execution was at Huntingdon, in 1716;" in Scotland, at Darnock, in

1722. The last person burned as a witch was Maria Sanger, at Wurzburg, in Bavaria, 1749 (Ibid, p. 265). Such fruit has borne the command of God from Sinai. It was under these circumstances that God taught that any who sacrificed to any God but himself should be "utterly destroyed" (Ex. xxii. 20). The practical effect of this we shall presently see, in conjunction with other passages.

If we pass from these precepts, given with such special solemnity, to the other articles of the so-called Mosaic code, we shall find rules of an equally immoral character. Lev. xxiv. 16 commands that "he that blasphemeth the name of the Lord" shall be stoned. Lev. xxv. 44-46 directs the Hebrews to buy bondmen and bondwomen of the nations around them, "and ye shall take them as an inheritance for your children after you, to inherit them for a possession," thus sanctioning the slave-traffic. Leviticus xxvii. 29 distinctly commands human sacrifice, forbidding the redemption of any that are "devoted of men." Clear as the words are, their meaning has been hotly contested, because of the stain they affix on the Mosaic code. "[Hebrew: MOT VOMOT]" that he die. The commentators take much trouble to soften this terrible sentence. According to Raschi, it concerns a man condemned to death, in which case he must not be redeemed for money. According to others, it is necessary that the person shall be devoted by public authority, and not by private vow; and the Talmud speaks of Jephthah as a fanatic for having thought that a human being could serve as a victim, as a burnt-offering; but there are too many facts which prove the existence and the execution of this barbarous law; see, besides, the paraphrase of Ben Ouziel: [Hebrew: KL APRShA TMVL DDYN QShVL MYTChYYB] "all anathema which shall be anathematised of the human race cannot be redeemed neither by money, by vows, nor by sacrifices, neither by prayers for mercy before God, since he is condemned to death" (Lévitique, par Cahen, p. 143; ed. 1855). Thus Jephthah devoted to the Lord "whatsoever cometh out of the doors of my house to meet me," and, his daughter being the one who came, he "did with her according to his vow" (Judges xi. 30-40).

Kalisch, in his Commentary on the Old Testament, gives us an exhaustive essay on "Human Sacrifices among the Hebrews," endeavouring, as far as possible, to defend his people from the charge of offering such sacrifices to Jehovah by reducing instances of it to a minimum. He says, however: "Yet we have at least two clear and unquestionable instances of human sacrifices offered to Jehovah. The first is the immolation of Jephthah's daughter." He then analyses the account, pointing out that it was clearly a sacrifice to Jehovah, and that Jephthah's "intention of sacrificing his daughter was publicly known for two full months; no priest, no prophet, no elder, no magistrate interfered, or even remonstrated." Even further: "The event gave rise to a popular custom annually observed by the maidens of Israel; Jephthah's deed evidently met with universal approbation; it was regarded as praiseworthy piety; and indeed he could not have ventured to make his vow, had not human victims offered to Jehovah been deemed particularly meritorious in his time; otherwise he must have apprehended to provoke by it the wrath of God, rather than procure his assistance. Nothing can be clearer or more decided.... The fact stands indisputable that human sacrifices offered to Jehovah were possible among the Hebrews long after the time of Moses, without meeting a check or censure from the teachers and leaders of the nation—a fact for which the sad political confusion that prevailed in the period of the Judges is insufficient to account" (Leviticus, Part I., pp. 383-385; ed. 1867). Kalisch further points out that the vow of Jephthah promises a human sacrifice; the Hebrew expression signifies "whoever comes forth" (see p. 383), and "the Hebrew words, in fact, absolutely exclude any animal whatever; they admit none but a human being, who alone can be described as going out of the house to meet somebody; for, though the restrictive usage of the East binds girls generally to the seclusion of the house, it seems to have been a common custom for Hebrew women to proceed and meet returning conquerors with music and rejoicing; and the sacrifice of one animal, an extremely poor offering after a most signal and most important success, would certainly not have been promised by a previous vow solemnly pronounced" (Ibid, pp. 385, 386). Our commentator justly adds: "From the tenour of the narrative it is manifest that the deed was no isolated case, but that human sacrifices were on emergencies of peculiar moment habitually offered to God, and expected to secure his aid. One instance like that of Jephthah not only justifies, but necessitates, the influence of a general custom. Pious men slaughtered human victims not to Moloch, nor to any other foreign deity, but to the national God Jehovah" (Ibid, p. 390). "The second recorded instance of human sacrifices killed in honour of Jehovah forms a remarkable incident in the life of David" (Ibid, p. 390). We read in 2 Sam. xxi. that God said that a famine then prevailing was on account of Saul and of his bloody house; that David desired to make an "atonement;" that seven men of Saul's family were hanged "in the hill before the Lord;" that then they were buried, with Saul and Jonathan, "and, after that, God was intreated for the land." "It particularly concerns us to observe that the whole matter was, in the first instance, referred to Jehovah; that David was plainly informed of the intention of the Gibeonites of 'hanging up' the seven persons 'before Jehovah' as an 'atonement;' that he willingly surrendered them for that atrocity; that he evidently expected from that act a cessation of the famine; and that this calamity is reported to have really disappeared in consequence of the offering" (Ibid, p. 392). Kalisch, in his anxiety to diminish as far as possible the evidence that human sacrifices were enjoined by the law, urges that the passage in Leviticus (xxvii. 29) merely implies that "everything so devoted shall be destroyed. The extirpation of the men, as a rule heathen enemies in

Canaan, or Hebrew idolaters, is indeed referred to a command of Jehovah, but it is not intended as a sacrifice to him" (Ibid, p. 409). Surely this verges on quibbling, and is not even then borne out by the context. Leviticus xxvii. deals entirely with private "singular vows," and the "devoting" (Cherem) of "man and beast and of the field of his possession," is not the judicial devoting to destruction of an idolatrous city or individual, but a special voluntary offering from a pious worshipper. Besides, even if such judicial duties were "the rule," what of the exceptions? There are several indications of the practice of human sacrifice to Jehovah beyond the two related by Kalisch (the command to sacrifice Isaac is in itself a consecration by God of the abomination); the curious account of Aaron's death—whose garments are taken off and put on his son, and who thereupon dies at the top of the mount, having walked up there for that purpose, clearly indicates that he did not die a natural death (Numbers xx. 23-28). Many think that "the fire from the Lord" which devoured Nadab and Abihu (Lev. x. 1-5) denotes the sacrifice "before the Lord" of the offending priests. Kalisch demurs to these latter charges, and to some other additional ones, but says: "It is, therefore, undoubted that human sacrifices were offered by the Hebrews from the earliest times up to the Babylonian period, both in honour of Jehovah and of heathen deities, not only by depraved idolaters, but sometimes even by pious servants of God; they probably ceased to be presented to Jehovah not much before they ceased to be presented at all" (Leviticus, part i., p. 396). We cannot here omit to notice the command of God in Exodus xxii. 29, 30: "The first-born of thy sons shalt thou give to me. Likewise thou shalt do with thine oxen and with thy sheep," etc. As against this we read a command in chap. xiii. 13, "All the first-born of man among thy children thou shalt redeem." Here, as in many other instances, we get contradictory commands, best explained by the fact that the Pentateuch is the work of many hands. Kalisch says: "It is impossible to deny that the first-born sons were frequently sacrificed, not only by idolatrous Israelites, in honour of foreign gods, as Moloch and Baal, but by pious men in honour of Jehovah; but the Pentateuch, the embodiment of the more enlightened and advanced creed of the Hebrews, distinctly commanded the redemption of the first-born" (Ibid, p. 404). Kalisch—we may point out—considers the Pentateuch in its present form as post Babylonian, and regards it as a reforming agent in the Jewish community.

In Numbers v. 12-31 we find the command to practise the brutal and superstitious custom of the ordeal, the endorsement of the whole ordeal system of the Middle Ages. Deuteronomy xiii. is entirely devoted to commands of murder, and is the indulgence given beforehand to every persecuting priest. The prophet whom God uses to prove his people, is to be put to death for being God's instrument; anyone who tries to turn people aside from God is to be stoned, and the hand of the nearest and dearest is to be "first upon him to put him to death;" any city which becomes idolatrous is to be destroyed, the inhabitants and the cattle are to be slain, and everything else is to be burnt. Deuteronomy xvii. 2-7 is to the same effect. These commands have also borne abundant fruit. Who can reckon the millions of human lives that have been spilt in obedience to them? The slaughter of the Midianites, of the people of Jericho, Ai, Makkedah, Libnah, Lachish, and of many another city, marking with blood each step of the people of God, who smote "all the souls that were" in each, and "let none remain"—all these are but as the first-fruits of the great harvest of human slaughter, reaped for the glory of God. Right through the "sacred volume" runs the scarlet river, staining every page; when its record closes, the Church takes it up, and the river rolls on down the centuries; let the Inquisition tell over its victims; let Spain reckon her murdered ones, 31,912 burnt alive in that one land alone; let the Netherlands speak of their slain sons and daughters; let France and Italy swell the tale; nor let England and Scotland be forgotten, nor the blood-roll of Ireland be missed; Catholic murdering Arian; Arian slaying Catholic; Romanist burning Protestant; Protestant hanging Romanist. The names of those who obey God's command may be changed, but they all do the same accursed work, spreading religion everywhere with fire and sword; nor does the harm confine itself to Jews and Christians only, for Mahomet, the prophet of Arabia, catches up the teaching of Moses and re-echoes it, and the Moslem follows on the inspired path, and stains it once again with human blood. A God, a Bible, a priesthood—how have they ruined the world; how fair and bright might earth have been had there been no teachers of religion!

> "How powerless were the mightiest monarch's arm,
> Vain his loud threat and impotent his frown!
> How ludicrous the priest's dogmatic roar!
> The weight of his exterminating curse
> How light! and his affected charity,
> To suit the pressure of the changing times,
> What palpable deceit! but for thy aid,
> Religion! but for thee, prolific fiend,
> Who peoplest earth with demons, hell with men,
> And heaven with slaves!
> Thou taintest all thou look'st upon......."

—("Queen Mab," by P.B. Shelley; can. 6. Collected works, p. 12, edition 1839.)

Deuteronomy xxi. 10-14 instructs the Hebrew that if, after victory, he sees a beautiful woman and desires her, he may take her, and if later, "thou have no delight in her, then thou shalt let her go whither she will," to starvation, to misery, what matter, after God's chosen is satisfied. Deut. xxiii. 2 punishes a man for that which is no

164

fault of his, his illegitimate birth. We have omitted many absurd precepts found in this Mosaic code, and have only chosen those which are grossly immoral, and can be defended by no kind of reasoning as to "defective," or "imperfect" morality, "suited to a nation in a low stage of civilisation."

These laws not only fall short of a perfect morality, but they are distinctly and foully immoral, and tend directly to the brutalisation of the nation which should live under them. It is true that there is much pure morality in this code, and some refined feeling here and there. These jewels are curiously out of place in their surroundings. Imagine a people so savage as to need laws permitting all the abominations referred to above, and yet so cultivated as to be capable of appreciating the beauty of: "If thou see the ass of him that hateth thee lying under his burden, and wouldest forbear to help him; thou shalt surely help him" (Exodus xxiii. 5). It is time that it should be publicly acknowledged that the so-called Mosaic code is literally a mosaic of scattered fragments of legislation, of various ages, and various stages of civilisation, put together a few hundred years before Christ. At present, the whole code lies on the shoulders of Christianity, and is fairly pleaded against it by the Freethinker.

It is not necessary to speak here against the practical morality of Old Testament saints; the very names of Lot, Abraham, Isaac, Jacob, Moses, Joshua, Samuel, David, etc., bring before the mind's eye a list of crimes so foul, so cowardly, so bloody, that no enumeration of them can be needed. Of them, we may fairly say with Virgil:—

"Non ragioniam di lor, ma guarda e passa."

Turning to the New Testament morality, we may attack it in various ways: we may argue that the better part of it is not new, and therefore cannot be regarded as especially inspired, or that it leaves out of account many virtues necessary to the well-being of families and states; or we may contend that much of it is harmful, and much of it impracticable.

The better part is that which is NON-ORIGINAL. All that is fair and beautiful in Christian morality had been taught in the world ages before Christ was born. Buddha, Confucius, Lao-Tsze, Mencius, Zoroaster, Manu, taught the noble human morality found in some of the teaching ascribed to Christ (throughout this Section the morality put into Christ's mouth in the New Testament will be treated as his).

Christ taught the duty of returning good for evil. Buddha said: "A man who foolishly does me wrong I will return to him the protection of my ungrudging love; the more evil comes from him, the more good shall go from me" ("Anthology," by Moncure D. Conway, page 240). In the Buddhist Dhammapada we read: "Let a man overcome anger by love; let him overcome evil by good; let him overcome the greedy by liberality, the liar by truth" (Ibid, p. 307). Again: "Hatred does not cease by hatred at any time; hatred ceases by love; this is an old rule" (Ibid, p. 131). Lao-Tsze says: "The good I would meet with goodness. The not good I would meet with goodness also. The faithful I would meet with faith. The not faithful I would meet with faith also. Virtue is faithful. Recompense injury with kindness" (Ibid, p. 365). Confucius struck a yet higher and truer note: "Some one said, 'What do you say concerning the principle that injury should be recompensed with kindness?' The Sage replied, 'With what, then, will you recompense kindness? Recompense kindness with kindness, and injury with justice'" (Ibid, p. 6). Manu places "returning good for evil" in his tenfold system of duties; in his code also we find: "By forgiveness of injuries the learned are purified" (Ibid, p. 311). The "golden rule" is as old as the generous and just heart. The Saboean Book of the Law taught: "Let none of you treat his brother in a way which he himself would dislike" (Ibid, p. 7). "Tsze-Kung asked, 'Is there one word which may serve as a rule for one's whole life?' Confucius answered, 'Is not reciprocity such a word? What you do not wish done to yourself, do not to others. When you are labouring for others let it be with the same zeal as if it were for yourself'" (Ibid, pp. 6, 7).

If Christ taught humility, we read from Lao-Tsze: "I have three precious things which I hold fast and prize—Compassion, Economy, Humility. Being compassionate, I can therefore be brave. Being economical, I can therefore be liberal. Not daring to take precedence of the world, I can therefore become chief among the perfect ones. In the present day men give up compassion, and cultivate only courage. They give up economy and aim only at liberality. They give up the last place, and seek only the first. It is their death" (Ibid, p. 216). Lao-Tsze says again: "By undivided attention to the passion-nature and tenderness it is possible to be a little child. By putting away impurity from the hidden eye of the heart, it is possible to be without spot. There is a purity and quietude by which we may rule the whole world. To keep tenderness, I pronounce strength.... The fact that the weak can conquer the strong and the tender the hard, is known to all the world; yet none carry it out in practice. The reason of heaven does not strive, yet conquers well; does not call, yet things come of their own accord; is slack, yet plans well" (Ibid, pp. 323, 324). Again: "The sage ... puts himself last, and yet is first; abandons himself, and yet is preserved. Is not this through having no selfishness? Hereby he preserves self-interest intact. He is not self-displaying, and therefore he shines. He is not self-approving, and therefore he is distinguished. He is not self-praising, and therefore he has merit. He is not self-exalting, and therefore he stands high; and inasmuch as he does not strive, no one in all the world strives with him. That ancient saying, 'He that humbles himself shall be preserved entire'—oh, it is no vain utterance" (Ibid, pp. 327, 328).

Jesus is said to be pre-eminent as a moral teacher because he directed his teaching to the improvement of the heart, knowing that from a good heart a good life would flow; in Manu's code we read: "Action, either mental, verbal, or corporeal, bears good or evil fruit as itself is good or evil ... of that threefold action be it known in the world that the heart is the instigator" (Ibid, p. 4). Buddha said: "It is the heart of love and faith accompanying good actions which spreads, as it were, a beneficent shade from the world of men to the world of angels" (Ibid, p. 234). Jesus reminded the people that the ceremonial duties of religion were small compared with "the weightier matters of the law, justice, mercy, and truth;" Manu wrote: "To a man contaminated by sensuality, neither the Vedas, nor liberality, nor sacrifices, nor observances, nor pious austerities will procure felicity. A wise man must faithfully discharge his moral duties, even though he dares not constantly perform the ceremonies of religion. He will fall very low if he performs ceremonial acts only, and fails to discharge his moral duties" (Ibid, p. 3). Exactly parallel to a saying of Jesus is one in the Saboean Book of the Law: "Adhere so firmly to the truth that your yea shall be yea, and your nay, nay" (Ibid, p. 7).

In urging that all great moral duties were taught by pre-Christian thinkers, we do not mean that Christ took his moral sayings from the books of these great Eastern teachers; there was no necessity that he should go so far in search of them, for in the teachings of the Rabbis of his nation he found all of which he stood in need. Many of these teachings have been preserved in the more modern Talmud, grains of wheat amid much chaff, the moral thoughts of some of the purest Jewish minds. "Take the Talmud and study it, and then judge from what uninspired source Jesus drew much of his highest teaching. 'Whoso looketh on the wife of another with a lustful eye, is considered as if he had committed adultery'—(Kalah). 'With what measure we mete, we shall be measured again'—(Johanan). 'What thou wouldst not like to be done to thyself, do not to others; this is the fundamental law'—(Hillel). 'If he be admonished to take the splinter out of his eye, he would answer, Take the beam out of thine own'—(Tarphon). 'Imitate God in his goodness. Be towards thy fellow-creatures as he is towards the whole creation. Clothe the naked; heal the sick; comfort the afflicted; be a brother to the children of thy Father.' The whole parable of the houses built on the rock and on the sand is taken out of the Talmud, and such instances of quotation might be indefinitely multiplied" ("On Inspiration;" by Annie Besant; Scott Series, p. 20). From these founts Jesus drew his morality, and spoke as Jew to Jews, out of the Jewish teachings. To point out these facts is by no means to disparage the nobler part of Christian morality. It is rather to elevate Humanity by showing that pure thoughts and gracious words are human, not divine; that the so-called "inspiration" is in all races cultivated to a certain point, and not in one alone; that morality is a fair blossom of earth, not a heaven-transplanted exotic, and grows

167

naturally out of the rich soil of the loving human heart and the noble human brain.

What nobler or grander moral teachings can be found anywhere than breathe through the following passages, taken from the "bibles of all nations" so ably collected for us by Mr. Corway in the "Sacred Anthology" quoted from above? "Let a man continually take pleasure in truth, in justice, in laudable practices and in purity; let him keep in subjection his speech, his arm, and his appetites. Wealth and pleasures repugnant to law, let him shun; and even lawful acts which may cause pain, or be offensive to mankind. Let him not have nimble hands, restless feet, or voluble eyes; let him not be flippant in his speech, nor intelligent in doing mischief. Let him walk in the path of good men" (Manu, p. 7). "He who neglecteth the duties of this life is unfit for this, much less for any higher world" ("Bhagavat Gita," p. 26). "Charity is the free gift of anything not injurious. If no benefit is intended, or the gift is harmful, it is not charity. There must also be the desire to assist, or to show gratitude. It is not charity when gifts are given from other considerations, as when animals are fed that they may be used, or presents given by lovers to bind affection, or to slaves to stimulate labour. It is found where man, seeking to diffuse happiness among all men—those he loves, and those he loves not—digs canals and pools, makes roads, bridges, and seats, and plants trees for shade. It is found where, from compassion for the miserable and the poor, who have none to help them, a man erects resting-places for wanderers, and drinking-fountains, or provides food, raiment, medicine for the needy, not selecting one more than another. This is true charity, and bears much fruit" ("Katha Chari," pp. 219, 220). "Never will I seek, nor receive, private individual salvation—never enter into final peace alone; but for ever, and everywhere, will I live and strive for the universal redemption of every creature throughout the world" (Kwan-yin, p. 233). "All men have in themselves the feelings of mercy and pity, of shame and hatred of vice. It is for each one by culture to let these feelings grow, or to let them wither. They are part of the organisation of men, as much as the limbs or senses, and may be trained as well. The mountain Nicon-chau naturally brings forth beautiful trees. Even when the trunks are cut down, young shoots will constantly rise up. If cattle are allowed to feed there, the mountain looks bare. Shall we say, then, that bareness is natural to the mountain? So the lower passions are let loose to eat down the nobler growths of reverence and love in the heart of man; shall we, therefore, say that there are no such feelings in his heart at all? Under the quiet peaceful airs of morning and evening the shoots tend to grow again. Humanity is the heart of man; justice is the path of man. To know heaven is to develop the principle of our higher nature" (Mencius, pp. 275, 276). "The first requisite in the pursuit of virtue is, that the learner think of his own improvement, and do not act from a regard to (the admiration of) others" ("The She-King," p. 286).

"Benevolence, justice, fidelity, and truth, and to delight in virtue without weariness, constitute divine nobility" (Mencius, p. 339). "Virtue is a service man owes himself; and though there were no heaven, nor any God to rule the world, it were not less the binding law of life. It is man's privilege to know the right and follow it. Betray and prosecute me, brother men! Pour out your rage on me, O malignant devils! Smile, or watch my agony with cold disdain, ye blissful gods! Earth, hell, heaven, combine your might to crush me—I will still hold fast by this inheritance! My strength is nothing—time can shake and cripple it; my youth is transient—already grief has withered up my days; my heart—alas! it seems well nigh broken now! Anguish may crush it utterly, and life may fail; but even so my soul, that has not tripped, shall triumph, and dying, give the lie to soulless destiny, that dares to boast itself man's master" ("Ramayana," pp. 340, 341). What Christian apostle left behind him the records of such words as those of Confucius, boldly spoken to a king: "Ke K'ang, distressed about the number of thieves in his kingdom, inquired of Confucius how he might do away with them? The sage said, 'If you, sir, were not covetous, the people would not steal, though you should pay them for it.' Ke K'ang asked, 'What do you say about killing the unprincipled for the good of the principled?' Confucius said, 'In carrying out your government, why use killing at all? Let the rulers desire what is good, and the people will be good. The grass must bend when the wind blows across it.' How can men who cannot rectify themselves, rectify others?" ("Analects of Confucius," p. 358).

In "The Wheel of the Law," by Henry Alabaster, we find some most interesting information on the moral teaching of Buddhism, and the following quotation is taken from one of the Sutras: "On a certain occasion the Lord Buddha led a number of his disciples to a village of the Kalamachou, where his wisdom and merit and holiness were known. And the Kalamachou assembled, and did homage to him and said, 'Many priests and Brahmins have at different times visited us, and explained their religious tenets, declaring them to be excellent, but each abused the tenets of every one else, whereupon we are in doubt as to whose religion is right and whose wrong; but we have heard that the Lord Buddha teaches an excellent religion, and we beg that we may be freed from doubt, and learn the truth.' And the Lord Buddha answered, 'You were right to doubt, for it was a doubtful matter. I say unto all of you, Do not believe in what ye have heard; that is, when you have heard anyone say this is especially good or extremely bad; do not reason with yourselves that if it had not been true, it would not have been asserted, and so believe in its truth. Neither have faith in traditions, because they have been handed down for many generations and in many places. Do not believe in anything because it is rumoured and spoken of by many; do not think that it is a proof of its truth. Do not believe merely because the written statement of some old sage is produced; do not be sure that the writing has ever been revised by the said sage, or can be relied on. Do not believe in what you have fancied, thinking that because an idea is extraordinary it must have been implanted by a Dewa, or some wonderful being. Do not believe in guesses, that is, assuming some thing at haphazard as a starting-point, draw your conclusions from it; reckoning your two and your three and your four before you have fixed your number one. Do not believe because you think there is analogy, that is, a suitability in things and occurrences, such as believing that there must be walls of the world, because you see water in a basin, or that Mount Meru must exist because you have seen the reflection of trees: or that there must be a creating God because houses and towns have builders.... Do not believe merely on the authority of your teachers and masters, or believe and practise merely because they believe and practise. I tell you all, you must of your own selves know that 'this is evil this is punishable, this is censured by wise men, belief in this will bring no advantage to one, but will cause sorrow.' And when you know this, then eschew it. I say to all you dwellers in this village, answer me this. Lopho, that is covetousness, Thoso, that is anger and savageness, and Moho, that is ignorance and folly—when any or all of these arise in the hearts of men, is the result beneficial or the reverse?' And they answered, 'It is not beneficial, O Lord!' Then the Lord continued, 'Covetous, passionate, and ignorant men destroy life and steal, and commit adultery, and tell lies, and incite others to follow their example, is it not so?' And they answered, 'It is as the Lord says.' And he continued, 'Covetousness, passion, ignorance, the destruction of life, theft, adultery, and lying, are these good or bad, right or wrong? Do wise men praise or blame them? Are they not unprofitable, and causes of sorrow?' And they replied, 'It is as the Lord has spoken.' And the Lord said, 'For this I said to you, do not believe merely because you have heard, but when of your own consciousness you know a thing to be evil, abstain from it.' And then the Lord taught of that which is good, saying, 'If any of you know of yourselves that anything is good and not evil, praised by wise men, advantageous, and productive of happiness, then act abundantly according to your belief. Now I ask you, Alopho, absence of covetousness, Athoso, absence of passion, Amoho, absence of folly, are these profitable or not?' And they answered, 'Profitable.' The Lord continued, 'Men who are not covetous, or passionate, or foolish, will not destroy life, nor steal, nor commit adultery, nor tell lies; is it not so?' And they answered, 'It is as the Lord says.' Then the Lord asked, 'Is freedom from covetousness, passion, and folly, from destruction of life, theft, adultery, and lying, good or bad, right or wrong, praised or blamed by wise men, profitable, and tending to happiness or not?' And they replied, 'It is good, right, praised by the wise, profitable, and tending to happiness.' And the Lord said, 'For this I taught you, not to believe merely because you have heard, but when you believed of your own consciousness, then to act accordingly and

170

abundantly'" (pp. 35-38). In this wise fashion did Buddha found his morality, basing it on utility, the true measure of right and wrong. Buddhism has its Five Commandments, certainly equal in value to the Ten Commandments of Jews and Christians:—

"*First*. Thou shall abstain from destroying or causing the destruction of any living thing.

"*Second*. Thou shalt abstain from acquiring or keeping, by fraud or violence, the property of another.

"*Third*. Thou shalt abstain from those who are not proper objects for thy lust.

"*Fourth*. Thou shalt abstain from deceiving others either by word or deed.

"*Fifth*. Thou shalt abstain from intoxication" (Ibid, p. 57).

From Dr. Muir's translations of "religious and moral sentiments," already quoted from, we might fill page after page with purest morality. "Let a man be virtuous even while yet a youth; for life is transitory. If duty is performed, a good name will be obtained, as well as happiness, here and after death" ("Mahabharata," xii., 6538, p. 22). "Deluded by avarice, anger, fear, a man does not understand himself. He plumes himself upon his high birth, contemning those who are not well-born; and overcome by the pride of wealth, he reviles the poor. He calls others fools, and does not look to himself. He blames the faults of others, but does not govern himself. When the wise and the foolish, the rich and the poor, the noble and the ignoble, the proud and the humble, have departed to the cemetery and all sleep there, their troubles are at an end, and their bodies are stripped of flesh, little else than bones, united by tendons—other men then perceive no difference between them, whereby they could recognise a distinction of birth or of form. Seeing that all sleep, deposited together in the earth, why do men foolishly seek to treat each other injuriously? He who, after bearing this admonition, acts in conformity therewith from his birth onwards, shall attain the highest blessedness" (Ibid, xi. 116, p. 23).

Such are a few of the moral teachings current in the East before the time of Christ. Since that period, these non-Christian nations have gone on in their paths, and many a gem of pure morality might be culled from their later writings, but we have only here presented teachings that were pre-Christian, so as to prove how little need there was for a God to become incarnate to teach morality to the world. "Revealed morality" has nothing grander to say than this earth-born morality, nothing sublimer comes from Judæa than comes from Hindustan and from China. Just as the symbolism of Christianity comes from nature, and is common to many creeds, so does the morality of Christianity flow from nature, and is common to many faiths; when nations attain to a certain stage of civilisation, and inherit a certain amount of culture, they also develop a morality proportionate to the point they have reached, because morality is necessary to the stability of States, and utility formulates the code of moral laws. Christianity can no longer stand on a pinnacle as the sole possessor of a pure and high morality. The pedestal she has occupied is built out of the bricks of ignorance, and her apostles and her master must take rank among their brethren of every age and clime.

It is a serious fault in Christian morality that it has so many OMISSIONS in it. It is full of exhortations to bear, to suffer, to be patient; it sorely lacks appeals to patriotism, to courage, to self-respect. "The heroes of Paganism exemplified the heroism of enterprise. Patriotism, chivalrous deeds of valour, high-souled aspirations after glory, stern justice taking its course in their hands, while natural feeling was held in abeyance—this was the line in which they shone. Our blessed Lord illustrated all virtues indeed, but most especially the passive ones. His heroism took its colouring from endurance. Women, though inferior to men in enterprise, usually come out better than men in suffering; and it is always to be remembered that our blessed Lord held his humanity, not of the stronger, but of the weaker sex" ("Thoughts on Personal Religion," by Dean Goulburn, vol. ii., p. 99; ed. 1866). What is this but to say, in polite language, that Jesus was very effeminate? The Christian religion has all the vices of slavery, and encourages submission to evil instead of resistance to it; it has in it the pathetic beauty of the meekness of the bruised and beaten wife still loving the injurer, of the slave forgiving the slave-driver, but it is a beauty which perpetuates the wrong of which it is born. Better, far better, both for oppressor and for oppressed, is resistance to cruelty than submission to it; submission encourages the wrong-doer where resistance would check him, and Christianity fails in that it omits to value strong men and true patriots, rebels against authority which is unjust. Rome taught its citizens to reverence themselves, to love their country, to maintain freedom: the Roman would die gladly for his mother-country, and deemed his duty as a citizen the foremost of his obligations. The love of country, and the sense of service owed to the State, is the grandest and sublimest virtue of the Pagan world. All felt it, from the highest to the lowest: at Thermopylae the Spartans died gladly for the land they covered with their bodies, faithful unto death to the duty entrusted to them by their country; men and women equally felt the paramount claim of the State, and mothers gave their sons to death rather than that they should fail in duty there. The Roman was taught to value the Republic above its officers; to resist the highest if he grasped at unfair supremacy; to maintain inviolate the rights and the liberties of the people. Christianity undermined all these manly virtues; it preached obedience to "the powers that be," whether they were good or bad; it upheld the authority of a Nero as "ordained of God," and pronounced damnation on those who resisted him; and so it paved the way for the despotism of the Middle Ages, by crushing out the manhood of the nations, and fashioning them into Oriental slaves.

Little wonder that kings embraced Christianity, and forced it on their subjects, for it placed the nations bound at their footstools, and endorsed the tyranny of man with the authority of God. Throughout the New Testament what word is there of patriotism? The citizenship is in heaven. What incitement to heroism? Resist not the power. What appeal to self-reverence? In my flesh dwelleth no good thing. What cry against injustice and oppression? Honour the king, and give obedience to the froward. Christianity makes a paradise for tyrants and a hell for the oppressed.

Intertwined with the evil of omissions of duty is the direct injury of commanding NON-RESISTANCE, and of enforcing INDIFFERENCE TO EARTHLY CARES. "I say unto you that ye resist not evil: but whosoever shall smite thee on thy right cheek, turn to him the other also. And if any man will sue thee at the law, and take away thy coat, let him have thy cloak also. And whosoever shall compel thee to go a mile, go with him twain. Give to him that asketh thee, and from him that would borrow of thee turn not thou away" (Matt. v. 39-42). The surface meaning of these words is undeniable; they are the amplification of the command, "resist not evil." What effect would obedience to these injunctions have upon a State? None committing an assault would be punished; every unjust suit would succeed; every forced concession would be endorsed; every beggar would live in luxury; every borrower would spend at will. Nay more; those who did wrong would be rewarded, and would be thus encouraged to go on in their evil ways. Meanwhile, the man who was insulted would be again struck; the poor man who had lost one thing would lose two; the hard-working, frugal labourer would have to support the beggar and the borrower out of the fruits of his toil. Such is Christ's code of civil laws: he is deliberately abrogating the Mosaic code, "an eye for an eye and a tooth for a tooth," and is replacing it by his own. If the Mosaic law is to be taken literally—as it was—that which is to replace it must also be taken literally, or else one code would be abolished, and there would be none to succeed it, so that the State would be left in a condition of lawlessness. Suppose, however, that we allow that the passage is to be taken metaphorically, what then? A metaphor must mean something: what does this metaphor mean? It can scarcely signify the exact opposite of what it intimates, and yet the exact opposite is true morality. Only a system of taking Christ's words "contrariwise" can make them useful as civil rules, and even "oriental exaggeration" can scarcely be credited with saying the diametrically contrary of its real meaning. But it is urged that, if all men were Christians, then this teaching would be right, and Christ was bound to give a perfect morality. That is to say, if people were different to what they are, this teaching of Christ would not be injurious because—it would be unneeded! If there were no robbers, and no assaulters, and no borrowers, then the morality of the Sermon on the Mount would be most harmless. High praise, truly, for a legislator that his laws would not be injurious when they were no longer needed. Christ should have remembered that the "law is made for sinners," and that such a law as he gives here is a direct encouragement to sin.

We can scarcely wonder that, inculcating a course of conduct which must inevitably lead to poverty, Christ should hold up a state of poverty as desirable. We read in Matthew v. 3, "Blessed are the poor in spirit" and it is contended that it is poverty only of spirit which Christ blesses; if so, he blesses the source of much wretchedness, for poor-spirited people get trampled down, and are a misery to themselves and a burden to those about them. If, however, we turn to Luke vi. 20, we find the declaration: "Blessed are ye poor," addressed directly to his Apostles, who were anything but poor in spirit (Luke ix. 46, and xxii. 24); and we find it, further, joined with the announcement, "blessed are ye that hunger now," and followed by the curses: "Woe unto you that are rich ... woe unto you that are full." If "hunger" means "hunger after righteousness," the antithesis "full" must also mean "full of righteousness," a state on which Christ would surely not pronounce a woe. Mr. Bradlaugh well draws out the various thoughts in these most unfortunate sayings: "Is poverty of spirit the chief amongst virtues, that Jesus gives it the prime place in his teaching? Is poverty of spirit a virtue at all? Surely not. Manliness of spirit, honesty of spirit, fulness of rightful purpose, these are virtues; but poverty of spirit is a crime. When men are poor in spirit, then do the proud and haughty in spirit oppress and trample upon them, but when men are true in spirit and determined (as true men should be) to resist and prevent evil, wrong, and injustice whenever they can, then is there greater opportunity for happiness here, and no lesser fitness for the enjoyment of future happiness, in some may be heaven, hereafter. Are you poor in spirit, and are you smitten; in such case what did Jesus teach? 'Unto him that smiteth thee on the one cheek offer also the other' (Luke vi. 29). It were better far to teach that 'he who courts oppression shares the crime.' Rather say, if smitten once, take careful measures to prevent a future smiting. I have heard men preach passive resistance, but this teaches actual invitation of injury, a course degrading in the extreme ... the poverty of spirit principle is enforced to the fullest conceivable extent— 'Him that taketh away thy cloak, forbid not to take thy coat also. Give to every man that asketh of thee, and of him that taketh away thy goods ask them not again' (Luke vi. 29, 30). Poverty of person is the only possible sequence to this extraordinary manifestation of poverty of spirit. Poverty of person is attended with many unpleasantnesses; and if Jesus knew that poverty of goods would result from his teaching, we might expect some notice of this. And so there is—as if he wished to keep the poor content through their lives with poverty, he says, 'Blessed be ye poor, for yours is the kingdom of God' (Luke vi. 20) ... Poor in spirit and poor in pocket. With no courage to work for food, or money

174

to purchase it, we might well expect to find the man who held these doctrines with empty stomach also; and what does Jesus teach? 'Blessed are ye that hunger now, for ye shall be filled' ... Craven in spirit, with an empty purse and hungry mouth—what next? The man who has not manliness enough to prevent wrong, will probably bemoan his hard fate, and cry bitterly that so sore are the misfortunes he endures. And what does Jesus teach? 'Blessed are ye that weep now, for ye shall laugh' (Luke vi. 21) ... Jesus teaches that the poor, the hungry, and the wretched shall be blessed. This is not so. The blessing only comes when they have ceased to be poor, hungry, and wretched. Contentment under poverty, hunger, and misery is high treason, not to yourself alone but to your fellows. These three, like foul diseases, spread quickly wherever humanity is stagnant and content with wrong" ("What Did Jesus Teach?" pp. 1-3).

But Jesus did more than panegyrise poverty; he gave still more exact directions to his disciples as to how poverty should be attained. Matt. vi. 25-34 is as mischievous a passage as has been penned by any moralist. "Take no thought for your life, what ye shall eat or what ye shall drink; nor yet for your body, what ye shall put on." It is said that "take no thought" means, "be not over anxious;" if this be so, why does Christ emphasise it by quoting birds and lilies as examples, things, which, literally, take no thought? the argument is: birds do not store food in barns, yet God feeds them. You are more valuable than the birds. God will take equal care of you if you follow the birds' example. The lilies spin no raiment, yet God clothes them. So shall he clothe you, if you follow their example. The passage has no meaning, the illustrations no appositeness, unless Christ means that no thought is to be taken for the future. He makes the argument still stronger: "the Gentiles seek" meat, drink, and clothing. But God, your Father, knows your need for all these things. Therefore, "seek ye first the kingdom of God and his righteousness, and all these things shall be added unto you. Take, therefore, no thought for the morrow: for the morrow shall take thought for the things of itself. Sufficient unto the day is the evil thereof." If Christ only meant the common-place advice, "do not be over-anxious," he then lays the most absurd stress on it, and speaks in the most exaggerated way. Sensible Gentiles do not worry themselves by over-anxiety, after they have taken for the morrow's needs all the care they can; but they do not act like birds or like lilies, for they know that many a bird starves in a hard winter because it is not capable of gathering and storing food into barns, and that many a garbless lily is shrivelled up by the cold east wind. They notice that though men and women are "much better than" birds and lilies, yet God does not always feed and clothe them; that, on the contrary, many a poor creature dies of starvation and of winter's bitter cold; when our daily papers record no inquests on those who die from want, because none but God takes thought for them, then it will be time enough for us to cease from preparing for the morrow, and to trust that "heavenly Father" who at present "knoweth that" we "have need of these things," and, knowing, lets so many of his children starve for lack of them.

The true meaning of Christ is plainly shown by his injunctions to the twelve apostles and to the seventy when he sent them on a journey: "Take nothing for your journey, neither staves, nor scrip, neither bread, nor money; neither have two coats apiece" (Luke ix. 3); and: "Carry neither purse, nor scrip, nor shoes ... in the same house remain, eating and drinking such things as they give" (Ibid, x. 4, 7). The same spirit breathes in his injunction to the young man: "Go and sell that thou hast, and give to the poor, and thou shalt have treasure in heaven; and come and follow me" (Matt. xix. 21). The fact is that Jesus held the ascetic doctrine, that poverty was, in itself, meritorious; and, in common with many sects, he regarded the highest life as the life of the mendicant teacher. His doctrine of poverty passed on into the Church that bears his name, and one of the three vows taken by those who aspire to lead "the angelic life" is the vow of poverty. The mendicant friars of the Middle Ages, the "sturdy beggars," are the lineal descendants of the Eastern mendicants, and are the fruits of the morality taught by Christ. On this point, as on many others, the morality of the Epistles is far higher than that of the Gospels, and the common-sense and righteous law, "that if any would not work neither should he eat" is, however, incompatible with Christ's admiration for mendicancy, a far more wholesome and salutary kind of moral teaching than that which we have been considering.

The dogma of rewards and punishments as taught by Christ is fatal to all reality of virtue. To do right from hope of heaven: to avoid wrong for fear of hell: such virtue is only skin-deep, and will not stand rough usage. True virtue does right because it is right, and therefore beneficial, and not from hope of a personal reward, or from dread of a personal punishment, hereafter. Christianity is the apotheosis of selfishness, gilded over with piety; self is the pivot on which all turns: "What shall it profit a man if he gain the whole world, and lose his own soul?" (Mark viii. 36). "He that receiveth a prophet in the name of a prophet shall receive a prophet's reward; and he that receiveth a righteous man in the name of a righteous man shall receive a righteous man's reward. And whosoever shall give to drink unto one of these little ones a cup of cold water only in the name of a disciple, verily I say unto you, he shall in nowise lose his reward" (Matt. x. 41, 42). "Whosoever therefore shall confess me before men, him will I confess also before my Father which is in heaven. But whosoever shall deny me before men, him will I also deny before my Father which is in heaven" (Ibid, 32, 33). "Pray to thy Father which is in secret; and thy Father, which seeth in secret, shall reward thee openly" (Ibid, vi. 6). "We have forsaken all and followed thee: what shall we have therefore?... When the Son of man shall sit in the throne of his glory, ye also shall sit upon twelve thrones" (Matt. xix. 27, 28). The passages might be multiplied; but these are sufficient to show the thorough selfishness inculcated. All is done with an eye to personal gain in the future; even the cold water is to be given, not because the "little one" is thirsty and needs it, but for the reward promised therefore to the giver. Pure, generous love is excluded: there is a taint of selfishness in every gift.

The thought of Heaven is also injurious to human welfare, because men learn to disregard earth for the sake of "the glory to be revealed." People whose "citizenship is in heaven," make but sorry citizens of earth, for they regard this world as "no continuing city," while they "seek one to come." Hence, as all history shows us, they are apt to despise this world while dreaming about another, to trouble little about earth's wrongs while thinking of the mansions in the skies; to acquiesce in any assertion that "the whole world lieth in wickedness," and to trouble themselves but little as to the means of improving it. From this line of thought follows the long list of monasteries and nunneries, wherein people "separate" themselves from this world in order to "prepare" for another. All this evil flows directly from the Christian morality which teaches that all hopes, efforts, and aims should be turned towards laying up treasures in heaven, where also the heart should be. One need scarcely add a word of reprobation as to the horrible doctrine of eternal torture, although that, too, is part of the teaching of Christ. The whole conscience of civilised mankind is so turning against that shameful and cruel dogma, that it is only now believed among the illiterate and uncultured of the Christians, and soon will be too savage even for them. It has, however, hardened the hearts of many in days gone by, and has made the burning of heretics seem an appropriate act of faith, since men only began on earth the roasting which God was to continue to all eternity.

The morality of Christ is also faulty because it shares in the persecuting spirit of the Mosaic code. The disciples are told: "Whosoever shall not receive you, nor hear your words, when ye depart out of that house or city, shake off the dust of your feet. Verily, I say unto you, It shall be more tolerable for the land of Sodom and Gomorrah in the day of judgment, than for that city" (Matt. x. 14, 15). Christ proclaims openly: "Think not that I am come to send peace on earth: I came not to send peace, but a sword. For I am come to set a man at variance against his father, and the daughter against her mother, and the daughter-in-law against her mother-in-law. And a man's foes shall be they of his own household" (Ibid, 34-36). To a man whom he calls to follow him, and who asks to be allowed first to bury his father, Christ gives the brutal reply: "Let the dead bury their dead: but go thou and preach the kingdom of God" (Luke x. 60). Another time he says: "If any man come to me, and hate not his father, and mother, and wife, and children, and brethren, and sisters, yea, and his own life also, he cannot be my disciple" (Ibid, xiv. 26). A religion that destroys the home, that introduces discord into the family, that bids its votaries hate all else save Christ, acts as a disintegrating force in human life, and cannot be too strongly opposed.

Neither must we forget the teaching of Christ regarding marriage. He deliberately places virginity above marriage, and counsels self-mutilation to those capable of making the sacrifice. "All men cannot receive this saying, save they to whom it is given ... there be eunuchs which have made themselves eunuchs for the kingdom of heaven's sake. He that is able to receive it, let him receive it" (Matt. xix. 11, 12). Following this, 1 Cor. vii. teaches the superiority of an unmarried state, and threatens "trouble in the flesh" to those who marry. And in Rev. xiv. 1-4, we find, following the Lamb, with special privileges, 144,000 who "were not defiled with women; for they are virgins." This coarse and insulting way of regarding women, as though they existed merely to be the safety-valves of men's passions, and that the best men were above the temptation of loving them, has been the source of unnumbered evils. To this saying of Christ are due the self-mutilations of many, such as Origen, and the destruction of myriads of human lives in celibacy; monks and nuns innumerable owe to this evil teaching their shrivelled lives and withered hearts. For centuries the leaders of Christian thought spoke of women as of a necessary evil, and the greatest saints of the Church are those who despised women the most. The subjection of women in Western lands is wholly due to Christianity. Among the Teutons women were honoured, and held a noble and dignified place in the tribe; Christianity brought with it the evil Eastern habit of regarding women as intended for the toys and drudges of man, and intensified it with a special spite against them, as the daughters of Eve, who was first "deceived." Strangely different to the *general Eastern feeling and showing a truer and nobler view of life, is the precept of Manu: "Where women are honoured, there the deities are pleased; but where they are dishonoured, there all religious acts become fruitless" ("Anthology," p. 310).

Evil also is the teaching that repentance is higher than purity: "joy shall be in heaven over one sinner that repenth, more than over ninety and nine just persons which need no repentance" (Luke xv. 7, 10). The fatted calf is slain for the prodigal son, who returns home after he has wasted all his substance; and to the laborious elder son, during the many years of his service, the father never gave even a kid that he might make merry with his friends (Ibid, 29). What is all this but putting a premium upon immorality, and instructing people that the more they sin, the more joyous will be their welcome whenever they may choose to reform, and, like the prodigal, think to mend their broken fortunes by repentance?

Thoroughly immoral is the teaching contained in the two parables in Luke xvi. In the one, a steward who has wasted his master's goods, is commended because he went and bribed his employer's debtors to assist him, by suggesting to them that they should cheat his master by altering the amount of the bills they owed him. In the other, the parable of the rich man and Lazarus, the evil moral is taught that riches are in themselves deserving of punishment, and poverty of reward. The rich man is in hell simply because he was rich, and the poor man in Abraham's bosom simply because he was poor; it can scarcely add, one may remark, to the pleasure of heaven for the Lazaruses all to look at the Diveses, and be unable to reach them, even to give them a single drop of water.

Thus whether we see that the nobler part of the Christian morality is pre-Christian, and is neither Christian, nor Jewish, nor Hindu, nor Buddhist, but is simply human, and belongs to the race and not to one creed. Whether we note the omissions in its code, making it insufficient for human guidance; whether we mark its errors, mistakes, and injurious teachings; whichever point of view we take from which to consider it, we find in it nothing to distinguish it above other moral codes, or to prevent it from being classed among other moralities, as being a mixture of good and bad, and, therefore, not to be taken as an, unerring guide, being like them, all FALLIBLE.

SECTION IV

ITS HISTORY

This section does not pretend, within the short limits of some fifty pages, to give even a complete summary of Christian history. It proposes only to draw up an impeachment against Christianity from the facts of its history which occurred in the day of its power, from the time of Constantine, up to the time of the Reformation. If it be urged that Christianity was corrupt during this period, and ought not therefore to be judged by it, we can only reply that, corrupt or not, it is the only Christianity there was, and if only bad fruit is brought forth, it is fair to conclude that the tree which bears nothing else is also bad. If the bishops, and clergy, and missionaries were ignorant, sensual, tyrannical, and superstitious, they are none the less the representatives of Christianity, and if these are not true Christians, where are the true Christians from A.D. 324 to A.D. 1,500?

We propose, in this section, to practically condense the dark side of Mosheim's "Ecclesiastical History," as translated from the Latin by Dr. A. Maclaine (ed. 1847), only adding, here and there, extracts from other writers; all extracts, therefore, except where otherwise specified, will be taken from this valuable history, a history which, perhaps from its size and dryness, is not nearly so much studied by Freethinkers as it should be; its special worth for our object is that Dr. Mosheim is a sincere Christian, and cannot, therefore, be supposed to strain any point unduly against the religion to which he himself belongs.

During the second and third centuries the Christians appear to have grown in power and influence, and their faith, made up out of many older creeds and forming a kind of eclectic religion, gradually spread throughout the Roman empire, and became a factor in political problems. In the struggles between the opposing Roman emperors, A.D. 310-324, the weight of the Christian influence was thrown on the side of Constantine, his rivals being strongly opposed to Christianity; Maximin Galerius was a bitter persecutor, and his successor, Maximin, trod in his steps in A.D. 312, and 313, Maxentius was defeated by Constantine, and Maximin by Licinius, and in A.D. 312 Constantine and Licinius granted liberty of worship to the Christians; in the following year, according to Mosheim, or in A.D. 314 according to Eusebius, a second edict was issued from Milan, by the two emperors, which granted "to the Christians and to all, the free choice to follow that mode of worship which they may wish ... that no freedom at all shall be refused to Christians, to follow or to keep their observances or worship; but that to each one power be granted to devote his mind to that worship which he may think adapted to himself" (Eusebius,

"Eccles. Hist." p. 431). Licinius, however, renewed the war against Constantine, who immediately embraced Christianity, thus securing to himself the sympathy and assistance of the faith which now for the first time saw its votary on the imperial throne of the world, and Licinius, by allying himself with Paganism, and persecuting the Christians, drove them entirely over to Constantine, and was finally defeated and dethroned, A.D. 324. From that date Christianity was supreme, and became the established religion of the State. Dr. Draper regards the conversion of Constantine from the point of view taken above. He says: "It had now become evident that the Christians constituted a powerful party in the State, animated with indignation at the atrocities they had suffered, and determined to endure them no longer. After the abdication of Diocletian (A.D. 305), Constantine, one of the competitors for the purple, perceiving the advantages that would accrue to him from such a policy, put himself forth as the head of the Christian party. This gave him, in every part of the empire, men and women ready to encounter fire and sword in his behalf; it gave him unwavering adherents in every legion of the armies. In a decisive battle, near the Milvian bridge, victory crowned his schemes. The death of Maximin, and subsequently that of Licinius, removed all obstacles. He ascended the throne of the Cæsars—the first Christian emperor. Place, profit, power—these were in view of whoever now joined the conquering sect. Crowds of worldly persons, who cared nothing about its religious ideas, became its warmest supporters. Pagans at heart, their influence was soon manifested in the Paganisation of Christianity that forthwith ensued. The emperor, no better than they, did nothing to check their proceedings. But he did not personally conform to the ceremonial requirements of the Church until the close of his evil life, A.D. 337" ("History of the Conflict between Religion and Science," p. 39; ed. 1875). Constantine, in fact, was not baptised until a few days before his death.

The character of the first Christian emperor is not one which strikes us with admiration. As emperor he sank into "a cruel and dissolute monarch, corrupted by his fortune, or raised by conquest above the necessity of dissimulation ... the old age of Constantine was disgraced by the opposite yet reconcilable vices of rapaciousness and prodigality" (Gibbon's "Decline and Fall," vol. ii., p. 347). He was as effeminate as he was vicious. "He is represented with false hair of various colours, laboriously arranged by the skilful artists of the time; a diadem of a new and more expensive fashion; a profusion of gems and pearls, of collars and bracelets, and a variegated flowing robe of silk, most curiously embroidered with flowers of gold." To his other vices he added most bloodthirsty cruelty. He strangled Licinius, after defeating him; murdered his own son Crispus, his nephew Licinius, and his wife Fausta, together with a number of others. It must indeed have needed an efficacious baptism to wash away his crimes; and "future tyrants were encouraged to believe that the innocent blood which they might shed in a long reign would instantly be washed away in the waters of regeneration" (Ibid, pp. 471, 472).

The wealth of the Christian churches was considerable during the third century, and the bishops and clergy lived in much pomp and luxury. "Though several [bishops] yet continued to exhibit to the world illustrious examples of primitive piety and Christian virtue, yet many were sunk in luxury and voluptuousness, puffed up with vanity, arrogance, and ambition, possessed with a spirit of contention and discord, and addicted to many other vices that cast an undeserved reproach upon the holy religion of which they were the unworthy professors and ministers. This is testified in such an ample manner by the repeated complaints of many of the most respectable writers of this age, that truth will not permit us to spread the veil which we should otherwise be desirous to cast over such enormities among an order so sacred.... The example of the bishops was ambitiously imitated by the presbyters, who, neglecting the sacred duties of their station, abandoned themselves to the indolence and delicacy of an effeminate and luxurious life. The deacons, beholding the presbyters deserting thus their functions, boldly usurped their rights and privileges; and the effects of a corrupt ambition were spread through every rank of the sacred order" (p. 73). During this century also we find much scandal caused by the pretended celibacy of the clergy, for the people—regarding celibacy as purer than marriage, and considering that "they, who took wives, were of all others the most subject to the influence of malignant demons"—urged their clergy to remain celibate, "and many of the sacred order, especially in Africa, consented to satisfy the desires of the people, and endeavoured to do this in such a manner as not to offer an entire violence to their own inclinations. For this purpose, they formed connections with those women who had made vows of perpetual chastity; and it was an ordinary thing for an ecclesiastic to admit one of these fair saints to the participation of his bed, but still under the most solemn declarations, that nothing passed in this commerce that was contrary to the rules of chastity and virtue" (p. 73). Such was the morality of the clergy as early as the third century!

The doctrine of the Church in these primitive times was as confused as its morality was impure. In the first century (during which we really know nothing of the Christian Church), Dr. Mosheim, in dealing with "divisions and heresies," points to the false teachers mentioned in the New Testament, and the rise of the Gnostic heresy. Gnosticism (from [Greek: gnosis] knowledge), a system compounded of Christianity and Oriental philosophy, long divided the Church with the doctrines known as orthodox. The Gnostics believed in the existence of the two opposing principles of good and evil, the latter being by many considered as the creator of the world. They held that from the Supreme God emanated a number of Æons—generally put at thirty;

182

(see throughout "Irenæus Against Heresies")—and some maintained that one of these, Christ, descended on the man Jesus at his baptism, and left him again just before his passion; others that Jesus had not a real, but only an apparent, body of flesh. The Gnostic philosophy had many forms and many interdivisions; but most of the "heresies" of the first centuries were branches of this one tree: it rose into prominence, it is said, about the time of Adrian, and among its early leaders were Marcion, Basilides, and Valentinus. In addition to the various Gnostic theories, there was a deep mark of division between the Jewish and the Gentile Christians; the former developed into the sects, of Nazarenes and Ebionites, but were naturally never very powerful in the Church. In the second century, as the Christians become more visible, their dissensions are also more clearly marked; and it is important to observe that there is no period in the history of Christianity wherein those who laid claim to the name "Christian" were agreed amongst themselves as to what Christianity was. Gnosticism we see now divided into two main branches, Asiatic and Egyptian. The Asiatic believed that, in addition to the two principles of good and evil, there was a third being, a mixture of both, the Demiurgus, the creator, whose son Jesus was; they maintained that the body of Jesus was only apparent; they enforced the severest discipline against the body, which was evil, in that it was material; and marriage, flesh, and wine were forbidden. The Elcesaites were a judaising branch of this Asiatic Gnosticism; Saturninus of Antioch, Ardo of Syria, and Marcion of Pontus headed the movement, and after them Lucan, Severus, Blastes, Apelles, and Bardesanes formed new sects. Tatian (see ante, pp. 259, 260) had many followers called Tatianists, and in connection with him and his doctrines we hear of the Eucratites, Hydroparastates (the water-drinkers), and Apotactites. The Eucratites appear to have been in existence before Tatian professed Gnosticism, but he so increased their influence as to be sometimes regarded as their founder. The Egyptian Gnostics were less ascetic, and mostly favoured the idea that Jesus had a real body on which the Æon descended and joined himself thereunto. They regarded him as born naturally of Joseph and Mary. Basilides, and Valentinus headed the Egyptians, and then we have as sub-divisions the Carpocratians, Ptolemaites, Secundians, Heracleonites, Marcosians, Adamites, Cainites, Sethites, Florinians, Ophites, Artemonites, and Hermogenists; in addition to these we have the Monarchians or Patripassians, who maintained that there was but one God, and that the Father suffered (whence this name) in the person of Christ. This long list may be closed with the Montanists, a sect joined by Tertullian (see his account of the orthodox after he became a Montanist, ante, p. 225); they held that Montanes, their founder, was the Paraclete promised by Christ, missioned to complete the Christian code; he forbade second marriages, the reception into the Church of those who had been excommunicated for grievous sin, and inculcated

183

the sternest asceticism. He opposed all learning as anti-Christian, a doctrine which was rapidly spreading among Christians, and which seems, indeed, to have been an integral part of the religion from its very beginning (Matt. xi. 25, 1 Cor. i. 26, 27). In the third century the heretic camp received a new light in the person of Manes, or Manichæus, a Persian magus; he appears to have been a man of great learning, a physician, an astronomer, a philosopher. He taught the old Persian creed tinctured with Christianity, Christ being identical with Mithras (see ante, p. 362), and having come upon earth in an apparent body only to deliver mankind. Manes was the paraclete sent to complete his teaching; the body was evil, and only by long struggle and mortification could man be delivered from it, and reach final blessedness. Those who desired to lead the highest life, the elect, abstained from flesh, eggs, milk, fish, wine, and all intoxicating drink, and remained in the strictest celibacy; they were to live on bread, herbs, pulse, and melons, and deny themselves every comfort and every gratification (see pp. 80-82). The Hieracites in Egypt were closely allied with the Manichæans. The Novatians differed from the orthodox only in their refusal to receive again into the Church any who had committed grievous crimes, or who had lapsed during persecution. The Arabians denied the immortality of the soul, maintaining that it died with the body, and that body and soul together would be revivified by God. The controversies on the persons of the Godhead now increased in intensity. Noctus of Smyrna maintained the doctrine of the Patripassians, that God was one and indivisible, and suffered to redeem mankind; Sabellius also taught that God was one, but that Jesus was a man, to whom was united a "certain energy only, proceeding from the Supreme Parent" (p. 83). He also denied the separate personality of the Holy Ghost. Paul of Samosata, Bishop of Antioch, taught a cognate doctrine, and founded the sect of the Paulians or Paulianists, and was consequently degraded from his office. Thus we see that the history of the Church, before it came to power, is a mass of quarrels and divisions, varied by ignorance and licentiousness. If we exclude Origen, whose writings contain much that is valuable, the works produced by Christian writers in these centuries might be thrown into the sea, and the world would be none the poorer for the loss.

CENTURY IV

Constantine attained undisputed and sole authority A.D. 324, and in the year 325 he summoned the first general council, that of Nicea, or Nice, which condemned the errors of Arius, and declared Christ to be of the same substance as the Father. This council has given its name to the "Nicene Creed," although that creed, as now recited, differs somewhat from the creed issued at Nice, and received its present form at the Council of Constantinople, A.D. 381. During the reign of Constantine, the Church grew swiftly in power and influence, a growth much aided by the penal laws passed against Paganism. The moment Christianity was able to seize the sword, it wielded it remorselessly, and cut its way to supremacy in the Roman world. Bribes and penalties shared together in the work of conversion. "The hopes of wealth and honours, the example of an emperor, his exhortations, his irresistible smiles, diffused conviction among the venal and obsequious crowds which usually fill the apartments of a palace. The cities, which signalised a forward zeal by the voluntary destruction of their temples, were distinguished by municipal privileges and rewarded with popular donatives; and the new capital of the East gloried in the singular advantage that Constantinople was never profaned by the worship of idols. As the lower ranks of society are governed by imitation, the conversion of those who possessed any eminence of birth, of power, or of riches, was soon followed by dependent multitudes. The salvation of the common people was purchased at an easy rate, if it be true, that, in one year, twelve thousand men were baptised at Rome, besides a proportionable number of women and children; and that a white garment, with twenty pieces of gold, had been promised by the emperor to every convert" (Gibbon's "Decline and Fall," vol. ii. pp. 472, 473). With Constantine began the ruinous system of dowering the Church with State funds. The emperor directed the treasurers of the province of Carthage to pay over to the bishop of that district £18,000 sterling, and to honour his further drafts. Constantine also gave his subjects permission to bequeath their fortunes to the Church, and scattered public money among the bishops with a lavish hand. The three sons of Constantine followed in his steps, "continuing to abrogate and efface the ancient superstitions of the Romans, and other idolatrous nations, and to accelerate the progress of the Christian religion throughout the empire. This zeal was no doubt, laudable; its end was excellent; but, in the means used to accomplish it, there were many things worthy of blame" (p. 88). Julian succeeded to part of the empire in A.D. 360, and to sole authority in A.D. 361. He was educated as a Christian, but reverted to philosophic Paganism, and during his short reign he revoked the special privileges granted to Christianity, and placed all creeds on the most perfect civil equality. Julian's dislike of Christianity, and his philosophic writings directed against it, have gained for him, from Christian writers, the title of "the Apostate." The emperors who succeeded were, however, all Christian, and used their best endeavours to destroy Paganism. Christianity spread apace; "multitudes were drawn into the profession of Christianity, not by the power of conviction and argument, but by the prospect of gain, and the fear of punishment" (p. 102). "The zeal and diligence with which Constantine and his successors exerted themselves in the cause of Christianity, and in extending the limits of the Church, prevent our surprise at the number of barbarous and uncivilised nations, which received the Gospel" (p. 90); and Dr. Mosheim admits that: "There is no doubt but that the victories of Constantine the Great, the fear of punishment, and the desire of pleasing this mighty conqueror and his imperial successors, were the weighty arguments that moved whole nations, as well as particular persons, to embrace Christianity" (p. 91). Fraud, as well as force and favour, lent its aid to the progress of "the Gospel." We hear of the "imprudent methods employed to allure the different nations to embrace the Gospel" (p. 98): "disgraceful" would be a fitter term whereby to designate them, for Dr. Mosheim speaks of "the endless frauds of those odious impostors, who were so far destitute of all principles, as to enrich themselves by the ignorance and errors of the people. Rumours were artfully spread abroad of prodigies and miracles to be seen in certain places (a trick often practised by the heathen priests), and the design of these reports was to draw the populace, in multitudes, to these places, and to impose upon their credulity ... Nor was this all; certain tombs were falsely given out for the sepulchres of saints and confessors. The list of the saints was augmented by fictitious names, and even robbers were converted into martyrs. Some buried the bones of dead men in certain retired places, and then affirmed that they were divinely admonished, by a dream, that the body of some friend of God lay there. Many, especially of the monks, travelled through the different provinces; and not only sold, with most frontless impudence, their fictitious relics, but also deceived the eyes of the multitude with ludicrous combats with evil spirits or genii. A whole volume would be requisite to contain an enumeration of the various frauds which artful knaves practised, with success, to delude the ignorant, when true religion was almost entirely superseded by horrid superstition" (p. 98). When to all these weapons we add the forgeries everywhere circulated (see ante, pp. 240-243), we can understand how rapidly Christianity spread, and how "the faithful" were rendered pliable to those whose interests lay in deceiving them. During this century flourished some of the greatest fathers of the Church, pre-eminent among whom we note Ambrose, of Milan, Augustine, of Hippo, and the great ecclesiastical doctor, Jerome. Already, in this century, we find clear traces of the supremacy of the bishop of Rome, and "when a new pontiff was to be elected by the suffrages of the presbyters and the people, the city of Rome was generally agitated with dissensions, tumults, and cabals, whose consequences were often deplorable and fatal" (p. 94). By a decree of the Council of Constantinople, the bishop of that city was given precedence next after the Roman prelate, and the jealousy which arose between the bishops of the two imperial cities fomented the disputes which ended, finally, in the separation of the Eastern and Western

Churches. Of the officers of the Church in this century we read that: "The bishops, on the one hand, contended with each other, in the most scandalous manner, concerning the extent of their respective jurisdictions, while, on the other, they trampled upon the rights of the people, violated the privileges of the inferior ministers, and imitated, in their conduct, and in their manner of living, the arrogance, voluptuousness, and luxury of magistrates and princes" (pp. 95, 96).

In this century is the first instance of the burning alive of a heretic, and it was Spain who lighted that first pile. Theodosius, of all the emperors of this age, was the bitterest persecutor of the heretic sects. "The orthodox emperor considered every heretic as a rebel against the supreme powers of heaven and of earth; and each of those powers might exercise their peculiar jurisdiction over the soul and body of the guilty.... In the space of fifteen years [A.D. 380-394], he promulgated at least fifteen severe edicts against the heretics; more especially against those who rejected the doctrine of the Trinity; and to deprive them of every hope of escape, he sternly enacted, that if any laws or rescripts should be alleged in their favour, the judges should consider them as the illegal productions either of fraud or forgery.... The heretical teachers ... were exposed to the heavy penalties of exile and confiscation, if they presumed to preach the doctrine, or to practise the rites of their accursed sects.... Their religious meetings, whether public or secret, by day or by night, in cities or in the country, were equally proscribed by the edicts of Theodosius: and the building or ground, which had been used for that illegal purpose, was forfeited to the imperial domain. It was supposed, that the error of the heretics could proceed only from the obstinate temper of their minds; and that such a temper was a fit object of censure and punishment.... The sectaries were gradually disqualified for the possession of honourable or lucrative employments; and Theodosius was satisfied with his own justice, when he decreed, that as the Eunonians distinguished the nature of the Son from that of the Father, they should be incapable of making their wills, or of receiving any advantages from testamentary donations" (Gibbon's "Decline and Fall," vol. iii. pp. 412, 413).

One important event of this century must not be omitted, the dispersion of the great Alexandrine library, collected by the Ptolemies. In the siege of Alexandria by Julius Cæsar, the Philadelphian library in the museum, containing some 400,000 volumes, had been burned; but there still remained the "daughter library" in the Serapion, containing about 300,000 books. During the episcopate of Theophilus, predecessor of Cyril, a riot took place between the Christians and the Pagans, and the latter "held the Serapion as their head-quarters. Such were the disorder and bloodshed that the emperor had to interfere. He despatched a rescript to Alexandria, enjoining the bishop, Theophilus, to destroy the Serapion; and the great library, which had been collected by the Ptolemies, and had escaped the fire of Julius Cæsar, was by that fanatic dispersed" ("Conflict of Religion and Science," p. 54), A.D. 389. To Christian bigotry it is that we owe the loss of these rich treasures of antiquity.

Heresies grew and strengthened during this fourth century. Chief leader in the heretic camp was Arius, a presbyter of Alexandria; he asserted that the Son, although begotten of the Father before the creation of aught else, was not "of the same substance" as the Father, but only "of like substance;" a vast number of the Christians embraced his definition, and thus began the long struggle between the Arians and the Catholics. Arius also "took the ground that there was a time when, from the very nature of sonship, the Son did not exist, and a time at which he commenced to be, asserting that it is the necessary condition of the filial relation that a father must be older than his son. But this assertion evidently denied the co-eternity of the three persons of the Trinity; it suggested a subordination or inequality among them, and indeed implied a time when the Trinity did not exist. Hereupon the bishop, who had been the successful competitor against Arius [for the episcopate], displayed his rhetorical powers in public debates on the question, and, the strife spreading, the Jews and Pagans, who formed a very large portion of the population of Alexandria, amused themselves with theatrical representations of the contest on the stage—the point of their burlesques being the equality of age of the Father and his Son" (Ibid, p. 53). Gibbon quotes an amusing passage to show how widely spread was the interest in the subject debated between the rival parties: "This city is full of mechanics and slaves, who are all of them profound theologians, and preach in the shops and in the streets. If you desire a man to change a piece of silver, he informs you wherein the Son differs from the Father; if you ask the price of a loaf, you are told, by way of reply, that the Son is inferior to the Father; and if you inquire whether the bath is ready, the answer is, that the Son was made out of nothing" (Gibbon's "Decline and Fall," vol. iii. p. 402). Arius maintained that "the Logos was a dependent and spontaneous production, created from nothing by the will of the Father. The Son, by whom all things were made, had been begotten before all worlds, and the longest of the astronomical periods could be compared only as a fleeting moment to the extent of his duration; yet this duration was not infinite, and there had been a time which preceded the ineffable generation of the Logos.... He governed the universe in obedience to the will of his Father and Monarch" (Ibid, pp. 18,19). The "Nicene creed" of the Prayer-book consists of the creed promulgated by the Council of Nice, with the anathema at the end omitted, and with the addition of some phrases joined to it at the Council at Constantinople, and the insertion of the Filioque. At the Council of Nice, Arius was condemned and banished, to the triumph of his great opponent, Athanasius; but he was recalled in A.D. 330, obtained the banishment of Athanasius in A.D. 335, and died suddenly, under very suspicious circumstances, in A.D. 336.

Throughout this century the struggle proceeded furiously, each party in turn getting the upper hand, as the emperor of the time inclined towards Catholicism or towards Arianism, and each persecuting the adherents of the other. Among Arian subdivisions we find Semi-Arians, Eusebians, Aetians, Eunomians, Acasians, Psathyrians, etc. Then we have the Apollinarians, who maintained that Christ had no human soul, the divinity supplying its place; the Marcellians, who taught that a divine emanation descended on Christ. Allied to the Manichæan heresy were the Priscillians, the Saccophori, the Solitaries, and many others; and, in addition, the Messalians or Euchites, the Luciferians, the Origenists, the Antidicomarianites, and the Collyridians. A quarrel about the consecration of a bishop gave rise to fierce struggles not connected with the doctrine, so much as with the discipline of the Church. The Bishops of Numidia were angered by not having been called to the consecration of Cæcilianus Bishop of Carthage, and, assembling together, they elected and consecrated a rival bishop to that see, and declared Cæcilianus incompetent for the episcopal office. Donatus, Bishop of Casa Nigra, was the foremost of these Numidian malcontents, and from him the sect of Donatists took its name; they denied the orders of those ordained by Cæcilianus, and hence the validity of the Sacraments administered by them. Excommunicated themselves, "they boldly excommunicated the rest of mankind who had embraced the impious party of Cæcilianus, and of the traditors, from whom he derived his pretended ordination. They asserted with confidence, and almost with exultation, that the apostolical succession was interrupted, that all the bishops of Europe and Asia were infected by the contagion of guilt and schism, and that the prerogatives of the Catholic Church were confined to the chosen portion of the African believers, who alone had preserved inviolate the integrity of their faith and discipline. This rigid theory was supported by the most uncharitable conduct. Whenever they acquired a proselyte, even from the distant provinces of the east, they carefully repeated the sacred rites of baptism and ordination; as they rejected the validity of those which he had already received from the hands of heretics or of schismatics" (Gibbon's "Decline and Fall," vol. iii. pp. 5, 6). A number of Donatists, known as Circumcelliones, "maintained their cause by the force of arms, and overrunning all Africa, filled that province with slaughter and rapine, and committed the most enormous acts of perfidy and cruelty against the followers of Caecilianus" (p. 109). To complete the darkly terrible picture of the Church in the fourth century, we need only note the various orders of fanatical monks, filthy in their habits, densely ignorant, hopelessly superstitious, amongst whom may be numbered the travelling mendicants called Sarabaites. "Many of the Coenobites were chargeable with vicious and scandalous practices. This order, however, was not so universally corrupt as that of the Sarabaites, who were, for the most part, profligates of the most abandoned kind"

(p. 102). The pen wearies over the list of scandals of these early Christian ages; we can but sketch the outline here; let the student fill the picture in, and he will find even blacker shades needed to darken it enough.

CENTURY V

This century sees the destruction of the Roman Empire of the West, and the rise into importance of the great Gothic monarchies. The Christian emperors of the East put down paganism with a strong hand, conferring state offices on Christians only, and forbidding pagan ceremonies [unless under Christian names]. The sons of Constantine had pronounced the penalty of death and confiscation against any who sacrificed to the old gods; and Theodosius, in A.D. 390, had forbidden, under heavy penalties, all pagan rites. This work of repression was rigorously carried on. Clovis, king of the Franks, embraced Christianity, finding its profession "of great use to him, both in confirming and enlarging his empire" (p. 117); and many of the barbarous tribes were "converted to the faith" by means of pretended miracles, "pious frauds ... very commonly practised in Gaul and in Spain at this time, in order to captivate, with more facility, the minds of a rude and barbarous people, who were scarcely susceptible of a rational conviction" (pp. 117, 118). The supremacy of the see of Rome advanced with rapid strides during this century. The people depending, in their superstitious ignorance, on the clergy, and the clergy on the bishops, it became the interest of the savage kings to be on friendly terms with the latter, and to increase their influence; and as the bishops, in their turn, leant upon the central authority of Rome, the power of the pontiff rapidly increased. This power was still further augmented by the struggles for supremacy among the Eastern bishops, for by favouring sometimes one and sometimes another, he fostered the habit of looking to Rome for aid. In the East, five "patriarchs" were raised over the rest of the bishops, the Patriarch of Constantinople standing at their head. Thus, East and West drifted ever more apart. Mosheim speaks of "the ambitious quarrels and the bitter animosities that rose among the patriarchs themselves, and which produced the most bloody wars, and the most detestable and horrid crimes. The Patriarch of Constantinople distinguished himself in these odious contests. Elated with the favour and proximity of the Imperial Court, he cast a haughty eye on all sides, where any objects were to be found on which he might exercise his lordly ambition. On the one hand, he reduced under his jurisdiction the Patriarchs of Alexandria and Antioch, as prelates only of the second order; and on the other, he invaded the diocese of the Roman Pontiff, and spoiled him of several provinces. The two former prelates, though

190

they struggled with vehemence and raised considerable tumults by their opposition, yet they struggled ineffectually, both for want of strength, and likewise on account of a variety of unfavourable circumstances. But the Roman Pontiff, far superior to them in wealth and power, contended also with more vigour and obstinacy; and, in his turn, gave a deadly wound to the usurped supremacy of the Byzantine Patriarch. The attentive inquirer into the affairs of the Church, from this period, will find, in the events now mentioned, the principal source of those most scandalous and deplorable dissensions which divided first the Eastern Church into various sects, and afterwards separated it entirely from that of the West. He will find that these ignominious schisms flowed chiefly from the unchristian contentions for dominion and supremacy which reigned among those who set themselves up for the fathers and defenders of the Church" (p. 123).

Learning during this century fell lower and lower, in spite of the schools established and fostered by the emperors, and while knowledge diminished, vice increased. "The vices of the clergy were now carried to the most enormous lengths; and all the writers of this century, whose probity and virtue render them worthy of credit, are unanimous in their accounts of the luxury, arrogance, avarice, and voluptuousness of the sacerdotal orders. The bishops, particularly those of the first rank, created various delegates or ministers, who managed for them the affairs of their dioceses, and a sort of courts were gradually formed, where these pompous ecclesiastics gave audience, and received the homage of a cringing multitude" (p. 123). Superstition performed its maddest freak in the Stylites, men "who stood motionless on the tops of pillars;" the original maniac being one Simon, a Syrian, who actually spent thirty-seven years of his life on pillars, the last of which was forty cubits high. Another of the same class spent sixty-eight years in this useful manner (see pp. 128, 129, and note). The Agapae were abolished, and auricular confession was established, during this century.

Among the bishops of this century, one name deserves an immortality of infamy. It is that of Cyril, Bishop of Alexandria. Under his rule took place the terrible murder of Hypatia, that pure and beautiful Platonic teacher, who was dragged by a fanatic mob, headed by Peter the Reader, into the great church of Alexandria, and tortured to death on the steps of the high altar. Cyril's "hold upon the audiences of the giddy city [Alexandria] was, however, much weakened by Hypatia, the daughter of Theon, the mathematician, who not only distinguished herself by her expositions of the doctrines of Plato and Aristotle, but also by her comments on the writings of Apollonius and other geometers. Each day, before her academy, stood a long train of chariots; her lecture-room was crowded with the wealth and fashion of Alexandria.... Hypatia and Cyril! Philosophy and bigotry. They cannot exist together. So Cyril felt, and on that feeling he acted. As Hypatia repaired to her academy, she was assaulted by Cyril's mob—a mob of

191

many monks. Stripped naked in the street, she was dragged into a church, and there killed by the club of Peter the Reader [A.D. 415]. The corpse was cut to pieces, the flesh was scraped from the bones with shells, and the remnants cast into a fire. For this frightful crime Cyril was never called to account. It seemed to be admitted that the end sanctified the means" (Draper's "Conflict between Religion and Science," p. 55).

The heresies of the last century were continued in this, and various new ones arose. Chief among these was the heresy of Nestorius, a Bishop of Constantinople, who distinguished so strongly between the two natures in Christ as to make a double personality, and he regarded the Virgin Mary as mother of Christ, but not mother of God. The Council of Ephesus (A.D. 431) was called to decide the point, and was presided over by the great antagonist of Nestorius, Cyril, Bishop of Alexandria. The matter was settled very quickly. Church Councils vote on disputed points, and the vote of the majority constitutes orthodoxy. The Council was held before the arrival of the bishops who sympathised with Nestorius, and thus, by the simple expedient of getting everything over before the opponents arrived, it was settled for evermore that Christ is one person with two natures. A heresy of the very opposite character was that of Eutyches, abbot of the monastery in Constantinople. He maintained that in Christ there was only one nature, "that of the incarnate word," and his opinion was endorsed by a council called at Ephesus, A.D. 449; but this decree was annulled by the Council of Chalcedon (reckoned the fourth OEcumenical), A.D. 451, wherein it was again declared that Christ had two natures in one person. It was at the Council of Ephesus, in A.D. 449, that Flavianus, Bishop of Constantinople, was so beaten by the other bishops that he died of his wounds, and the bishops who held with him hid themselves under benches to get out of the way of their infuriate brothers in Christ (see notes on pp. 136, 137). The Theopaschites were a branch of the Eutychian heresy, and the Monophysites were a cognate sect; from these arose the Acephali, Anthropomorphites, Barsanuphites, and Esaianists. Not less important than the heresy of Eutyches was that of Pelagius, a British monk, who taught that man did not inherit original sin on account of Adam's fall, but that each was born unspotted into the world, and was capable of rising to the height of virtue by the exercise of his natural faculties. The semi-Pelagians held that man could turn to God by his own strength, but that divine grace was necessary to enable him to persevere.

One heretic of this period deserves a special word of record. Vigilantius was a Gallic priest, remarkable for his eloquence and learning, and he devoted himself to an effort to reform the Church in Spain. "Among other things, he denied that the tombs and the bones of the martyrs were to be honoured with any sort of homage or worship; and therefore censured pilgrimages that were made to places that were reputed holy. He turned into derision the prodigies which were said to be wrought in the temples consecrated to martyrs, and condemned the custom of performing vigils in them. He asserted, and indeed with reason, that the custom of burning tapers at the tombs of the martyrs in broad day, was imprudently borrowed from the ancient superstition of the Pagans. He maintained, moreover, that prayers addressed to departed saints were void of all efficacy; and treated with contempt fastings and mortifications, the celibacy of the clergy, and the various austerities of the monastic life. And finally he affirmed that the conduct of those who, distributing their substance among the indigent, submitted to the hardships of a voluntary poverty, or sent a part of their treasures to Jerusalem for devout purposes, had nothing in it acceptable to the Deity" (p. 129). Under these circumstances we can scarcely wonder that Vigilantius was scouted as a heretic by all orthodox, lucre-loving clerics. He is the forerunner of a long line of protesters against the ever-growing strength and superstition of the Church.

CENTURY VI

The darkness deepens as we proceed. Christianity spread among the barbarous tribes of the East and West, but "it must, however, be acknowledged, that of these conversions, the greatest part were owing to the liberality of the Christian princes, or to the fear of punishment, rather than to the force of argument or to the love of truth. In Gaul, the Jews were compelled by Childeric to receive the ordinance of baptism; and the same despotic method of converting was practised in Spain" (p. 141). "They required nothing of these barbarous people that was difficult to be performed, or that laid any remarkable restraint upon their appetites and passions. The principal injunctions they imposed upon these rude proselytes were that they should get by heart certain summaries of doctrine, and to pay the images of Christ and the saints the same religious services which they had formerly offered to the statues of the gods" (p. 142). Libraries were formed in many of the monasteries, and schools were opened, but apparently only for those who intended to enter the monastic life; these, however, did not flourish, for many bishops showed "bitter aversion" towards "every sort of learning and erudition, which they considered as pernicious to the progress of piety" (p. 144). "Greek literature was almost everywhere neglected.... Philosophy fared still worse than literature; for it was entirely banished from all the seminaries which were under the inspection and government of the ecclesiastical order" (Ibid). The wealth of the Church grew apace. "The arts of a rapacious priesthood were practised upon the ignorant devotion of the simple; and even the

193

remorse of the wicked was made an instrument of increasing the ecclesiastical treasure. For an opinion was propagated with industry among the people, that the remission of their sins was to be purchased by their liberalities to the churches and monks" (p. 146). "The monastic orders, in general, abounded with fanatics and profligates; the latter were more numerous than the former in the Western convents, while in those of the East the fanatics were predominant" (ibid). It was in this century (A.D. 529) that the great Benedictine rule was composed by Benedict of Nursia. The Council of Constantinople, A.D. 553, is reckoned as the fifth general Council. It is said to have condemned the doctrines of Origen, thus summarised by Mosheim:—"1. That in the Trinity the Father is greater than the Son, and the Son than the Holy Ghost. 2. The pre-existence of souls, which Origen considered as sent into mortal bodies for the punishment of sins committed in a former state of being. 3. That the soul of Christ was united to the word before the incarnation. 4. That the sun, moon, and stars, etc., were animated and endowed with rational souls. 5. That after the resurrection all bodies will be of a round figure. 6. That the torments of the damned will have an end; and that as Christ had been crucified in this world to save mankind, he is to be crucified in the next to save the devils" (p. 151, note). Among the various notabilities of this age none are specially worthy attention, save Brethius, Cassiodorus, Gregory the Great, Benedict of Nursia, Gregory of Tours, and Isidore of Seville. The heresies of former centuries continued during this, and several unimportant additional sects sprang up. The Monophysites gained in strength under Jacob, Bishop of Edessa, and became known as Jacobites, and exist to this day in Abyssinia and America. Six small sects grew up among the Monophysites and died away again, which held varying opinions about the nature of the body of Christ We find also the Corrupticolæ, Agnoetæ, Tritheists, Philoponists, Cononites, and Damianists, the four last of which differed as to the nature of the Trinity. Thus was rent into innumerable factions the supposed-to-be-indivisible Christianity, and the most bloody persecutions disgraced the uppermost party of the moment.

CENTURY VII

Many are the missionary enterprises of this century, and we find the missionaries grasping at temporal power, and exercising a "princely authority over the countries where their ministry had been successful" (p. 157). Learning had almost vanished; "they, who distinguished themselves most by their taste and genius, carried their studies little farther than the works of Augustine and Gregory the Great; and it is of scraps collected out of these two writers, and patched together without much uniformity, that the best productions of this century are entirely composed.... The schools which had been committed to the care and inspection of the bishops, whose ignorance and indolence were now become enormous, began to decline apace, and were in many places, fallen into ruin. The bishops in general were so illiterate, that few of that body were capable of composing the discourses which they delivered to the people. Such of them as were not totally destitute of genius, composed out of the writings of Augustine and Gregory a certain number of insipid homilies, which they divided between themselves, and their stupid colleagues, that they might not be obliged through incapacity to discontinue preaching the doctrines of Christianity to their people" (p. 159). "The progress of vice among the subordinate rulers and ministers of the Church was, at this time, truly deplorable.... In those very places, that were consecrated to the advancement of piety and the service of God, there was little else to be seen than ghostly ambition, insatiable avarice, pious frauds, intolerable pride, and a supercilious contempt of the natural rights of the people, with many other vices still more enormous" (p. 161). The wealth of the Church increased rapidly; it grew fat on the wages of sin. "Abandoned profligates, who had passed their days in the most enormous pursuits, and whose guilty consciences filled them with terror and remorse, were comforted with the delusive hopes of obtaining pardon, and making atonement for their crimes by leaving the greatest part of their fortune to some monastic society. Multitudes, impelled by the unnatural dictates of a gloomy superstition, deprived their children of fertile lands and rich patrimonies in favour of the monks, by whose prayers they hoped to render the Deity propitious" (p. 161). The only new sect of any importance in this century is that of the Monothelites, later known as Maronites; they taught that Christ had but one will, but the doctrine is wrapped up in so many subtleties as to be almost incomprehensible. They were condemned, in the sixth General Council, held at Constantinople, A.D. 680. It was during this century that "Boniface V. enacted that infamous law, by which the churches became places of refuge to all who fled thither for protection; a law which procured a sort of impunity to the most enormous crimes, and gave a loose rein to the licentiousness of the most abandoned profligates" (p. 164). The effect of this law was that the monasteries became the refuge of bandits and murderers, who issued from them to plunder and to destroy, and paid for the security of their persons by bestowing on their hosts a portion of the spoil they had collected during their raids. Such were the civilizing and purifying effects of Christianity.

CENTURY VIII

Winfred, better known as Boniface, "the Apostle of Germany," is, perhaps, the chief ecclesiastical figure of this century. He taught Christianity right through Germany; was consecrated bishop in A.D. 723, created archbishop in A.D. 738, and Primate of Germany and Belgium in A.D. 746; in A.D. 755 he was murdered in Friesland, with fifty other ecclesiastics. Much stress is laid upon his martyrdom by Christian writers, but Boniface, after all, only received from the Frieslanders the measure he had meted out to their brethren, and there seems no good reason why Christian missionaries should claim a monopoly of the right to kill. Mosheim allows that he "often employed violence and terror, and sometimes artifice and fraud" (p. 169) in order to gain converts, and he was supported by Charles Martel, the enemy of Friesland, and appeared among the Germans as the friend and agent of their foes. A few years later, Charlemagne spread Christianity among the Saxons with great vigour. For "a war broke out, at this time, between Charlemagne and the Saxons, which contributed much to the propagation of Christianity, though not by the force of a rational persuasion. The Saxons were, at this time, a numerous and formidable people, who inhabited a considerable part of Germany, and were engaged in perpetual quarrels with the Franks concerning their boundaries, and other matters of complaint. Hence Charlemagne turned his armies against this powerful nation, A.D. 772, with a design not only to subdue that spirit of revolt with which they had so often troubled the empire, but also to abolish their idolatrous worship, and engage them to embrace the Christian religion. He hoped, by their conversion, to vanquish their obstinacy, imagining that the divine precepts of the Gospel would assuage their impetuous and restless passions, mitigate their ferocity, and induce them to submit more tamely to the government of the Franks. These projects were great in idea, but difficult in execution; accordingly, the first attempt to convert the Saxons, after having subdued them, was unsuccessful, because it was made without the aid of violence, or threats, by the bishops and monks, whom the victor had left among that conquered people, whose obstinate attachment to idolatry no arguments nor exhortations could overcome. [Mark the naïveté of this confession.] More forcible means were afterwards used to draw them into the pale of the Church, in the wars which Charlemagne carried on in the years 775, 776, and 780, against that valiant people, whose love of liberty was excessive, and whose aversion to the restraints of sacerdotal authority was inexpressible. During these wars their attachment to the superstition of their ancestors was so warmly combated by the allurements of reward, by the terror of punishment, and by the imperious language of victory, that they suffered themselves to be baptised, though with inward reluctance, by the missionaries, which the emperor sent among them for that purpose" (p. 170). Rebellion broke out once more, headed by the two most powerful Saxon chiefs, but they were won over by Charlemagne, who persuaded them "to make a public and solemn profession of Christianity, in the year 785, and to promise an adherence to that divine religion for the rest of their days. To prevent, however, the Saxons from renouncing a religion which they had embraced with reluctance, several bishops were appointed to reside among them, schools also were erected, and monasteries founded, that the means of instruction might not be wanting. The same precautions were employed among the Huns in Pannonia, to maintain in the profession of Christianity that fierce people whom Charlemagne had converted to the faith, when, exhausted and dejected by various defeats, they were no longer able to make head against his victorious arms, and chose rather to be Christians than slaves" (p. 170). The grateful Church canonized Charlemagne, the brutal soldier who had so enlarged her borders; "not to enter into a particular detail of his vices, whose number counter-balanced that of his virtues, it is undeniably evident that his ardent and ill-conducted zeal for the conversion of the Huns, Frieslanders, and Saxons, was more animated by the suggestions of ambition, than by a principle of true piety; and that his main view in these religious exploits was to subdue the converted nations under his dominion, and to tame them to his yoke, which they supported with impatience, and shook off by frequent revolts. It is, moreover, well known, that this boasted saint made no scruple of seeking the alliance of the infidel Saracens, that he might be more effectually enabled to crush the Greeks, notwithstanding their profession of the Christian religion" (p. 171). Thus was Christianity spread by fire and sword, and where-ever the cross passed it left its track in blood. While the soldiers thus converted the heathen, "the clergy abandoned themselves to their passions without moderation or restraint; they were distinguished by their luxury, their gluttony, and their lust" (p. 173). To these evils was added that of gross deception, for a bad clergy used bad weapons; false miracles abounded in every direction; "the corrupt discipline that then prevailed admitted of those fallacious stratagems, which are very improperly called pious frauds; nor did the heralds of the gospel think it at all unlawful to terrify or to allure to the profession of Christianity, by fictitious prodigies, those obdurate hearts which they could not subdue by reason and argument" (p. 171). The wealth of the Church increased year by year. "An opinion prevailed universally at this time, though its authors are not known, that the punishment which the righteous judge of the world has reserved for the transgressions of the wicked, was to be prevented and annulled by liberal donations to God, to the saints, to the churches and clergy. In consequence of this notion, the great and opulent—who were, generally speaking, the most remarkable for their flagitious and abominable lives—offered, out of

197

the abundance which they had received by inheritance or acquired by rapine, rich donations to departed saints, their ministers upon earth, and the keepers of the temples that were erected in their honour, in order to avoid the sufferings and penalties annexed by the priests to transgression in this life, and to escape the misery denounced against the wicked in a future state. This new and commodious method of making atonement for iniquity was the principal source of those immense treasures which, from this period, began to flow in upon the clergy, the churches, and monasteries, and continued to enrich them through succeeding ages down to the present time" (p. 174). Another source of wealth is to be found in the desire of the kings of the various warring tribes to attach to themselves the bishop and clergy in their dominions; by bestowing on these lands and dignities they secured to themselves the aid which the Church officials had it in their power to render, for not only could bishops bring to the support of their suzerain the physical succour of armies, but they could also launch against his enemies that terrible bolt of mediaeval times, excommunication, which, "rendered formidable by ignorance, struck terror into the boldest and most resolute hearts" (p. 174). In these latter gifts we see the origin of the temporalities and titles attached to episcopal sees and to cathedral chapters. During this century the power of the Roman Pontiff swelled to an enormous degree, and his sway extended into civil and political affairs: so supreme an authority had he become that, in A.D. 751, the Frankish states of the realm—convoked by Pepin to sanction his design of seizing on the French throne, then occupied by Childeric III.—directed that an embassy should be sent to the Pope Zachary, to ask whether it was not right that a weak monarch should be dethroned; and on the answer of the Pope in the affirmative being received, Childeric was dethroned without opposition, and Pepin was crowned in his stead.

In the East, the Church was torn with dissensions, while the imperial throne was rocking under the repeated attacks of the Turks—a tribe descended from the Tartars—who entered Armenia, struggled with the Saracens for dominion, subdued them partially, and then turned their arms against the Greek empire. The great controversy of this century is that on the worship of images, between the Iconoduli or Iconolatrae (image worshippers), and the Iconomachi or Iconoclastae (image breakers). The Emperor Bardanes, a supporter of the Monothelite heresy, ordered that a picture representing the sixth general council should be removed from the Church of St. Sophia, because that council had condemned the Monothelites. Not content with doing this (A.D. 712), Bardanes sent an order to Rome that all pictures and images of the same nature should be removed from places of worship. Constantine, the Pope, immediately set up six pictures, representing the six general councils, in the porch of St. Peter's, and called a council at Rome, which denounced the Emperor as an apostate. Bardanes was dethroned by a revolution, but his successor, Leo, soon took up the quarrel. In A.D. 726, he issued an imperial edict commanding the removal of all images from the churches and forbidding all image worship, save only those representing the crucifixion of Christ. Pope Gregory I. excommunicated the Emperor, and insurrections broke out all over the empire in consequence; the Emperor retorted by calling a council at Constantinople, which deposed the bishop of that city for his leanings towards image worship, and put a supporter of the Emperor in his place. The contest was carried on by Constantine, who succeeded his father, Leo, in A.D. 741, and who, in A.D. 754, called a council, at Constantinople—recognised by the Greek Church as the seventh general council—which condemned the use and worship of images. Leo IV. (A.D. 775) issued penal laws against image worshippers, but he was poisoned by Irene, his wife, in A.D. 780, and she entered into an alliance with Pope Adrian, so that the Iconoduli became triumphant in their turn. While this controversy raged, a second arose as to the procession of the Holy Ghost. The creed of Constantinople (see ante, p. 434) ran—"I believe in the Holy Ghost, the Lord and Giver of Life, who proceedeth from the Father;" to this phrase the words, "and the Son," had been added in the West, originally by some Spanish bishops; the Greeks protested against an unauthorised addition being inserted into a creed promulgated by a general council, and received by the universal Church as the symbol of faith. Thus arose the celebrated controversy on the "Filioque," which was one of the chief causes of the great schism between the Eastern and Western Churches in the ninth century.

The Arian, Manichæan, Marcionite, and Monothelite heresies spread, during this century, through the Greek Church, and, where the Arabians ruled, the Nestorians and Monophysites also flourished. In the Latin Church a phase of the Nestorian heresy made its way, under the name of Adoptianism, a name given because its adherents regarded Christ, so far as his manhood was concerned, as the Son of God by adoption only.

CENTURY IX

Christendom, during this century, as during the preceding one, was threatened and harassed by the inroads of Mahommedan powers, and the first gleams of returning light began to penetrate its thick darkness—light proceeding from the Arabians and the Saracens, the restorers of knowledge and of science. It is not here our duty to trace that marvellous work of the revival of thought—thought which Christianity had slain, but which, revived by Mahommedanism, was destined to issue in the new birth of heretic philosophy. While this work was proceeding among the Saracens, the Arabians, and the Moors, Christendom went on its way, degraded, vicious, and superstitious; only here and there an effort at learning was made, and some few went to the Arabian schools, and returned with some tincture of knowledge. John Scotus Erigena, a subtle and acute thinker, left behind him works which have made some regard him as the founder of the Realist school of the middle ages, the school which followed Aristotle, in opposition to the Nominalists, who held with Zeno and the Stoics. Erigena taught that the soul would be re-absorbed into the divine spirit, from which it had originally emanated; from God all things had come—to Him would they ultimately return; God alone was eternal, and in the end nothing but God would exist. Some of Erigena's works naturally fell under the displeasure of the Church, and were duly burned: he was a philosopher, and therefore dangerous.

While this slight effort at thought was thus frowned upon, vice made its way unchecked and unrebuked by the authorities. "The impiety and licentiousness of the greater part of the clergy arose, at this time, to an enormous height, and stand upon record in the unanimous complaints of the most candid and impartial writers of this century. In the East, tumult, discord, conspiracies, and treason reigned uncontrolled, and all things were carried by violence and force. These abuses appeared in many things, but particularly in the election of the Patriarchs of Constantinople.... In the western provinces, the bishops were become voluptuous and effeminate to a very high degree. They passed their lives amidst the splendour of courts, and the pleasures of a luxurious indolence, which corrupted their taste, extinguished their zeal, and rendered them incapable of performing the solemn duties of their function; while the inferior clergy were sunk in licentiousness, minded nothing but sensual gratifications, and infected with the most heinous vices the flock whom it was the very business of their ministry to preserve, or to deliver from the contagion of iniquity. Besides, the ignorance of the sacred order was, in many places, so deplorable that few of them could either read or write, and still fewer were capable of expressing their wretched notions with any degree of method or perspicuity" (p. 193). "Many other causes also contributed to dishonour the Church, by introducing into it a corrupt ministry. A nobleman who, through want of talents, activity, or courage, was rendered incapable of appearing with dignity in the cabinet, or with honour in the field, immediately turned his views towards the Church, aimed at a distinguished place among its chiefs and rulers, and became, in consequence, a contagious example of stupidity and vice to the inferior clergy. The patrons of churches, in whom resided the right of election, unwilling to submit their disorderly conduct to the keen censure of zealous and upright pastors, industriously looked for the most abject, ignorant, and worthless ecclesiastics, to whom they committed the cure of souls" (p. 193). Of the Roman pontiffs, Mosheim says: "The greatest

200

part of them are only known by the flagitious actions that have transmitted their names with infamy to our times" (p. 194). And "the enormous vices that must have covered so many pontiffs with infamy in the judgment of the wise, formed not the least obstacle to their ambition in these memorable times, nor hindered them from extending their influence and augmenting their authority both in church and state" (p. 195). Among the vast mass of forgeries which gradually built up the supremacy of the Roman see, the famous Isidorian Decretals deserve a word of notice. They were issued about A.D. 845, and consisted of "about one hundred pretended decrees of the early Popes, together with certain spurious writings of other church dignitaries and acts of synods. This forgery produced an immense extension of the papal power. It displaced the old system of church government, divesting it of the republican attributes it had possessed, and transforming it into an absolute monarchy. It brought the bishops into subjection to Rome, and made the pontiff the supreme judge of the clergy of the whole Christian world. It prepared the way for the great attempt, subsequently made by Hildebrand, to convert the states of Europe into a theocratic priest kingdom, with the Pope at its head" (Draper's "Conflict of Religion and Science," p. 271). We note during this century a remarkable growth of saints. Everyone wanted a saint through whom to approach God, and the supply kept pace with the demand. "This preposterous multiplication of saints was a new source of abuses and frauds. It was thought necessary to write the lives of these celestial patrons, in order to procure for them the veneration and confidence of a deluded multitude; and here lying wonders were invented, and all the resources of forgery and fable exhausted to celebrate exploits which had never been performed, and to perpetuate the memory of holy persons who had never existed" (p. 200). The contest on images still raged furiously, success being now on the one side, now on the other; various councils were called by either party, until, in A.D. 879, a council at Constantinople, reckoned by the Greeks as the eighth general council, sanctioned the worship of images, which thereafter triumphed in the East. In the West, the opposition to image-worship gradually died away. The Filioque contest also continued hotly and widened the breach between East and West yet more. The final separation was not long delayed. The ever-increasing jealousy between Rome and Constantinople had at last reached a height which made even nominal union impossible, and the smouldering fire burst into sudden flame. In A.D. 858 Photius was made Patriarch of Constantinople, by the Emperor Michael, in the room of Ignatius, deprived and banished by that prince. A council, held at Constantinople in A.D. 861, endorsed the appointment of the emperor; but Ignatius appealed to Rome, and Pope Nicholas I. readily took up his quarrel. A council was held at Rome, in A.D. 862, in which the pontiff excommunicated Photius and his adherents. It was answered by one at Constantinople, in A.D. 866, wherein Nicholas was pronounced unworthy of his office and outside the pale of Christian communion. Yet another council of Constantinople, A.D. 869, approved the action of Basilius, the new emperor, who recalled Ignatius, and imprisoned Photius. When Ignatius died, Photius was reinstated (A.D. 878), and he was acknowledged by the Roman pontiff, John VIII., at another council of Constantinople, A.D. 879, on the understanding that the jurisdiction over Bulgaria, claimed both by Pope and Patriarch, should be definitely yielded to Rome. This, however, was not done; and the Pope sent a legate to Constantinople, recalling his declaration in favour of Photius. The legate, Marinus, was cast into prison; and when he was later raised to the pontificate, he remembered the outrage, and anew excommunicated Photius. A.D. 886 saw the fall and imprisonment of Photius, and union might have been maintained but for the extravagant demands of the Roman pontiff, who required the degradation of all priests and bishops ordained by Photius. The Greeks indignantly refused, and at last the great schism took place, which severed from each other entirely the Eastern and the Western Churches.

The ancient heresy of the Paulicians had not yet died out, spite of having suffered much persecution at Catholic hands, and under the Emperors Michael and Leo, a fierce attack upon these unfortunate beings took place. They were hunted down and executed without mercy, and at last they turned upon their persecutors, and revenged themselves by murdering the bishop, magistrates, and judges in Armenia, after which they fled to the countries under Saracen rule. After a while, they gradually returned to the Greek empire; but when the Empress Theodora was regent, during her son's minority, she issued a stern decree against them. "The decree was severe, but the cruelty with which it was put in execution, by those who were sent into Armenia for that purpose, was horrible beyond expression; for these ministers of wrath, after confiscating the goods of above a hundred thousand of that miserable people, put their possessors to death in the most barbarous manner, and made them expire slowly in a variety of the most exquisite tortures" (p. 212).

In addition to the heresies inherited from the previous centuries, three new ones, important in their issues, arose to divide yet more the divided indivisible Church. A monk, named Pascasius Radbert, wrote a treatise (A.D. 831 and 845), in which he maintained that, at the Eucharist, the substance of the bread and wine became changed, by consecration, into the body and blood of Christ, and that this body "was the same body that was born of the Virgin, that suffered upon the cross, and was raised from the dead" (p. 205). Charles the Bald bade Erigena and Ratramn (or Bertramn) draw up the true doctrine of the Church, and the long controversy began which is continued even in the present day. The second great dispute arose on the question of predestination and divine grace. Godeschalcus, an eminent Saxon monk, returning from Rome in A.D. 847, resided for a space in Verona, where he spoke much on predestination, affirming that God had, from all eternity, predestined some to heaven and others to hell. He was condemned at a council held in Mayence, A.D. 848, and in the following year, at another council, he was again condemned, and was flogged until he burned, with his own hand, the apology for his opinions he had presented at Mayence. The third great controversy regarded the manner of Christ's birth, and monks furiously disputed whether or no Christ was born after the fashion of other infants. The details of this dispute need not here be entered into.

CENTURY X

"The deplorable state of Christianity in this century, arising partly from that astonishing ignorance that gave a loose rein both to superstition and immorality, and partly from an unhappy concurrence of causes of another kind, is unanimously lamented by the various writers who have transmitted to us the history of these miserable times" (p. 213). Yet "the gospel" spread. The Normans embraced "a religion of which they were totally ignorant" (p. 214), A.D. 912, because Charles the Simple of France offered Count Rollo a large territory on condition that he would marry his daughter and embrace Christianity: Rollo gladly accepted the territory and its encumbrances. Poland came next into the fold of the Church, for the Duke of Poland, Micislaus, was persuaded by his wife to profess Christianity, A.D. 965, and Pope John III. promptly sent a bishop and a train of priests to convert the duke's subjects. "But the exhortations and endeavours of these devout missionaries, who were unacquainted with the language of the people they came to instruct [how effective must have been their arguments!] would have been entirely without effect, had they not been accompanied with the edicts and penal laws, the promises and threats of Micislaus, which dejected the courage and conquered the obstinacy of the reluctant Poles" (p. 214). "The Christian religion was established in Russia by means every way similar to those that had occasioned its propagation in Poland" (p. 215); the Greek wife of the Russian duke persuaded him to adopt her creed, and he was baptized A.D. 987. Mosheim assumes that the Russian people followed their princes of their own accord, since "we have, at least, no account of any compulsion or violence being employed in their conversion" (p. 215); if the Russians adopted Christianity without compulsion or violence, all we can say is, that their conversion is unique. The Danes were converted in A.D. 949, Otto the Great having defeated them, and having made it an imperative condition of peace, that they should profess Christianity. The Norwegians accepted the religion of Jesus on the same terms. Thus the greater part of Europe became Christian, and we even hear a cry raised by Pope Sylvester II. for the deliverance of Palestine from the Mahommedans—for a holy war. Christianity having now become so strong, learning had become proportionately weak; it had been sinking lower and lower during each succeeding epoch, and in this tenth century it reached its deepest stage of degradation. "The deplorable ignorance of this barbarous age, in which the drooping arts were entirely neglected, and the sciences seemed to be upon the point of expiring for want of encouragement, is unanimously confessed and lamented by all the writers who have transmitted to us any accounts of this period of time" (p. 218). In vain a more enlightened emperor in the East strove to revive learning and encourage study: "many of the most celebrated authors of antiquity were lost, at this time, through the sloth and negligence of the Greeks" (p. 219). "Nor did the cause of philosophy fare better than that of literature. Philosophers, indeed, there were; and, among them, some that were not destitute of genius and abilities; but none who rendered their names immortal by productions that were worthy of being transmitted to posterity" (p. 219). So low, under the influence of Christianity, had sunk the literature of Greece—Greece Pagan, which once brought forth Pythagoras, Socrates, Plato, Euclid, Zenophon, and many another mighty one, whose fame rolls down the ages—that Greece had become Greece Christian, and the vitality of her motherhood had been drained from her, and left her without strength to conceive men. In the West things were yet worse—instead of Rome Pagan, that had spread light and civilization—the Rome of Cicero, of Virgil, of Lucretius—we have Rome Christian, spreader of darkness and of degradation, the Rome of the Popes and the monks. The Latins "were, almost without exception, sunk in the most brutish and barbarous ignorance, so that, according to the unanimous accounts of the most credible writers, nothing could be more melancholy and deplorable than the darkness that reigned in the western world during this century.... In the seminaries of learning, such as they were, the seven liberal sciences were taught in the most unskilful and miserable manner, and that by the monks, who esteemed the arts and sciences no further than as they were subservient to the interests of religion, or, to speak more properly, to the views of superstition" (p. 219). But the light from Arabia was struggling to penetrate Christendom. Gerbert, a native of France, travelled into Spain, and studied in the Arabian schools of Cordova and Seville, under Arabian doctors; he developed mathematical ability, and returned into Christendom with some amount of learning: raised to the papal throne, under the name of Sylvester II., he tried to restore the study of science and philosophy, and found that his geometrical figures "were regarded by the monks as magical operations," and he himself "as a magician and a disciple of Satan" (p. 220).

The vice of the clergy was something terrible. "These corruptions were mounted to the most enormous height in that dismal period of the Church which we have now before us. Both in the eastern and western provinces, the clergy were, for the most part, composed of a most worthless set of men, shamefully illiterate and stupid, ignorant, more especially in religious matters, equally enslaved to sensuality and superstition, and capable of the most abominable and flagitious deeds. This dismal degeneracy of the sacred order was, according to the most credible accounts, principally owing to the pretended chiefs and rulers of the universal Church, who indulged themselves in the commission of the most odious crimes, and abandoned themselves to the lawless impulse of the most licentious passions without reluctance or remorse—who confounded, in short, all difference between just and unjust, to satisfy their impious ambition, and whose spiritual empire was such a diversified scene of iniquity and violence as never was exhibited under any of those temporal tyrants who have been the scourges of mankind" (p. 221). Such is the verdict passed on Christian rule by a Christian historian. In the East we see such men as Theophylact; "this exemplary prelate, who sold every ecclesiastical benefice as soon as it became vacant, had in his stable above 2000 hunting horses, which he fed with pignuts, pistachios, dates, dried grapes, figs steeped in the most exquisite wines, to all which he added the richest perfumes. One Holy Thursday, as he was celebrating high-mass, his groom brought him the joyful news that one of his favourite mares had foaled; upon which he threw down the Liturgy, left the church, and ran in raptures to the stable, where, having expressed his joy at that grand event, he returned to the altar to finish the divine service, which he had left interrupted during his absence" (p. 221, note). We shall see, in a moment, how the masses of the people were housed and fed while such insane luxury surrounded horses. In the west, the weary tale of the Roman pontiffs cannot all be narrated here. Take the picture as drawn by Hallam: "This dreary interval is filled up, in the annals of the papacy, by a series of revolutions and crimes. Six popes were deposed, two murdered, one mutilated. Frequently two, or even three, competitors, among whom it is not always possible by any genuine criticism to distinguish the true shepherd, drove each other alternately from the city. A few respectable names appear thinly scattered through this darkness; and sometimes, perhaps, a pope who had acquired estimation by his private virtues may be distinguished by some encroachment on the rights of princes, or the privileges of national churches. But, in general, the pontiffs of that age had neither leisure nor capacity to perfect the great system of temporal supremacy, and looked rather to a vile profit from the sale of episcopal confirmations, or of exemptions to monasteries. The corruption of the head extended naturally to all other members of the Church. All writers concur in stigmatizing the dissoluteness and neglect of decency that prevailed among the clergy. Though several codes of ecclesiastical

205

discipline had been compiled by particular prelates, yet neither these nor the ancient canons were much regarded. The bishops, indeed, who were to enforce them, had most occasion to dread their severity. They were obtruded upon their sees, as the supreme pontiffs were upon that of Rome, by force or corruption. A child of five years old was made Archbishop of Rheims. The see of Narbonne was purchased for another at the age of ten" ("Europe during the Middle Ages," p. 353, ed. 1869). John X. made pope at the solicitation of his mistress Theodora, the mother-in-law of the sovereign, and murdered at the instance of Theodora's daughter, Marozia; John XI., illegitimate son of the same Marozia, and of the celibate pontiff, Sergius III.; Boniface VII. expelled, banished, returning and murdering the reigning pope: what avails it to chronicle these monsters? Below the popes, a clergy as vicious as their rulers, squandering money, plundered from the people in dissoluteness and luxury. And the people, what of them?

As late as A.D. 1430 the houses of the peasantry were "constructed of stones put together without mortar; the roofs were of turf—a stiffened bull's-hide served for a door. The food consisted of coarse vegetable products, such as peas, and even the bark of trees. In some places they were unacquainted with bread. Cabins of reeds plastered with mud, houses of wattled stakes, chimneyless peat fires, from which there was scarcely an escape for the smoke, dens of physical and moral pollution swarming with vermin, wisps of straw twisted round the limbs to keep off the cold, the ague-stricken peasant with no help except shrine-cure," i.e., cure by the touching bone of saint, or image of virgin (Draper's "Conflict between Religion and Science," p. 265). Even among the wealthy, the life was coarse and rough; carpets were unknown; drainage never thought of. The Anglo-Saxon "'nobles, devoted to gluttony and voluptuousness, never visited the church, but the matins and the mass were read over to them by a hurrying priest in their bed-chambers, before they rose, themselves not listening. The common people were a prey to the more powerful; their property was seized, their bodies dragged away to distant countries; their maidens were either thrown into a brothel or sold for slaves. Drinking, day and night, was the general pursuit: vices, the companions of inebriety, followed, effeminating the manly mind.' The baronial castles were dens of robbers. The Saxon chronicler [William of Malmesbury, from whom the quotation above] records how men and women were caught and dragged into those strongholds, hung up by their thumbs or feet, fire applied to them, knotted strings twisted round their heads, and many other torments inflicted to extort ransom" (Ibid, p. 266). When the barons had nearly finished their evil lives, the church stepped in, claiming her share of the plunder and the wealth thus amassed, and opening the gates of paradise to the dying thief. The cities were as wretched as their inhabitants: no paving, no cleaning, no lighting. In the country the old Roman roads were unmended, unkept;

Europe was slipping backwards into uttermost barbarism. Meanwhile things were very different where the blighting power of Christianity was not in the ascendant. "Europe at the present day does not offer more taste, more refinement, more elegance, than might have been seen, at the epoch of which we are speaking, in the capitals of the Spanish Arabs. Their streets were lighted and solidly paved. The houses were frescoed and carpeted; they were warmed in winter by furnaces, and cooled in summer with perfumed air brought by underground pipes from flower-beds. They had baths, and libraries, and dining-halls, fountains of quicksilver and water. City and country were full of conviviality, and of dancing to the lute and mandolin. Instead of the drunken and gluttonous wassail orgies of their northern neighbours, the feasts of the Saracens were marked by sobriety. Wine was prohibited.... In the tenth century, the Khalif Hakem II. had made beautiful Andalusia the paradise of the world. Christians, Mussulmans, Jews, mixed together without restraint.... All learned men, no matter from what country they came, or what their religious views, were welcomed. The khalif had in his palace a manufactory of books, and copyists, binders, illuminators. He kept book-buyers in all the great cities of Asia and Africa. His library contained 400,000 volumes, superbly bound and illuminated" (Ibid, pp. 141, 142). When the Christians in the fifteenth century seized "beautiful Andalusia," they erected the Inquisition, burned the books, burned the people, banished the Jews and the Moors, and founded the miserable land known as modern Spain.

There was but little heresy during this melancholy century; people did not think enough even to think badly. The Paulicians spread through Bulgaria, and established themselves there under a patriarch of their own. Some Arians still existed. Some Anthropomorphites gave some trouble, maintaining that God sat on a golden throne, and was served by angels with wings: their "heresy" is, however, directly supported by the Scriptures. A.D. 999, a man named Lentard began to speak against the worship of images, and the payment of tithes to priests, and asserted that in the Old Testament prophecies truth and falsehood are mingled. His disciples seem to have merged into the Albigenses in the next century.

The year A.D. 1000 deserves a special word of notice. Christians fancied that the world was to last for but one thousand years after the birth of Christ, and that it would therefore come to an end in A.D. 1000. "Many charters begin with these words: 'As the world is now drawing to its close.' An army marching under the emperor Otho I. was so terrified by an eclipse of the sun, which it conceived to announce this consummation, as to disperse hastily on all sides" ("Europe during the Middle Ages," Hallam, P. 599) "Prodigious numbers of people abandoned all their civil connections, and their parental relations, and giving over to the churches or monasteries all their lands, treasures, and worldly effects, repaired with the utmost precipitation to Palestine, where they imagined that Christ would descend to judge the world. Others devoted themselves by a solemn and voluntary oath to the service of the churches, convents, and priesthood, whose slaves, they became in the most rigorous sense of that word, performing daily their heavy tasks; and all this from a notion that the Supreme Judge would diminish the severity of their sentence, and look upon them with a more favourable and propitious eye, on account of their having made themselves the slaves of his ministers. When an eclipse of the sun or moon happened to be visible, the cities were deserted, and their miserable inhabitants fled for refuge to hollow caverns, and hid themselves among the craggy rocks, and under the bending summits of steep mountains. The opulent attempted to bribe the Deity and the saintly tribe, by rich donations conferred upon the sacerdotal and monastic orders, who were looked upon as the immediate vicegerents of heaven" (p. 226). Thus the Church still reaped wealth out of the fear of the people she deluded, and while fields lay unsown, and houses stood unrepaired, and the foundations of famine were laid, Mother Church gathered lands and money into her capacious lap, and troubled little about the starving children, provided she herself could wax fat on the good things of the world which she professed to have renounced.

CENTURY XI

The Prussians, during this century, were driven into the fold of the Church. A Christian missionary, Adalbert, bishop of Prague, had been murdered by the "fierce and savage Prussians," and in order to show the civilising results of the gentle Christian creed, Boleslaus, king of Poland, entered "into a bloody war with the Prussians, and he obtained, by the force of penal laws and of a victorious, army, what Adalbert could not effect by exhortation and argument. He dragooned this savage people into the Christian Church" (p. 230). Some of his followers tried a gentler method of conversion, and were murdered by the Prussians, who clearly saw no reason why Christians should do all the killing. We have already seen that Sylvester II. called upon the Christian princes to commence a "holy war" against "the infidels" who held the holy places of Christianity. Gregory VII. strove to stir them up in like fashion, and had gathered together an army of upwards of 50,000 men, whom he proposed to lead in person into Palestine. The Pope, however, quarrelled with Henry IV., emperor of Germany, and his project fell through. At the close of this century, the long-talked of effort was made. Peter the Hermit, who had travelled through Palestine, came into Europe and related in all directions tales of the sufferings of the Christians under the rule of the "barbarous" Saracens. He appealed to Urban II., the then Pope, and Urban, who at first discouraged him, seeing that Peter had succeeded in rousing the most warlike nations of Christian Europe into enthusiasm, called a council at Placentia, A.D. 1095, and appealed to the Christian princes to take up the cause of the Cross. The council was not successful, and Urban summoned another at Clermont, and himself addressed the assembly. "It is the will of God" was the shout that answered him, and the people flew to arms. "Every means was used to excite an epidemical frenzy, the remission of penance, the dispensation from those practices of self-denial which superstition imposed or suspended at pleasure, the absolution of all sins, and the assurance of eternal felicity. None doubted that such as persisted in the war received immediately the reward of martyrdom. False miracles and fanatical prophecies, which were never so frequent, wrought up the enthusiasm to a still higher pitch. [Mosheim states, p. 231, that Peter the Hermit carried about with him a letter from heaven, calling on all true Christians to deliver their brethren from the infidel yoke.] And these devotional feelings, which are usually thwarted and balanced by other passions, fell in with every motive that could influence the men of that time, with curiosity, restlessness, the love of licence, thirst for war, emulation, ambition. Of the princes who assumed the cross, some, probably from the beginning, speculated upon forming independent establishments in the East. In later periods, the temporal benefits of undertaking a crusade undoubtedly blended themselves with less selfish considerations. Men resorted to Palestine, as in modern times they have done to the colonies, in order to redeem their time, or repair their fortune. Thus Gui de Lusignan, after flying from France for murder, was ultimately raised to the throne of Jerusalem. To the more vulgar class were held out inducements which, though absorbed in the more overruling fanaticism of the first crusade, might be exceedingly efficacious when it began rather to flag. During the time that a crusader bore the cross, he was free from suit for his debts, and the interest of them was entirely abolished; he was exempted, in some instances, at least, from taxes, and placed under the protection of the Church, so that he could not be impleaded in any civil court, except on criminal charges, or disputes relating to land" ("Europe during the Middle Ages," Hallam, pp. 29, 30). Thus fanaticism and earthly pleasures and benefits all pushed men in the same direction, and Europe flung itself upon Palestine. Men, women, and children, poured eastwards in that first crusade, and this mixed vanguard of the coming army of warriors was led by Peter the Hermit and Gaultier Sans-Avoir. This vanguard was "a motley assemblage of monks, prostitutes, artists, labourers, lazy tradesmen, merchants, boys, girls, slaves, malefactors, and profligate debauchees;" "it was principally composed of the lowest dregs of the multitude, who were animated solely by the prospect of spoil and plunder, and hoped to make their fortunes by this holy campaign" (p. 232). "This first division, in their march through Hungary and Thrace, committed the most flagitious crimes, which so incensed the inhabitants of the countries through which they passed, particularly those of Hungary and Turcomania, that they rose up in arms and massacred the greatest part of them" (Ibid). "Father Maimbourg, notwithstanding his immoderate zeal for the holy war, and that fabulous turn which enables him to represent it in the most favourable points of view, acknowledges frankly that the first division of this prodigious army committed the most abominable enormities in the countries through which they passed, and that there was no kind of insolence, in justice, impurity, barbarity, and violence, of which they were not guilty. Nothing, perhaps, in the annals of history can equal the flagitious deeds of this infernal rabble" (Ibid, note). Few of these unhappy wretches reached the Holy Land. "To engage in the crusade and to perish in it, were almost synonymous" (Hallam, p. 30), even for those who entered Palestine. The loss of life was something terrible. "We should be warranted by contemporary writers in stating the loss of the Christians alone during this period at nearly a million; but at the least computation, it must have exceeded half that number" (Ibid). The real army, under Godfrey de Bouillon, consisted of some 80,000 well-appointed horse and foot. But at Nice the crowd of crusaders numbered 700,000, after the great slaughter in Hungary. Jerusalem was taken, A.D. 1099, and it was there "where their triumph was consummated, that it was stained with the most atrocious massacre; not limited to the hour of resistance, but renewed deliberately even after that famous penitential procession to the holy sepulchre, which might have calmed their ferocious dispositions if, through the misguided enthusiasm of the enterprise, it had not been rather calculated to excite them" (Ibid, p. 31). The last crusade occurred A.D. 1270, and between the first in 1096 and the last in 1270, human lives were extinguished in numbers it is impossible to reckon, increasing ever the awful sum total of the misery lying at the foot of the blood-red cross of Christendom.

A collateral advantage accrued to the clergy through the crusades; "their wealth, continually accumulated, enabled them to become the regular purchasers of landed estates, especially in the time of the crusades, when the fiefs of the nobility were constantly in the market for sale or mortgage" (Ibid, p. 333).

The last vestiges of nominal paganism were erased in this century, and it remained only under Christian names. Capital punishment was proclaimed against all who worshipped the old deities under their old titles, and "this dreadful severity contributed much more towards the extirpation of paganism, than the exhortations and instructions of ignorant missionaries, who were unacquainted with the true nature of the gospel, and dishonoured its pure and holy doctrines by their licentious lives and their superstitious practices" (p. 236). Learning began to revive, as men, educated in the Arabian schools, gradually spread over Europe; thus: "the school of Salernum, in the kingdom of Naples, was renowned above all others for the study of physic in this century, and vast numbers crowded thither from all the provinces of Europe to receive instruction in the art of healing; but the medical precepts which rendered the doctors of Salernum so famous were all derived from the writings of the Arabians, or from the schools of the Saracens in Spain and Africa" (p. 237). "About the year 1050, the face of philosophy began to change, and the science of logic assumed a new aspect. This revolution began in France, where several of the books of Aristotle had been brought from the schools of the Saracens in Spain, and it was effected by a set of men highly renowned for their abilities and genius, such as Berenger, Roscellinus, Hildebert, and after them by Gilbert de la Porre, the famous Abelard and others" (p. 238). Thus we see that in science, in philosophy, in logic, we alike owe to Arabia the revival of thought in Christendom. Progress, however, was very slow, and the thought was not yet strong enough to arouse the fears of the Church, so it spread for a while in peace.

Hallam sums up for us the state of learning, or rather of ignorance, during the eighth, ninth, tenth and eleventh centuries, and his account may well find its place here. "When Latin had thus ceased to be a living language, the whole treasury of knowledge was locked up from the eyes of the people. The few who might have imbibed a taste for literature, if books had been accessible to them, were reduced to abandon pursuits that could only be cultivated through a kind of education not easily within their reach. Schools confined to cathedrals and monasteries, and exclusively designed for the purposes of religion, afforded no encouragement or opportunities to the laity. The worst effect was that, as the newly-formed languages were hardly made use of in writing, Latin being still preserved in all legal instruments and public correspondence, the very use of letters, as well as of books, was forgotten. For many centuries, to sum up the account of ignorance in a word, it was rare for a layman, of whatever rank, to know how to sign his name. Their charters, till the use of seals became general, were subscribed with the mark of the cross. Still more extraordinary it was to find one who had any tincture of learning. Even admitting every indistinct commendation of a monkish biographer (with whom a knowledge of church music would pass for literature), we could make out a very short list of scholars. None certainly were more distinguished as such than Charlemagne and Alfred. But the former, unless we reject a very plain testimony, was incapable of writing; and Alfred found difficulty in making a translation from the pastoral instruction of St. Gregory, on account of his imperfect knowledge of Latin. Whatever mention, therefore, we find of learning and the

211

learned, during these dark ages, must be understood to relate only to such as were within the pale of clergy, which indeed was pretty extensive, and comprehended many who did not exercise the offices of religious ministry. But even the clergy were, for a long period, not very materially superior, as a body, to the uninstructed laity. An inconceivable cloud of ignorance overspread the whole face of the Church, hardly broken by a few glimmering lights, who owe almost the whole of their distinction to the surrounding darkness.... Of this prevailing ignorance it is easy to produce abundant testimony. Contracts were made verbally, for want of notaries capable of drawing up charters; and these, when written, were frequently barbarous and ungrammatical to an incredible degree. For some considerable intervals, scarcely any monument of literature has been preserved, except a few jejune chronicles, the vilest legends of saints, or verses equally destitute of spirit and metre. In almost every council the ignorance of the clergy forms a subject for reproach. It is asserted by one held in 992, that scarcely a single person was to be found in Rome itself who knew the first element of letters. Not one priest of a thousand in Spain, about the age of Charlemagne, could address a common letter of salutation to another. In England, Alfred declares that he could not recollect a single priest south of the Thames (the most civilised part of England) at the time of his accession who understood the ordinary prayers, or could translate Latin into his mother-tongue. Nor was this better in the time of Dunstan, when it is said, none of the clergy knew how to write or translate a Latin letter. The homilies which they preached were compiled for their use by some bishops, from former works of the same kind, or the writings of the Christian fathers.... If we would listen to some literary historians, we should believe that the darkest ages contained many individuals, not only distinguished among their contemporaries, but positively eminent for abilities and knowledge. A proneness to extol every monk of whose productions a few letters or a devotional treatise survives, every bishop of whom it is related that he composed homilies, runs through the laborious work of the Benedictines of St. Maur, the 'Literary History of France,' and, in a less degree, is observable even in Tiraboschi, and in most books of this class. Bede, Alcuin, Hincmar, Raban, and a number of inferior names, become real giants of learning in their uncritical panegyrics. But one might justly say, that ignorance is the smallest defect of the writers of these dark ages. Several of these were tolerably acquainted with books; but that wherein they are uniformly deficient is original argument or expression. Almost every one is a compiler of scraps from the fathers, or from such semi-classical authors as Boethius, Cassiodorus, or Martinus Capella. Indeed, I am not aware that there appeared more than two really considerable men in the republic of letters from the sixth to the middle of the eleventh century—John, surnamed Scotus, or Erigena, a native of Ireland, and Gerbert, who became pope by the name of Sylvester II.: the first endowed with a bold and acute metaphysical genius, the second excellent, for the time when he lived, in mathematical science and useful mechanical invention" ("Europe during the Middle Ages," Hallam, pp. 595-598).

If we look at the ministers of the Church, the old story of tyranny and vice is told over again during this century. Among its popes is numbered Benedict IX., deposed for his profligacy, restored and again deposed, restored by force of arms, and selling the pontificate, so that three popes at once claimed the tiara, and were all three declared unworthy, and a fourth placed on the throne. Fresh disturbances followed, and new usurpers, until in A.D. 1059 the election of the pope was taken out of the hands of the people and transferred to the college of cardinals, a change which was much struggled against, but which was ultimately adopted. In A.D. 1073 Hildebrand was elected pope under the title of Gregory VII.; this man, perhaps, more than any other, augmented the temporal power of the papacy. It was he who moulded the church into the form of an absolute monarchy, and fought against all local privileges and national freedom of the churches in each land; it was he who claimed rule over all kings and princes, and treated them as vassals of the Roman see; it was he who, in 1074, calling a council at Rome, caused it to decree the celibacy of the clergy, so that priests having no home, and no family ties, might feel their only home in the Church, and their only tie to Rome; it was he who struggled against Germany, and who kept the excommunicated emperor standing barefoot and almost naked in the snow for three days, in the courtyard of his castle. A bold bad man was this Hildebrand, but a man of genius and a master-mind, who conceived the mighty idea of a universal Church, wherein all princes should be vassals, and the head of the Church absolute monarch of the world.

It was at the annual council of Rome, A.D. 1076, that Pope Gregory VII. recited and proclaimed "all the ancient maxims, all the doubtful traditions, all the excessive pretensions, by which he could support his supremacy. It was, in a manner, the abridged code of his domination—the laws of servitude that he proposed to the world at large. Here are the terms of this charter of theocracy: 'The Roman Church is founded by God alone. The Roman pontiff alone can legitimately take the title of universal ... There shall be no intercourse whatever held with persons excommunicated by the Pope, and none may dwell in the same house with them.... He alone may wear the imperial insignia. All the princes of the earth shall kiss the feet of the Pope, but of none other.... He has the right of deposing emperors.... The sentence of the Pope can be revoked by none, and he alone can revoke the sentences passed by others. He can be judged by none. None may dare to pronounce sentence on one who appeals to the See Apostolic. To it shall be referred all major causes by the whole Church. The Church of Rome never has erred, and never can err, as Scripture warrants. A Roman pontiff, canonically ordained, at once becomes, by the merit of Saint Peter, indubitably holy. By his order and with his permission it is lawful for subjects to accuse princes.... The Pope can loose subjects from the oath of fealty.' Such are the fundamental articles promulgated by Gregory VII. in the Council of Rome, which the official historian of the Church reproduced in the commencement of the seventeenth century as being authentic and legitimate, and Rome has never disavowed it. Borrowed in part from the false Decretals, resting, most of them, on the fabulous donation of Constantine, and on the successive impostures and usurpations of the first barbarous ages, they received from the hand of Gregory VII. a new character of force and unity. That pontiff stamped them with the sanction of his own genius. Such authority had never before been created: it made every other power useless and subaltern" ("Life of Gregory VII.," by Villemain, trans. by Brockley, vol. ii., pp. 53-55). Thus the struggle became inevitable between the temporal and the spiritual powers. "In every country there was a dual government:—1. That of a local kind, represented by a temporal sovereign. 2. That of a foreign kind, acknowledging the authority of the Pope. This Roman influence was, in the nature of things, superior to the local; it expressed the sovereign will of one man over all the nations of the continent conjointly, and gathered overwhelming power from its compactness and unity. The local influence was necessarily of a feeble nature, since it was commonly weakened by the rivalries of conterminous states and the dissensions dexterously provoked by its competitor. On not a single occasion could the various European states form a coalition against their common antagonist. Whenever a question arose, they were skilfully taken in detail, and commonly mastered. The ostensible object of papal intrusion was to secure for the different peoples, moral well-being; the real object was to obtain large revenues and give support to large bodies of ecclesiastics. The revenues thus abstracted were not unfrequently many times greater than those passing into the treasury of the local power. Thus, on the occasion of Innocent IV. demanding provision to be made for three hundred additional Italian clergy by the Church of England, and that one of his nephews, a mere boy, should have a stall in Lincoln Cathedral, it was found that the sum already annually abstracted by foreign ecclesiastics from England was thrice that which went into the coffers of the king. While thus the higher clergy secured every political appointment worth having, and abbots vied with counts in the herds of slaves they possessed—some, it is said, owned not fewer than twenty thousand—begging friars pervaded society in all directions, picking up a share of what still remained to the poor. There was a vast body of non-producers, living in idleness and owning a foreign allegiance, who were subsisting on the fruits of the toil of the labourers" ("Conflict between Religion and Science," Draper, pp. 266, 267).

The struggle between the Greek and Latin Churches, hushed for awhile, broke out again fiercely A.D. 1053, and in 1054 Rome excommunicated Constantinople, and Constantinople excommunicated Rome. The disputes as to transubstantiation continued, and shook the Roman Church with their violence. Outside orthodoxy, some of the old heresies lingered on. The Paulicians wandered throughout Europe, and became known in Italy as the Paterini and the Cathari, in France as the Albigenses, Bulgarians, or Publicans. The Council of Orleans condemned them to be burned alive, and many perished.

CENTURY XII

The wars which spread Christianity were not yet entirely over, but we only hear of them now on the outskirts, so to speak, of Europe, except where some tribes apostatized now and then, and were brought back to the true faith by the sword. The struggles between the popes and the more stiff-necked princes as to their relative rights and privileges continued, and we sometimes see the curious spectacle of a pontiff on the side of the people, or rather of the barons, against the king: whenever this is so, we find that the king is struggling against Roman supremacy, and that the pope uses the power of the nation to subdue the rebellious monarch. We do not find Rome interfering to save the people from oppression when the oppressor is a faithful and obedient son of Holy Church.

Fresh heresies spread during this century, and we everywhere met with one corrective—death. Most of them appear to have grown out of the old Manichæan heresy, and taught much of the old asceticism. The Cathari were hunted down and put to death throughout Italy. Arnold of Brescia, who loudly protested against the possessions of the Church, and maintained that church revenues should be handed over to the State, proved himself so extremely distasteful to the clergy that they arrested him, crucified him and burned his dead body (A.D. 1155). Peter de Bruys, who objected to infant baptism, and may be called the ancestor of the Baptists, was burnt A.D. 1130. Many other reformers shared the same fate, and one large sect must here be noted. Peter Waldus, its founder, was a merchant of Lyons, who (A.D. 1160) employed a priest to translate the Gospels for him, together with other portions of the Bible. Studying these, he resolved to abandon his business and distribute his wealth among the poor, and, in A.D. 1180, he became a public preacher, and formed an association to teach the doctrines of the Gospel, as he conceived them, against the doctrines of the Church. The sect first assumed only the simple name of "the poor men of Lyons," but soon became known as the Waldenses, one of the most powerful and most widely spread sects of the Middle Ages. They

215

were, in fact, the precursors of the Reformation, and are notable as heretics protesting against the authorty of Rome because that authority did not commend itself to their reason; thus they asserted the right of private judgment, and for that assertion they deserve a niche in the great temple of heretic thought.

CENTURY XIII

In the far west of Europe paganism still struggled against Christianity, and from A.D. 1230 to 1280 a long, fierce war was waged against the Prussians, to confirm them in the Christian faith; the Teutonic knights of St. Mary succeeded finally in their apostolic efforts, and at last "established Christianity and fixed their own dominion in Prussia" (p. 309), whence they made forays into the neighbouring countries, and "pillaged, burned, massacred, and ruined all before them." In Spain, Christianity had a yet sadder triumph, for there the civilized Moors were falling under the brutal Christians, and the "garden of the world" was being invaded by the hordes of the Roman Church. The end, however, had not yet come. In France, we see the erection of THE INQUISITION, the most hateful and fiendish tribunal ever set up by religion. The heretical sects were spreading rapidly in southern provinces of France, and Innocent III., about the commencement of this century, sent legates extraordinary into the southern provinces of France to do what the bishops had left undone, and to extirpate heresy, in all its various forms and modifications, without being at all scrupulous in using such methods as might be necessary to effect this salutary purpose. The persons charged with this ghostly commission were Rainier, a Cistercian monk, Pierre de Castelnau, archdeacon of Maguelonne, who became also afterwards a Cistercian friar. These eminent missionaries were followed by several others, among whom was the famous Spaniard, Dominic, founder of the order of preachers, who, returning from Rome in the year 1206, fell in with these delegates, embarked in their cause, and laboured both by his exhortations and actions in the extirpation of heresy. These spiritual champions, who engaged in this expedition upon the sole authority of the pope, without either asking the advice, or demanding the succours of the bishops, and who inflicted capital punishment upon such of the heretics as they could not convert by reason and argument, were distinguished in common discourse by the title of inquisitors, and from them the formidable and odious tribunal called the Inquisition derived its origin (pp. 343, 344). In A.D. 1229, a council of Toulouse "erected in every city a council of inquisitors consisting of one priest and two laymen" (Ibid). In A.D. 1233, Gregory IX. superseded this tribunal by appointing the Dominican monks as inquisitors, and the pope's legate in France thereupon went from city to city, wherever these monks had a monastery, and there appointed some of their number "inquisitors of heretical pravity." The princes of Europe were then persuaded to lend the aid of the State to the work of blood, and to commit to the flames those who were handed over as heretics to the civil power by the inquisitors. The plan of working was most methodical.

The rules of torture were carefully drawn out: the prisoner was stripped naked, the hair cut off, and the body then laid on the rack and bound down; the right, then the left, foot tightly bound and strained by cords; the right and left arm stretched; the fleshy part of the arm compressed with fine cords; all the cords tightened together by one turn; a second and third turn of the same kind: beyond this, with the rack, women were not to be tortured; with men a fourth turn was employed. These directions were written in a Manual, used by the Grand Inquisitor of Seville as late as A.D. 1820. An analysis is given by Dr. Rule, in his "History of the Inquisition," Appendix to vol. i., pp. 339-359, ed. 1874. Then we hear, elsewhere, of torture by roasting the feet, by pulleys, by red-hot pincers—in short, by every abominable instrument of cruelty which men, inspired by religion, could conceive. Let the student take Llorente and Dr. Rule alone, and he will learn enough of the Inquisition horrors to make him shudder at the sight of a cross—at the name of Christianity.

Llorente gives the most revolting details of the torture of Jean de Salas, at Valladolid, A.D. 1527, and this one case may serve as a specimen of Inquisition work during these bloodstained centuries. Stripped to his shirt, he was placed on the chevalet (a narrow frame, wherein the body was laid, with no support save a pole across the middle), and his feet were raised higher than his head; tightly twisted cords cut through his flesh, and were twisted yet tighter and tighter as the torture proceeded; fine linen, thrust into his mouth and throat, added to the unnatural position, made breathing well nigh impossible, and on the linen water slowly fell, drop by drop, from a suspended vessel over his head, till every struggling breath stained the cloth with blood (see "Histoire critique de l'Inquisition d'Espagne," t. II., pp. 20-23, ed. 1818). This Spanish Inquisition, during its existence, punished heretics as follows:—

Burnt Alive 31,912
Burnt in effigy 17,659
Heavily punished 291,450
Total 341,021

(Ibid, t. IV. p. 271). Add to this list the ruined families, some of whose members fell victims to the Inquisition, and then—remembering that Spain was but one of the countries which it desolated—let the student judge of the huge total of human agony caused by this awful institution. Nor must it be forgotten that its dungeons did not gape only for those who opposed the pretensions of Rome; men of science, philosophers, thinkers, all these were its foes; Llorente gives a list of no less than 119 learned and eminent scientific men who, in Spain alone, fell under the scourge of the Inquisition (see t. II. pp. 417-483).

One special crime of the Church in this age must not be forgotten: her treatment of Roger Bacon. Roger Bacon was a Franciscan monk, who not only studied Greek, Hebrew, and Oriental languages, but who devoted himself to natural science, and made many discoveries in astronomy, chemistry, optics, and mathematics. He is said to have discovered gunpowder, and he proposed a reform of the calendar similar to that introduced by Gregory XIII., 300 years later. His reward was to be hooted at as a magician, and to be confined in a dungeon for many years.

The heretics spread and increased in this century, spite of the terrible weapon brought to bear against them. The "Brethren and Sisters of the Free Spirit," known also as Beghards, Beguttes, Bicorni, Beghins, and Turlupins, were the chief additional body. They believed that all things had emanated from God, and that to Him they would return; and to this Eastern philosophy they added practical fanaticism, rushing wildly about, shouting, yelling, begging. The Waldenses and Albigenses multiplied, and diversity of opinion spread in every direction.

CENTURY XIV

This fourteenth century is one of the epochs that sorely test the ingenuity of believers in papal infallibility; for the cardinals, having elected one pope in A.D. 1378, rapidly took a dislike to him, and elected a second. The first choice, Urban VI., remained at Rome; the second, Clement VII., betook himself to Avignon. They duly excommunicated each other, and the Latin Church was rent in twain. "The distress and calamity of these times is beyond all power of description; for not to insist upon the perpetual contentions and wars between the factions of the several popes, by which multitudes lost their fortunes and lives, all sense of religion was extinguished in most places, and profligacy arose to a most scandalous excess. The clergy, while they vehemently contended which of the reigning popes was the true successor of Christ, were so excessively corrupt as to be no longer studious to keep up even an appearance of religion or decency" ("Europe During the Middle Ages," Hallam, p. 359).

Meanwhile, the struggle between Rome and the heretics went on with ever-increasing fury. In England, Dr. John Wickcliff, rector of Lutterworth, became famous by his attack on the mendicant orders in A.D. 1360, and from that time he raised his voice louder and louder, till he spoke against the pope himself. He translated the Bible into English, attacked many of the prevailing superstitions, and although condemned as holding heretical opinions, he yet died in peace, A.D. 1387. Rome revenged itself by digging up his bones and burning them, about thirteen years later. Rebellion spread even among the monks of the Church, and a vast number of some nonconformist Franciscan monks, termed Spirituals, were burned for their refusal to obey the pope on matters of discipline. The intense hatred between the Franciscan and Dominican orders made the latter the willing instrument of the papacy; and, in their character as inquisitors, they hunted down their unfortunate rivals as heretics. The Flagellants, a sect who wandered about flogging themselves to the glory of God, fell also under the merciless hands of the inquisitors, as did also the Knights Templars in France. A new body, known as the Dancers, started up in A.D. 1373, and spread through Flanders; but the priests prayed them away by exorcising the dancing devils that, they said, inhabited the members of this curious sect. Among the sufferers of this century one name must not be forgotten: it is that of Ceccus Asculanus. This man was an Aristotelian philosopher, an astrologer, a mathematician, and a physician. "This unhappy man, having performed some experiments in mechanics that seemed miraculous to the vulgar, and having also offended many, and among the rest his master [the Duke of Calabria], by giving out some predictions which were said to have been fulfilled, was universally supposed to deal with infernal spirits, and burned for it by the inquisitors, at Florence, in the year 1337" (p. 355). There seems no green spot on which to rest the eye in this weary stretch of blood and fire.

CENTURY XV

In this fifteenth century the knell of the Church rang out; it is memorable evermore in history for the discovery of the New World, and the consequent practical demonstration of the falsehood of the whole theory of the patristic and ecclesiastical theology. In the flood only "Noah and his three sons, with their wives, were saved in an ark. Of these sons, Sham remained in Asia and repeopled it. Ham peopled Africa; Japhet, Europe. As the fathers were not acquainted with the existence of America, they did not provide an ancestor for its people" ("Conflict between Religion and Science," Dr. Draper, p. 63). Lactantius, indeed, inveighed against the folly of those who believed in the existence of the antipodes, and Augustine maintained that it was impossible there should be people living on the other side of the earth. Besides, "in the day of judgment, men on the other side of a globe could not see the Lord descending through the air" (Ibid, p. 64). Clearly there was no other side, theologically; only Columbus sailed there. Another fatal blow was struck at the Church by the invention of the printing press, about A.D. 1440, an invention which made knowledge possible for the many, and by diffusion of knowledge made heresy likewise certain. It is not for me, however, to trace here the progress of heretic thought; that brighter task is for another pen; mine only to turn over the bloodstained and black pages of the Church. One name stands out in the list of the pontiffs of this century, which is almost unparalleled in its infamy; it is that of Roderic Borgia, Pope Alexander VI. Foully vicious, cruel, and bloodthirsty, he is startlingly bad, even for a pope. Among his children are found the names of Cæsar and Lucretia Borgia, names whose very mention recalls a list of horrible crimes. Alexander died A.D. 1503, from swallowing, by mistake, a poison which he and his son Cæsar had prepared for others. Turning to the heretics, we see great lives cut short by the terrible blows of the inquisition:— Savanarola, the brave Italian preacher, the reformer monk, tortured and burned A.D. 1498; John Huss, the enemy of the papacy, burned A.D. 1415, in direct violation of the safe conduct granted him; Jerome, of Prague, the friend and companion of Huss, burned A.D. 1416. Myriads of their unhappy followers shared their fate in every European land. But to Spain belongs the terrible pre-eminence of cruelty in this last century before the Reformation. In the year 1478 a bull of Pope Sixtus IV. established the Inquisition in Spain. "In the first year of the operation of the Inquisition, 1481, two thousand victims were burnt in Andalusia; besides these, many thousands were dug up from their graves and burnt; seventeen thousand were fined or imprisoned for life. Whoever of the persecuted race could flee, escaped for his life. Torquemada, now appointed Inquisitor-General for Castile and Leon, illustrated his office by his ferocity. Anonymous accusations were received, the accused was not confronted by witnesses, torture was relied upon for conviction; it was inflicted in vaults where no one could hear the cries of the tormented. As, in pretended mercy, it was forbidden to inflict torture a second time, with horrible duplicity it was affirmed that the torment had not been completed at first, but had only been suspended out of charity until the following day! The families of the convicted were plunged into irretrievable ruin.... This frantic priest destroyed Hebrew Bibles wherever he could find them, and burnt six thousand volumes of Oriental literature at Salamanca, under an imputation that they inculcated Judaism" (Draper's "Conflict of Science and Religion," p. 146). Torquemada was, indeed, a worthy successor of Moses. During his eighteen years of power, his list of victims is as follows:—

Burnt at the stake alive 10,220

Burnt in effigy, the persons having died in prison or fled the country 6,860

Punished with infamy, confiscation, perpetual imprisonment, or loss of civil rights 97,321

Total 114,401

—("History of the Inquisition," by Dr. W.H. Rule, vol. i., p. 150. Full details of numbers are given in the "Histoire critique de l'Inquisition d'Espagne," Llorente, t. I., pp. 272-281).

Cardinal Ximenes was not quite so successful as Torquemada, but still his roll is long:

Burnt at the stake alive   3,564

Burnt in effigy   1,232

Punished heavily 48,059

Total 52,855

In A.D. 1481, in the bishoprics of Seville and Cadiz, "two thousand Judaizers were burnt in person, and very many in effigy, of whom the number is not known, besides seventeen thousand subject to cruel penance" (Ibid, p. 133). In A.D. 1485, no less than 950 persons were burned at Villa Real, now Ciudad Real.

Spite of all this awful suffering, heretics and Jews remained antagonistic to the church, and in March, A.D. 1492, the edict of the expulsion of the Jews was signed. "All unbaptized Jews, of whatever age, sex, or condition, were ordered to leave the realm by the end of the following July. If they revisited it, they should suffer death. They might sell their effects, and take the proceeds in merchandise or bills of exchange, but not in gold or silver. Exiled thus, suddenly from the land of their birth, the land of their ancestors for hundreds of years, they could not in the glutted market that arose sell what they possessed. Nobody would purchase what could be got for nothing after July. The Spanish clergy occupied themselves by preaching in the public squares sermons filled with denunciations against their victims, who, when the time for expatriation came, swarmed in the roads, and filled the air with their cries of despair. Even the Spanish onlookers wept at the scene of agony. Torquemada, however, enforced the ordinance that no one should afford them any help.... Thousands, especially mothers with nursing children, infants, and old people, died by the way—many of them in the agonies of thirst" (Ibid, p. 147). Thus was a peaceable, industrious, thoughtful population, driven out of Spain by the Church. Nor did her hand stay even here. Ferdinand, alas! had completed the conquest of the Moors; true, Granada had only yielded under pledge of liberty of worship, but of what value is the pledge of the Christian to the heretic? The Inquisition harried the land, until, in February 1502, word went out that all unbaptized Moors must leave Spain by the end of April. "They might sell their property, but not take away any gold or silver; they were forbidden to emigrate to the Mahommedan dominions; the penalty of disobedience was death. Their condition was thus worse than that of the Jews, who had been permitted to go where they chose" (Ibid, p. 148). And so the Moors were driven out, and Spain was left to Christianity, to sink down to what she is to-day. 3,000,000 persons are said to have been expelled as Jews, Moors and Moriscoes. The Moors departed,—they who had made the name of Spain glorious, and had spread science and thought through Europe from that focus of light,—they who had welcomed to their cities all who thought, no matter what their creed, and had covered with an equal protection Mahommedan, Christian, and Jew.

Nor let the Protestant Christian imagine that these deeds of blood are Roman, not Christian. The same crimes attach to every Church, and Rome's black list is only longer because her power is greater. Let us glance at Protestant communions. In Hungary, Giska, the Hussite, massacred and bruised the Beghards. In Germany, Luther cried, "Why, if men hang the thief upon the gallows, or if they put the rogue to death, why should not we, with all our strength, attack these popes and cardinals, these dregs of the Roman Sodom? Why not wash our hands in their blood?" ("The Spanish Inquisition," Le Maistre, p. 67, ed. 1838). Sandys, Bishop of London, wrote in defence of persecution. Archbishop Usher, in an address signed by eleven other bishops, said: "Any toleration to the papists is a grievous sin." Knox said, "The people are bound in conscience to put to death the queen, along with all her priests." The English Parliament said, "Persecution was necessary to advance the glory of God." The Scotch Parliament decreed death against Catholics as idolaters, saying "it was a religious obligation to execute them" (Ibid, pp. 67, 68). Cranmer, A.D. 1550, condemned six anabaptists to death, one of whom, a woman, was burned alive, and in the following year another was committed to the flames; this primate held a commission with "some others, to examine and search after all anabaptists, heretics, or contemners of the book of Common Prayer" ("Students' History of England," D. Hume, p. 291, ed. 1868).

In Switzerland, Calvin burned Servetus. In America, the Puritans carried on the same hateful tradition, and whipped the harmless Quakers from town to town. Wherever the cross has gone, whether held by Roman Catholic, by Lutheran, by Calvinist, by Episcopalian, by Presbyterian, by Protestant dissenter, it has been dipped in human blood, and has broken human hearts. Its effect on Europe was destructive, barbarising, deadly, until the dawning light of science scattered the thick black clouds which issued from the cross. One indisputable fact, pregnant with instruction, is the extremely low rate of increase of the population of Europe during the centuries when Christianity was supreme. "What, then, does this stationary condition of the population mean? It means, food obtained with hardship, insufficient clothing, personal uncleanness, cabins that could not keep out the weather, the destructive effects of cold and heat, miasm, want

222

of sanitary provisions, absence of physicians, uselessness of shrine cure, the deceptiveness of miracles, in which society was putting its trust; or, to sum up a long catalogue of sorrows, wants and sufferings in one term—it means a high death-rate. But, more, it means deficient births. And what does that point out? Marriage postponed, licentious life, private wickedness, demoralized society" (Draper's "Conflict of Religion and Science," p. 263). "The surface of the Continent was for the most part covered with pathless forests; here and there it was dotted with monasteries and towns. In the lowlands and along the river courses were fens, sometimes hundreds of miles in extent, exhaling their pestiferous miasms, and spreading agues far and wide." In towns there was "no attempt made at drainage, but the putrefying garbage and rubbish were simply thrown out of the door. Men, women, and children slept in the same apartment; not unfrequently domestic animals were their companions; in such a confusion of the family it was impossible that modesty and morality could be maintained. The bed was usually a bag of straw; a wooden log served as a pillow. Personal cleanliness was utterly unknown; great officers of state, even dignitaries so high as the Archbishop of Canterbury, swarmed with vermin; such, it is related, was the condition of Thomas à Becket, the antagonist of an English king. To conceal personal impurity, perfumes were necessarily and profusely used. The citizen clothed himself in leather, a garment which, with its ever-accumulating impurity, might last for many years. He was considered to be in circumstances of ease, if he could procure fresh meat once a week for his dinner. The streets had no sewers; they were without pavement or lamps. After night-fall, the chamber-shutters were thrown open, and slops unceremoniously emptied down, to the discomfiture of the wayfarer tracking his path through the narrow streets, with his dismal lantern in his hand" (Ibid, p. 265). Little wonder indeed, that plagues swept through the cities, destroying their inhabitants wholesale. The Church could only pray against them, or offer shrines where votive offerings might win deliverance; "not without a bitter resistance on the part of the clergy, men began to think that pestilences are not punishments inflicted by God on society for its religious shortcomings, but the physical consequences of filth and wretchedness; that the proper mode of avoiding them is not by praying to the saints, but by ensuring personal and municipal cleanliness. In the twelfth century it was found necessary to pave the streets of Paris, the stench in them was so dreadful. At once dysenteries and spotted fever diminished; a sanitary condition, approaching that of the Moorish cities of Spain, which had been paved for centuries, was attained" (Ibid, p. 314). The death-rate was still further diminished by the importation of the physician's skill from the Arabs and the Moors; the Christians had depended on the shrine of the saint, and the bone of the martyr, and the priest was the doctor of body as well as of soul. "On all the roads pilgrims were

223

wending their way to the shrines of saints, renowned for the cures they had wrought. It had always been the policy of the Church to discourage the physician and his art; he interfered too much with the gifts and profits of the shrines.... For patients too sick to move or be moved, there were no remedies except those of a ghostly kind—the Paternoster and the Ave" (Ibid, p. 269). Thus Christianity set itself against all popular advancement, against all civil and social progress, against all improvement in the condition of the masses. It viewed every change with distrust, it met every innovation with opposition. While it reigned supreme, Europe lay in chains, and even into the new world it carried the fetters of the old. Only as Christianity has grown feebler has civilization strengthened, and progress has been made more and more rapidly as a failing creed has lost the power to oppose. And now, day by day, that progress becomes swifter; now, day by day, the opposition becomes fainter, and soon, passing over the ruins of a shattered religion, Free Thought shall plant the white banner of Liberty in the midst of the temple of Humanity; that temple which, long desecrated by priests and overshadowed by gods, shall then be consecrated for evermore to the service of its rightful owner, and shall be filled with the glory of man, the only god, and shall have its air melodious with the voice of the prayer which is work.

9 781618 959898